If Only We Knew

How Ignorance Creates and Amplifies
the Greatest Risks Facing Society

Peter S. Baron

Praise For
If Only We Knew

"The ubiquitous waves of post-theatric disinformation that now permeate our 21st century lives undermine human connectivity and resilience in individuals and communities, local and global. Communication technology that was genuinely unthinkable only a few years ago, now connects our species in revolutionary ways that our human neurology simply can't keep up with. After all, for our 7 million years as upright walking apes, we all lived within small bands until that started to change some 12,000 years ago with the origins of agriculture, surplus and sedentary living. In other words, we're simply not wired to process all the social relations and endless stimuli that now influence our conscious and subconscious understanding of what it means to be human. So what are we to do? Well, we'll do what hominins have done for millions of years—we adapt—but we'll need to deploy our cultural DNA (e.g. languages, knowledge, epistemologies) to expedite this critical adaptation. In *If Only We Knew*, emerging scholar Peter S. Baron embraces a generational project to contemplate the theoretical foundations necessary for building individual and cultural resilience through community-, species-, and planet-level consciousness."

– **Scott M. Lacy, Ph.D.**
Associate Dean, College of Arts & Sciences
Faculty Chair, Community Engaged Research
Fairfield University

"In *If Only We Knew*, Peter S. Baron's passionate and informed voice speaks to the foundational ignorance that underlies America's persistent stagnation amid climate change, racism, mass incarceration, gun violence, health problems, poverty and privilege. His call for a more compassionate and loving culture amid our varied everyday violence gives me hope. While the issues he addresses in *If Only We Knew* are not new, Baron's voice is, and remarkably, it's a voice that's 'just' twenty years old as the book is released."

– Reggie Marra, cofounder, Fully Human at Work, and author, *Enough with the Talking Points, Killing America,* **and (forthcoming in 2022)** *Healing America's Narratives: Owning and Integrating Our National Shadow.*

"*If Only We Knew* is a timely analysis of social systems and problems that affect us all (as individuals and members of a society). Peter Baron's work provides hope that a better way is possible if we think more deeply about our own relationship to information, language, and knowledge. *If Only We Knew* provides an option for how we can mitigate our (collective) ignorance and embrace, rather than resist, the subjects and topics we need to learn more about. We all, regardless of credentials or training, can learn something new."

– Dr. Tiffany Wilgar
Professor of Rhetoric and Composition
Fairfield University

"Baron's well written exploration for what is just, leaves us all thinking about one critically significant question: have we all been manipulated to contribute to society's flaws or inspired to reengineer old standards and modernize systems that give rise to humanity and individual capacity in today's age of personalization?"

– Glenn Llopis, President of GLLG, Founder of the Age of Personalization Movement and Leadership Strategy Contributor to *Forbes*

Dedicated to my parents
Thank you for believing in me

First published by Ultimate World Publishing 2021
Copyright © 2021 Peter S. Baron

ISBN

Hardcover: 978-1-922597-93-9
Ebook: 978-1-922597-94-6

Peter S. Baron has asserted his rights under the Copyright, Designs and Patents Act 1988 to be identified as the author of this work. The information in this book is based on the author's experiences and opinions. The publisher specifically disclaims responsibility for any adverse consequences which may result from use of the information contained herein. Permission to use information has been sought by the author. Any breaches will be rectified in further editions of the book.

All rights reserved. No part of this publication may be reproduced, stored in or introduced into a retrieval system, or transmitted in any form, or by any means (electronic, mechanical, photocopying, recording or otherwise) without the prior written permission of the author. Any person who does any unauthorized act in relation to this publication may be liable to criminal prosecution and civil claims for damages. Enquiries should be made through the publisher.

Cover design: Ultimate World Publishing
Layout and typesetting: Ultimate World Publishing
Editor: Isabelle Russell
Cover image license: alphaspirit.it-Shutterstock.com
Photos: Brian Bogdanowich from Madison Ave Photo

Ultimate World Publishing
Diamond Creek,
Victoria Australia 3089
www.writeabook.com.au

Contents

Preface	xiii
Introduction	1
1. The Creation Of Ignorance: The Elite's Control Of Politics And Media	17
2. The Risk Of Climate Change	49
3. The Risk Of Racism	81
4. The Risk Of Mass Incarceration	127
5. The Risk Of Gun Violence	167
6. The Risk Of Poor Health	195
7. The Risk Of Poverty And Privilege	235
8. Building A Culture For Others	273
About the Author	287
Acknowledgments	289

Not ignorance, but ignorance of ignorance is the death of knowledge.
– Alfred North Whitehead (attributed)

Preface

> *Recognizing your ignorance is*
> *the beginning of all wisdom.*
> — Socrates

When I made the decision to write this book, I sought out to answer one question: *why are there so many crises facing society, and why are the dangers posed by these crises escalating?* I thought about wealth and income inequality, climate change, and the obesity epidemic. I saw no end in sight to the amplification of the risks facing our national and global society. This didn't make sense to me. I was especially perplexed because many solutions to these crises were presented in easy-to-access forums, such as Ted Talks. Yet practically none of them were being implemented. I asked myself, *how can there be so many solutions available but so little action taken?* Intrigued, I embarked on a more extensive research journey. What I found led me to the conclusion that serves as the thesis of this book: the creation, preservation, and manipulation of public ignorance creates and amplifies every risk facing society.

Okay, what does that mean? Well, as large corporations have consolidated the media industry and gained legal reach and power in the political sphere, a group of ultra-wealthy Americans—the "elite class"—has been granted unmatched influence over the ideas and beliefs held by the public. I argue that this elite class has leveraged their influence to intentionally spread false ideas among the public. The acceptance of these false ideas creates "public ignorance", which, in turn, creates and amplifies the dangers posed by social problems. While this creation and amplification of the dangers of social problems threatens and exploits the well-being of the public, it deliberately serves the socioeconomic interests of the elite. Throughout the book, I refer to the dangers of these social problems as risks (a term borrowed from late German sociologist Ulrich Beck) because the elite are taking a "risk" when they intentionally create and exacerbate social problems in an attempt to profit.

Every risk is an outgrowth of ignorance. Sometimes ignorance develops unintentionally, more often it is intentionally created, but ignorance always manifests itself in the form of a risk. In this book, I specifically address what I consider to be the six greatest risks facing our society. For each of these risks, I postulate that there is a causal relationship between the avarice of the elite class and the existence of these risks. The link between them? The elite class's ability to create and preserve public ignorance and then manipulate the resulting ignorant public in ways that spawn and perpetuate the risks that serve their vested socioeconomic interests. Hence, my thesis.

Now, it is important to clarify some of the terms and phrases mentioned in that last paragraph. I am not claiming that the entire public is "ignorant". However, I do maintain that intentionally created ignorance exists within a significant proportion of the public. It must also be acknowledged that there are many different variations of this "ignorant public". The people who are ignorant about the risk of racism are not the exact same people who are ignorant about the risk of climate change. While there is often overlap between the members of these "ignorant publics", there are innumerable "ignorant publics" that correspond to the existence of each and every risk.

As I will explain in the introduction and first chapter, when I mention the term "public ignorance", I am referring to people who are not just *uninformed*, but intentionally *misinformed*. I ask you to consider the substantial difference between the two terms. I further note that I am by no means arguing that every person holds the same ignorant beliefs. One person may believe Black *people* are biologically inferior whereas another person may believe Black *culture* is inferior; however, they are both still members of an ignorant public. Regardless of how one becomes ignorant, the argument I make throughout this book is that one does not reach false ideas and beliefs on their own accord. Rather, I argue that the elite class systematically imposes false ideas within the public consciousness. Subsequently, many in the public come to hold ignorant beliefs without ever realizing their strongest held beliefs are not the product of their own volition, but the product of manipulation.

That brings us to the next term we need to define: the "elite class". While I will explain who exactly these people are in greater detail in Chapter 1, it is important to clarify that I do not consider every person with wealth to be part of this class. When I refer to the elite class, I am referring to the class of people with enormous wealth and power who exert influence to shape the national agenda according to their vested interests. Again, I will explain how exactly they do this in Chapter 1, but for the sake of clarity, I want to reaffirm that I do not assume that *every* wealthy or influential person operates with this self-interested intent. No group is a monolith.

I do contend, however, that the elite class is culturally driven to go to great lengths to preserve their own interests. It's what they do. It's what they've always done. Creating and amplifying societal risks is the primary mechanism with which they enrich and empower themselves. If you take anything away from this book, remember this: the elite class is dependent on the existence and amplification of risks, so they create and preserve ignorance to do just that. While, of course, there are exceptions to this rule, we must recognize that the overwhelming majority of the elite class act in this self-interested manner.

If Only We Knew

Throughout this book, you will notice that I often use the term "conservative" to refer to those aiding and abetting the ignorance creating mission of the elite class. I purposely attempt to avoid using the terms "Republican" and "Democrat" when possible. I do this because I believe regardless of self-proclaimed party affiliation, everyone who acts to preserve the status quo that confers power and wealth upon the elite through the creation and amplification of risks should be considered a conservative. While, unsurprisingly, most conservatives are indeed Republicans, conservatives are present in both parties, and this cannot be ignored.

I wrote this book to identify how the elite class's intentional creation, preservation, and manipulation of public ignorance is at the root of the existence of risks.

To be as transparent as possible, I would like to address some of the reasons for which I *did not* write this book. I did not write this book to be a comprehensive guide to understanding all the risks that our society faces, nor did I attempt to address the ignorance of every existing risk, for if I did this book would have no end. I also did not attempt to comprehensively cover all the intricate, complex details of the risks I do address.

While I hope each chapter will prove very informative, and while I include significant historical scope of the development of each risk, please do not mistake my book for an all-encompassing description and explanation of every societal risk. Despite having conducted extensive research regarding each risk discussed in this book, there are instances where I do not provide references to the academic literature from which my ideas originate. This is because many of the concepts I discuss, such as in the overview I give on the history behind racist ideas in the United States, are widely accepted facts in the academic environment, not controversial topics that require citations to prove their accuracy. Please keep in mind that this book is not an academic text, but a popular press book. Therefore, please read it as a presentation of a new theoretical framework for understanding and working to mitigate the risks facing society.

Preface

This book also does not venture to deeply understand the complex psychological reasons for why some people fall victim to the elite class's manipulation and adopt ignorant beliefs, while others can see past them. While I briefly touch on this topic, my aim in this book is not to provide a truly sufficient understanding of what makes people susceptible to these false ideas and what leads to political divisions; this requires its own dedicated inquiry into moral and social psychology, sociology, and political theory, among other areas. Instead, this book is more concerned with the process of how the elite class creates and preserves ignorance and the consequences that ensue when people are manipulated according to this ignorance.

In addition to highlighting the relationship between the greed of the elite class and the existence of inequities, my book also aims to present a guide towards creating a more equitable, happier, less "risky" future. From the outset, one of my main intentions when writing this book was to demonstrate that creating a society that works for all is possible. I hope to show that the reversal of public ignorance will enable society to recognize and implement the solutions necessary to significantly reduce (or eradicate) existing risks and create a culture that does not produce future risks at a significant rate, but rather creates favorable conditions for widespread public happiness. Accordingly, at the end of each chapter, I identify what I consider to be essential solutions that we must implement to reduce or eradicate the threat posed by a given risk. Further, I conclude this book with a chapter calling for a massive social movement to build a "culture for others", as opposed to our current "me-first" culture. The flawed values of our current culture are not only at the root of the elite's motivation to preserve and amplify risks, they are also at the root of the public's vulnerability in accepting false ideas spread by the elite.

The solutions I offer are by no means the only solutions to the identified risks. There are numerous other solutions that I do not propose in this book. My goal in mentioning these solutions is not to offer a comprehensive "one-and-done" package, but rather to provide the reader with concrete ideas of how we can approach tackling these risks. More importantly, I hope the inclusion of these solution sections illustrates the power of reversing ignorance. I do strongly believe that, if implemented, the solutions I offer will result in significant transformational improvements in the lives of countless people and will dramatically reduce the threat posed by these risks. However, I reiterate that these solutions are not the "be-all and end-all". There may very well be better solutions that I do not mention. In any event, reversing ignorance is paramount to eradicating any risk.

In a nutshell, by applying a general theory to six specific risks, this book identifies problems and presents a guide to solving these problems. This general theory proceeds as follows:

1. Ignorance spawns risks;
2. Risks, by their nature, serve the interests of the elite class;
3. The elite class is primarily concerned with maintaining and enhancing their wealth, power, and status;
4. Thus, the elite class exerts their power and influence to create and preserve public ignorance so that they can manipulate an ignorant public into behaving in a way that perpetuates risks, which confers more power and wealth upon the elites;
5. This we can label "the problem of ignorance";
6. To create a society that does not produce and amplify risks at high rates (or in other words, which is not burdened with the problem of ignorance), we must commit as a society to reverse ignorance;
7. The best way to create a society that is committed to reversing ignorance is to create a "culture for others" in which individuals prioritize the well-being of their neighbor;
8. Therefore, to solve the problem of ignorance, we must build a culture for others.

Preface

When you finish reading my book, I hope you emerge with a renewed sense of hope for the future. While there may be times when you feel an overwhelming sense of doom and gloom, please remember to never disregard the potential within us to create a less risky, happier world. No matter the problem, there are always solutions. To find them, we must reverse ignorance.

Introduction

For Socrates, the worst kind of ignorance was the kind that masquerades as knowledge. Better a wide and honest ignorance than a narrow and suspect knowledge.
— Eric Weiner

Self-protection is inherent in our human nature. Throughout human history, people have protected themselves from physical and emotional harm in myriad ways. In today's "Information Age" of the internet and social media,[1] the instinct to protect oneself includes protecting one's virtual self-image as well. Many have come to believe that how their virtual persona is perceived reflects how others think of them in real life. Hence, to not look "dumb", or to avoid being labeled as "not woke", many often attempt to hide their ignorance of certain topics from public view. Perhaps worse, many simply deflect any and all criticisms of their opinions, claiming that they know *the singular* truth and anyone who disagrees with them must be wrong.

In this era where being wrong about anything has the potential to become a social catastrophe, it is simply not viable to acknowledge that you do not know something or that your knowledge and beliefs are inaccurate. Unsurprisingly, we have seen the concept of "truth"

---

[1] Nichols, T. *America's Cult of Ignorance* (The Daily Beast, 2017). https://www.thedailybeast.com/americas-cult-of-ignorance.

become increasingly subjectivized with many holding "alternative facts" as equal to plain old mainstream facts.

Today, being perceived as ignorant is a feared social risk.[2] This fear creates an environment ripe for the elite class's intentional imposition of ignorance among the public. Since there is a fear of being perceived as ignorant, people are afraid to seek to uncover and reverse their own ignorance. This environment enables ignorance to spread rapidly and become deeply rooted in the public consciousness.[3]

Ignorance is creating and amplifying large-scale societal risks at an alarming rate.[4] The non-recognition of public ignorance regarding these risks, society's complacency with ever-present widespread ignorance, and the existence of a "call-out/cancel culture" that disincentivizes uncovering and reversing individual ignorance is not just unfortunate, it is dangerous too.

I will explore why this ignorance exists in the first place—who creates and preserves it. I will then argue that the intentional creation and preservation of ignorance perpetuates societal risks that serve the interests of elite members of society at the expense of the masses.[5]

The elite class's power to create and weaponize ignorance is partially derived from the aforementioned social factors that lead people to accept and normalize the ignorance that exists in themselves and others. However, even if those social factors had no effect on the public, widespread public ignorance would still

---

[2] For the entirety of this book, a risk will be defined as any social, economic, environmental, or biological condition or institution that produces harm to a large group of relatively powerless people but reaps enormous benefits for a small group of powerful people.

[3] I am drawing from the same logic used by, Ijeoma Oluo in *So You Want to Talk About Race* (New York, 2018). She posits that people's fear of being called racist leads to more racism.

[4] Throughout this book, I will identify the existence of public ignorance primarily by citing polling statistics and the correlation between what I label as "ignorance creating mechanisms" and voting tendencies and widespread behavior.

[5] In Chapter 1, I will define who comprises this elite class and how exactly they impose ignorance upon the masses.

Introduction

exist in our society. This is because public ignorance is inevitable when an ill-intentioned elite class has unchecked control over the political and media spheres.

It is crucial to recognize the intimate connection between the existence of risks and the creation of ignorance. *Risks exist because of ignorance.* Ignorance is not simply created to distract the masses from the true causes of risks, rather the development of ignorance precedes the development of risk. Ignorance is intentionally created or preserved because it creates risks, and risks are created because their existence serves the socioeconomic interests of the elite. Ignorance then amplifies the danger posed by the same risks it spawns. Thus, ignorance is both the creator and amplifier of risks.

I will cover what I deem to be the most critical risks threatening our society and examine how ignorance amplifies the danger posed by these risks. For example, in Chapter 2, I will refer to the issue of climate change, where ignorance is preventing us from acting to protect our home on this planet. The danger posed by climate change is immense, but widespread ignorance leads to the inaction that exponentially amplifies the risk.

What you have read so far may have stirred some anxiety in you, but please do not worry too much. This is a hopeful book! Acknowledging the existence of widespread public ignorance is the first and most significant step to launching a pursuit of informed solutions to important issues. If we admit our ignorance and commit as a society to pursuing the unknown and becoming more educated on risks and their possible solutions, we can reverse the risk-creating-and-amplifying-ignorance that exists. We can create a better, "less-risky" future.

WHAT IS IGNORANCE?

Before we go any further, let's take a deeper look at what ignorance really is. You see, the dictionary definition of ignorance fails to capture the totality of how ignorance develops and functions in society.[6] What matters is not only what ignorance is, but also what it *does*. Throughout this book, when I mention "ignorance", I will be referring to more than what people do not know. Rather, I will focus primarily on the public's acceptance of misinformation as truth and will explore how this type of ignorance creates and amplifies risks.

For example, those who are ignorant about the risk of mass incarceration often are simply unaware of the history behind the boon in the prison population. This is textbook ignorance. However, they have developed this textbook ignorance and have come to accept other false ideas about the risk of mass incarceration because they were intentionally misinformed by the elite class. The misguided belief that harsher prison sentences reduce crime is a form of ignorance that served to create, and currently serves to amplify, the risk of mass incarceration. This myth, as we will discuss in Chapter 4, was intentionally spread among the public by the elite class.

We must examine how ignorance originates if we want to truly understand why it is so dangerous. Ignorance is action oriented. As most people understand it, ignorance can be the result of an individual choice; one can choose to learn about something or stay ignorant. However, in this book we will primarily focus on the action of ignorance creation and preservation, which occurs when false ideas are intentionally and systematically imposed on one group of people by another.

Another fitting example is the intentionally created public ignorance regarding gun violence in the United States. Ignorance surrounding today's gun-violence epidemic was in large part solidified in the public consciousness when the National Rifle Association (NRA) lobbied Congress to pass the Dickey Amendment in 1996. The Amendment prevents the Center for Disease Control (CDC) from using funds to conduct research on gun violence that

---

[6] The definition of ignorance given by the Meriam-Webster Dictionary is "the state or fact of being ignorant: lack of knowledge, education, or awareness."

would potentially label it as a public health issue or promote gun control legislation.[7] As a result, the public has been kept ignorant about the nature of gun violence and Congress has been prevented from taking a public health approach to confront it. In fact, the Dickey Amendment has even created ignorance among the experts in this field by preventing them from conducting sufficient research to truly understand the nature of gun violence.

Those in power, such as the leaders of the NRA, preserve existing ignorance and create new ignorance among the public. This enables powerful people and organizations to maximize their own efforts and maintain the status quo for their survival and benefit.

As mentioned, public ignorance is sometimes developed *unintentionally*. However, this does not negate the action-oriented nature of ignorance. For example, the risk of gun violence is largely a product of unintentionally developed ignorance, as researchers have long overlooked what makes it a public health issue. This unintentional ignorance, however, was intentionally preserved (by the Dickey Amendment) while new ignorance regarding the risk of gun violence (which I will discuss in greater detail in Chapter 5) was simultaneously created.

It is vitally important that we do not excuse or discount unintentional ignorance merely because it developed absent of intent. When individual or collective ignorance of a risk exists, it does not matter if the ignorance was created intentionally or if it developed unintentionally. Risks are the product of ignorance; therefore, to mitigate risks, society must always be diligent, not apathetic, in identifying where ignorance exists and reversing it, regardless of how the ignorance has developed.

It is a mistake to claim that there is nothing we can do about the development of public ignorance. The development of widespread public ignorance is preventable. In fact, becoming a less ignorant society is a practical and attainable goal. The knowledge needed

---

[7] Kaplan, S. *Congress Quashed Research into Gun Violence. Since Then, 600,000 People Have Been Shot* (New York Times, 2018).

to mitigate large-scale risks is abundant. The tricky part is circumventing the obstacles laid out by the elite class who have a vested interest in maintaining ignorance.

THE DISMISSAL OF LOGIC, REASON, AND EVIDENCE

The dismissal of logic, reason, and evidence has become commonplace in the rhetoric used by influential people in society. This tendency has contributed greatly to the creation of public ignorance. Let's take a look.

In recent decades, rational thought has become more frequently bogged down by logical fallacies (errors in reasoning that invalidate an argument). These malignant manipulations of rhetoric are combined with negative emotional appeals, such as fear mongering, hatred, and vengefulness. It has become acceptable and normalized for politicians to dismiss clear, proven evidence if it doesn't align with their worldview (or their political aspirations).

Today, bad faith rhetorical approaches have become commonplace because they have proven successful. As mentioned earlier, everyday people clearly have followed the lead of these politicians, evidenced by the many people who choose to opt for alternative facts that better align with their beliefs. This shift has resulted in increasingly polarized politics, and it has stifled the public policy proceedings that are needed to alleviate the risks facing society. These two factors have created favorable political conditions for the elite who wish to maintain the existence of public ignorance and risks.

Donald Trump's 2016 presidential campaign provides an excellent, if egregious, example. The campaign he ran was grounded almost completely on deceptive emotional appeal and a blatant disregard for evidence. Trump offered virtually zero specifics about any policy he planned on enacting in office. Instead, he made controversial statements at every debate, rally, and fundraiser he

Introduction

held. Even his campaign slogan, "Make America Great Again", intentionally neglects logic, reason, and historical context. Of course, America was never truly "great" for everyone, but this call to the past creates a collective false nostalgia and a notion that the nation can "turn back the clock" to a better time (which, of course, it cannot). Since his campaign made for good TV, he received constant media attention. When misleading rhetoric is promoted and validated by the media, it creates ignorance.

Trump appealed to the fearful and hateful emotions of Americans and intentionally created ignorance among many, which he used to his benefit. Trump infuriated many, but he also inspired and built a strong coalition of voters who connected emotionally with his deceitful rhetoric. This dismissal of logic, reason, and evidence among voters and politicians alike led to a movement of "Trumpism", which has radically changed the (explicit) values of the Republican party.[8] Following Trump's lead, many conservatives in Congress and in state and local branches of government have begun to disregard facts and spew blatant lies with reckless abandon.

When those in powerful social and political positions choose to neglect logic, reason, and evidence, they contribute to the creation of an ignorant public. Whether they act intentionally–as part of an effort to influence voters—or unintentionally—when they speak about a topic they know little about—these actions always have consequences. This is because the ignorance they create, in turn, creates and amplifies risks. To see just how dangerous it is when powerful people dismiss logic, reason, and evidence, one needs to look no further than to the lies of election fraud that culminated in the insurrectionist mob that stormed the Capitol building on January 6th, 2021.

---

[8] Burmila, E. *How Trump is changing Republican Party values* (The Week, 2018) https://theweek.com/articles/785361/how-trump-changing-republican-party-values.

If Only We Knew

THE SPREAD OF IGNORANCE IN THE 21ST CENTURY

It seems ironic that in the current "Information Age"—an age in which all the information one could ever dream about acquiring is available at the click of a button—it appears as if the public is becoming increasingly more ignorant.[9] It's shocking that the age of information is also the age of ignorance. Yet, when we take a closer look at why this is the case, this paradox is resolved. The rise of social media and the ubiquitous use of the internet has led to a decline in intellectual curiosity and an increase in the ability of "fake news" to spread like wildfire.

The popular default of claiming that there is no point in learning information because it is so readily available online has led to a decline in intellectual curiosity.[10] This development has had grave repercussions: people have grown more and more apathetic to the seriousness of the risks facing our domestic and global society, and as a result, our society has lost its motivation to actively recognize and reverse ignorance.

For those who are still invested in politics and current events, however, social media and the age of the internet have been detrimental. To generate profit from advertisements, free to download social media platforms rely on algorithms that are designed to keep users on their social media accounts for as long as possible. As a result, the algorithms present users with the most eye-catching content. When this content comes in the form of a funny cat video, it is benign. Oftentimes, however, it comes in the form of fake news or conspiracy theory posts. Unsurprisingly, it becomes very easy for people to fall into rabbit holes of consuming media involving conspiracy theories and fake news.

The algorithms built into social media platforms and search engines recognize patterns in our online behavior. They then suggest

---

[9] Nichols, 2017.

[10] Gino, F. *The Business Case for Curiosity* (Harvard Business Review, 2018).

news and social media posts specifically tailored to our personalized profile to keep us glued to our screens. So, when someone goes to Google to search "climate change", Google will suggest different searches and links, depending on one's online behavioral pattern. For example, if one tends to click on links to conservative news stories more often than progressive news stories, Google will suggest more conservative websites when that person searches "climate change". These are phenomena illustrated brilliantly by the Netflix documentary, *The Social Dilemma*. These algorithms, combined with our natural tendency to have our interest piqued by sensational stories, have led to increased political polarization and an explosion in public ignorance of the threatening risks that we will discuss in this book.

The obsession with "eye-catching" news is not just a product of social media, however. As we will discuss in greater detail in Chapter 1, since the private news industry functions as a business, the truthfulness of news is irrelevant, if not a detriment, to big media corporations. All that matters to them is the revenue stream and profit margin. The elite class—whose members own the media companies—capitalizes on the broadcasting of sensational, untruthful news, which does not just create and preserve widespread public ignorance, but which is also a profit generating mechanism within itself.[11]

Another negative consequence that has arisen in the age of social media is the death of expertise. Today, social movements have become more frequent, more accessible, and more visible. In some respects, this has been a very positive development. The social movements that call for equality have intensified. These movements demand equal rights for women, people of color, LGBTQ+ people, and other marginalized groups, as many within society have reasoned that if the United States is to be a truly democratic and free nation, complete and total equality for all is needed.

---

[11] Hedges, C. *'Fake News' in America: Homegrown, and Far From New* (Truthdig, 2016). https://www.truthdig.com/articles/fake-news-in-america-homegrown-and-far-from-new/.

This social movement for equality in all aspects, however, has had unintended side-effects. Somewhere along the way, in the call for everyone to be equal, an assumed equality of expertise has been adopted as well. In this new notion of democracy, everyone's *opinions* are equal. The problem is that this new epistemological equality has led to a sharp decline in how much we value expertise.[12] It is important not to equate the goal for equity in human rights to an equity in expertise or knowledge base. Not all opinions are equally credible.

In the age of Twitter and other social media, everyone can share their opinion about virtually any subject. This may sound like a good thing on the surface, and it certainly can be entertaining, but it is important to recognize the rhetorical consequences of Twitter. Twitter and other social media have created a platform for uninformed people to equate their opinion with that of experts in every field. Uninformed tweeters can share their opinion on very significant matters, such as the existence of systemic racism. They then can have their opinion validated and spread by likes and retweets from other uninformed people. Meanwhile, the opinions of highly educated, informed people are given no more than a passing glance as Twitter users scroll through their feed.

Even more devastatingly, verified users with thousands or millions of followers freely share their opinion on topics that they know little about. For instance, a right-wing media personality with no background in African American studies can reply to a scholar in this field who tweeted about systemic racism by claiming systemic racism does not exist, and her millions of followers will take her word as truth instead of the scholar's. In our current social media climate, everyone's opinions and comments are of equal value; nobody's opinion is seen as more important than that of anyone else. As illustrated, this is a significant problem, especially when addressing topics like healthcare, racism, or gun violence.

---

[12] Nichols, 2017.

Introduction

IGNORANCE'S AMPLIFICATION OF RISKS

Ulrich Beck, the late German sociologist and author of the book, *Risk Society: Towards a New Modernity*, wrote about modern society as one defined by risks. In 1992, Beck argued that the exponential development of technology and science was combining with public ignorance, and he believed that this synthesis was leading society down a dangerous path of producing large-scale risks at accelerated rates. These risks, such as governments around the world taking minimal action to halt the climate crisis, have large scale consequences.[13] Three decades later, large-scale public ignorance is not just *producing* risks, it is also *amplifying* risks. Beck's dark outlook has become reality.

When taking a broad worldview of the risks facing global society, we can clearly see that the proliferation of ignorance has severe consequences for our planet.[14] As a consequence of the world failing to acknowledge and act on the science and hard data that have identified climate change, the crisis continues to progress at an alarming rate.[15] The power of the elite to intentionally impose ignorance has almost completely prohibited problem solving of global risks. Subsequently, we are facing serious crises.[16]

For Americans, a narrower domestic view exposes the consequences of risks that affect them constantly. The more one learns about the risks facing the United States, the clearer it becomes that an overwhelming number of Americans are woefully ignorant about what is going on. This, of course, is no coincidence. The existence of ignorance is crucial to the survival of risks that serve the interests of the elite. In most instances, the K-12 educational system

---

[13] Beck, U. *Risk Society: Towards a New Modernity* (Munich, 1992).

[14] Wallace, W. D. *How We Could Change the Planet's Climate Future* (TED, 2019).

[15] According to NASA, the level of atmospheric carbon dioxide is currently nearing 420 parts per million. In 1950, the level of atmospheric carbon dioxide was 310 parts per million, nasa.gov.

[16] Davenport, C., Lipton, E. *How G.O.P. Leaders Came to View Climate Change as Fake Science* (2017).

does not sufficiently teach racism, mass incarceration, money in politics, and the role of the media in shaping public opinion. Again, this is no coincidence. As a result of this intentionally deficient education, the country at large suffers the consequences of a failing system while those in the elite class consistently accumulate more wealth and more power.

At this point you might be thinking, *"Risks that serve the interests of the elites? Why does he keep saying that? What is he talking about?"* Don't worry, this concept will become clearer when it is applied to specific risks in each chapter.

THE WEAPONIZATION OF IGNORANCE

Ignorance is not just created and preserved by powerful people and organizations; it is weaponized. For example, in recent years it has become clear to the Republican Party that they stand to benefit from suppressing the vote of African Americans and other minority groups who usually vote for Democrats. Therefore, they have been redrawing districts through the process of gerrymandering,[17] and they have been calling for and implementing stricter voter ID laws.[18] Some of these laws are so blatantly intended to suppress voters it's astonishing that Republicans have been able to pull off this sleight of hand.

Yet, while the laws themselves may be explicitly anti-democratic, the creation of ignorance that has occurred simultaneously has insulated the Republicans from losing a significant amount of support; as these laws are passed, conservatives have created ignorance among the public by telling voters these laws are intended to keep elections safe, fair, and secure. Using these key words is

---

[17] Associated Press. *Analysis: Partisan gerrymandering has benefited Republicans more than Democrats* (Business Insider, 2017).

[18] Gross, T. *Republican Voter Suppression Efforts Are Targeting Minorities, Journalist Says* (2018).

Introduction

a mechanism of rhetorical framing, something we will discuss in greater detail in Chapter 1.

If the public understood the true intent and consequences behind these new voter ID laws, one might expect the Republican Party to lose large numbers of supporters. However, the average person knows practically nothing about gerrymandering and voter suppression, or they naïvely believe that the actions of Republicans must be justified because they believe politicians wouldn't undermine the democracy and well-being of this country for their own gain (at least not so blatantly). As a result, the country continues to suffer from created ignorance.

It is important to acknowledge that the weaponization of ignorance by those in power is not a recent development or limited to the political sphere. Rather, it is a mechanism powerful people (in both public and private sectors) have frequently deployed in their pursuit of power and profits throughout history.

For example, during World War I, radium products became very popular in the United States. They were flaunted as must-have gadgets for those fighting in the war, as toys for kids at home, and as essential components in everyday household items. But radium is a dangerous radioactive element, not a toy, gadget, or household necessity. The manipulative rhetoric used by the powerful leaders of the U.S. Radium company enabled the corporation to deceive its workers and consumers into thinking radium was safe when, in fact, they knew it was extremely dangerous. Radium was so dangerous that four young women who worked for U.S. Radium, known as the "radium girls", died of radium poisoning. Countless others suffered health complications, such as cancer, because of exposure to the element.[19] The leading radium-producing company, U.S. Radium, intentionally kept this information secret to maintain strength in their labor force and to increase sales; a powerful company sacrificed the health of the public and their workers for profits.

---

[19] Johnson, R. *Romancing the Atom: Nuclear Infatuation from the Radium Girls to Fukushima* (2012).

In this example, we can clearly see intentionally established ignorance being weaponized to create a risk, and then making it much more dangerous than it should be. All the while, we can plainly see how the creation of ignorance serves the interests of wealthy, powerful people.

As I have emphasized, ignorance creates risks, regardless of whether it is developed unintentionally (uninformed) or intentionally (misinformed). However, the intentional weaponizing of ignorance for the sake of profits or political gain *exponentially amplifies* risks, as shown in the two examples above. In this book, I will argue that the pursuits of power and profit are almost always the primary drivers of the weaponization of ignorance. This is extremely important to recognize because it aids in the understanding of why elites are motivated to create risks in the first place.

For example, the development of concepts about race and racism can only be understood if one examines the monetary motivations and societal aggrandizement of power, dating back to the emergence of the slave trade. Or, again, one can comprehend the logical conundrum that is mass incarceration by examining the profit motives behind the prison industrial complex and realizing the oppressive racial power grab at play. Recognizing that the elite class's primary motive to create and preserve risks is the pursuits of power and profit will enable us to understand the flaws in our culture and to envision the creation of a new type of culture.

REVERSING IGNORANCE TO CREATE POSITIVE CHANGE

If there is any lesson to be learned from history, it is that things can change. The systems and structures found in society are not binding or irrevocable, and none last forever. As Martin Luther King Jr. famously stated, "The arc of the moral universe is long, but it bends towards justice." To ignite the movements for change, however, the public, both collectively and individually, must be willing to admit their ignorance and seek to reverse it.

We need leaders who are not afraid to admit their own ignorance and who encourage us to do the same. We need our elected officials to lean heavily on the experts who study all the risks facing our society and who have devised solutions to solve them. Perhaps more importantly, to ensure we are ready to confront any risk that challenges our society, we must always invest in "ignorance-reversing" studies and projects. It is true that ignorance is at the root of all risks, is the greatest risk amplifier in society, and can be used as a dangerous weapon. However, the commitment to reverse our ignorance is society's greatest asset and catalyst for change.

History has shown time and time again that acknowledging ignorance is the key to progress. Near the time of the scientific revolution, the Chinese, the Ottoman Empire, and European nations all had roughly the same level of technology and military forces, but the world came to be ruled by the Europeans. *Why?* While many factors contributed to the rise of a European dominated world, it cannot be overlooked that Europeans were largely able to separate themselves because they valued uncovering, seeking, and correcting ignorance as part of a pursuit to create new knowledge; the Chinese and Ottomans did not share these same ideals.[20] This willingness of the Europeans to acknowledge and seek out ignorance led to the scientific revolution. It resulted in new, effective medicines; huge leaps in the advancement of technology; a greater understanding of the universe and space; and most importantly, the trust and willingness to invest in science.[21]

The world can be changed for the better if society acknowledges ignorance and commits to understanding the problems it faces. The existence of ignorance should bring hope. Where ignorance exists, ignorance can be reversed. With an informed, self-aware, critical-thinking public, we can build a better society. Things *can* change.

---

[20] Harari, Y. *Sapiens: A Brief History of Humankind* (Harper, 2019). 264, 284.
[21] Ibid.

Bias and racism can be combatted by reversing the ignorance about race and racist ideas and implementing transformative antiracist policies. A strong coalition can be built, and enough public support can be garnered to lead a movement to right the injustices of mass incarceration, poverty and economic inequality, and corruption in media and politics. Society can also increase its knowledge of scientific based risks such as climate change, obesity, and mental health simply by following the abundance of evidence already available and adopting known, proven solutions. If the COVID-19 pandemic can teach us anything, it is that sharing *factual, relevant* information about topics such as health will make society safer. Collective action is needed to create a society that understands the potential and actualized consequences of large-scale risks. When citizens become more aware of the nature of these risks, and the benefits of solving them, our potential to solve them increases significantly. A society that acknowledges the value of reversing ignorance can, in turn, create new knowledge and enact effective solutions.

Remember, this is a hopeful book. Every solution I propose can be achieved. The United States education system, which perpetuates inequality and, in many aspects, intentionally keeps the public ignorant, must be appropriately modified. We must begin teaching the dangers and opportunities presented by the existence of ignorance and we must provide a more comprehensive education for our children. Society must call for a shift in the cultural norms that have led to complacency and the tolerance of ignorance. The public must demand that politicians rely on research conducted by sociologists, Black History scholars, environmentalists, public health experts, and other academics. These are the experts who actually study the major risks in society and already have the solutions to fix them. We must listen to them! If society acknowledges that ignorance creates and amplifies the greatest risks facing individuals, communities, and countries, it will gain a greater understanding of how to reverse them with knowledge. Only then will society begin to correct the injustices that affect so many.

1

The Creation Of Ignorance: The Elite's Control Of Politics And Media

If we do not get a handle on money in politics and the degree to which big money controls the political process in this country, nobody is going to bring about the changes that [are] needed in this country for the middle class and working families.
– Bernie Sanders

Every risk that will be discussed in this book is created and amplified by ignorance. This relationship between risks and ignorance tells us something very important: an ignorant public is dangerous to everyone. *So, if ignorance is so dangerous, why would anyone, any company, or any political organization want to create ignorance?* Quite simply, greed. Powerful corporations, politicians, and ultra-wealthy citizens act (often in unison) to shape public opinion, craft legislation, and influence voting tendencies to further enrich themselves. By strategically manipulating the political and media spheres through the creation and preservation of public ignorance, those corporations, politicians, and ultra-wealthy citizens can preserve and enhance the profit capabilities currently provided by the economic system in place.

The above-mentioned corporations, politicians, and ultra-wealthy citizens act to create and preserve ignorance with the concept of "bounded rationality" in mind.[22] Essentially, "bounded rationality" states that humans act rationally, but they can only make rational decisions based on what they know. So, when *true* information has the potential to negatively affect wealthy corporations and citizens, money from corporate America is used to coerce politicians and media figures to withhold this information or spread misinformation among the public.

In the political and media spheres, ignorance is often created via the strategic framing of a topic, discussion, or argument in favor of corporate interests. Elites do this via media outlets owned by the corporations in which they are heavily invested. By controlling what is reported in the media, corporate interests create widespread public ignorance. This ignorance enables politicians to act with little to no opposition as they structure (or eliminate) corporate regulations, enact pro-corporate legislation, and push a "conservative" ideology based largely on false information. If no one knows the harm you are causing to the nation or if people are under the guise that you are working in their best interest, then it follows that there will be no serious backlash against your actions. Oftentimes, you will even be met with support. By controlling the rhetoric of politicians and media figures, corporate interests very effectively shape public opinion and influence voters.

---

[22] Bounded rationality is the theory that humans are rational actors, and they can only make rational decisions based on the information available to them. (Stanford Encyclopedia of Philosophy). https://plato.stanford.edu/entries/bounded-rationality/.

The Creation Of Ignorance: The Elite's Control Of Politics And Media

The current corruption rampant in business and politics is dependent on the existence of the public's ignorance of the profitable, risk-amplifying arrangements between corporate America, politicians, and the media. The creation and control of the rhetoric seen, read, and heard on corporate owned media outlets enables corporations to continue acting in a self-serving manner. The bottom line is that when corporations flex their fiscal muscle to ensure that political, economic, and social issues are framed in such a way that: 1) withholds information, 2) spreads misinformation, 3) limits discourse, and 4) condemns opposition, the average American has little chance to make any truly informed decisions that would lead to the reduction of risks. Since the average American is kept ignorant of the facts about risks, as well as about how risks are being created, only very modest political, economic, and social progress can be achieved. Subsequently, large-scale risks are amplified to extremely dangerous levels.

What seems ironic is that all this ignorance has been created in the "Information Age". In this era, all the information regarding the true nature and consequences of risks is available on the internet. *So, why isn't everyone appropriately informed about risks?* Despite the abundance of information ubiquitously available, it becomes clear that the elite's ability to create ignorance among the masses is as strong as ever when we understand how powerful monied interests control the information that we see, read, and hear.

CORPORATE CONSOLIDATION OF THE MEDIA

One of the main ways corporate interests create ignorance is through controlling what is reported in the media. They achieve this control through corporate consolidation. In 1983, there were 50 companies who dominated the media industry.[23] Today, just six

---

[23] Shah, A. *Media Conglomerates, Mergers, Concentration of Ownership Author and Page information* (2004).

companies control 90 percent of the industry. They are known as "The Big Six".[24] Six large corporations own almost all the media outlets from which you get your news. They control what is reported and how it is reported. *How and why did this happen?*

When Ronald Reagan took presidential office, one of his top priorities was to deregulate as many potentially competitive industries as possible.[25] Reagan and many other conservatives espoused the idea that less government regulation of potentially competitive industries would equal more economic efficiency.[26] Reaganism preached supply-side, trickle-down economics and deregulation while denouncing the "evils" of big government. While Reagan was able to convince many Americans that his economic policies would help the nation, in reality, his policies did much more harm than good. [27] Long-term studies have shown us that Reaganomics does not lead to economic growth, income growth, wage growth, or job creation as it has promised.[28] Rather, it has had far-reaching negative social consequences. Journalist William Greider elaborated on the social consequences of Reaganomics in a 1982 *Rolling Stone* article:

---

[24] Lutz, A. *These 6 Corporations Control 90% Of The Media In America* (Business Insider, 2012). https://www.businessinsider.com/these-6-corporations-control-90-of-the-media-in-america-2012-6; Intellectual Bubblegum: Analysis Of Media Issues, Politics And Current Events. *The Big Six of Media. The six companies that control most of the media you watch* (Intellectual Bubblegum, 2019). http://www.intellectualbubblegum.com/the-big-six-of-media-the-six-companies-that-control-most-of-the-media-you-watch/.html.

[25] Wiley, R., Patrick, D., Tisch, L., Blake, J. Breger, M. *Broadcast Deregulation: The Reagan Years and Beyond* (American Bar Association, 1998). 346.

[26] Ibid.

[27] Newport, F., Jones, J., Saad, L. *Ronald Reagan from the People's Perspective: A Gallup Poll Review* (Gallup, 2004).

[28] Etebari, M. *Trickle-Down Economics: Four Reasons Why It Just Doesn't Work* (United for a Fair Economy, 2003). http://www.faireconomy.org/trickle_down_economics_four_reasons.

The Creation Of Ignorance: The Elite's Control Of Politics And Media

Reaganism's attack on big government sounded reasonable, even desirable, in the abstract, but its practical application had dreadful consequences: it revived class warfare in American politics. Rich versus poor. Business versus labor and consumers. Powerful interests versus the weak and unprotected. Old arguments about equity and intolerance, which many thought history had settled, were suddenly before us again.[29]

Perhaps, the most lasting significant feature of Reaganomics, at least in terms of the creation of ignorance, has been the steady weakening of Federal Communications Commission (FCC) regulations. From Reagan to Trump, every Republican president has appointed an FCC chair who has weakened regulations concerning media consolidation. Consequently, corporations have been endowed with seemingly limitless consolidating powers. And with an increase in their consolidating powers comes an increase in their power to create ignorance.

A primary reason corporations consolidate, or merge, is to increase revenue. From a monetary standpoint consolidation is logically sound; the more space (market share) you occupy within an industry, the more revenue you reign in. If six corporations own 90 percent of the media instead of 50 corporations, each of those six will reap a larger share of the revenue generated in the industry. In the pursuit of profit, these companies have become very conscious of what sells (ratings) and what makes for "good news".

During the 2016 presidential race, Donald Trump received $5 billion of free media—more than double any other candidate—because he was unique, entertaining (to some), shocking, and quite frankly, he was the embodiment of sensational journalism.[30] There

---

[29] Greider, W. *What Reagan Has Done to America* (Rolling Stone Magazine, 1982).

[30] Stewart, E. *Donald Trump Rode $5 Billion in Free Media to the White House* (The Street, 2016).

was a high demand for Trump among viewers. While the extensive coverage of Donald Trump and his campaign was lucrative to the media companies, it also had a significant impact on viewers. The media coverage of Donald Trump's campaign played a large role in his eventual victory. This example is a testament to the power media has on our democracy. Democracy is dependent on an informed electorate, yet, when the electorate is only exposed to and sufficiently informed about one candidate, public ignorance is created, and democracy is undermined.

Besides simply increasing profit from ratings, corporate consolidation also increases the power of corporations to influence the political world and preserve the economic policies that allow them to profit greatly. As conglomerates, these companies have substantial power to control the flow of information and shape public opinion. Using this power, corporate interests have used the rhetorical method of framing to spread a conservative ideology (among people of all economic backgrounds) that exalts and glorifies the rich. This ideology depicts the wealthy as benevolent economic actors, morally deserving of their wealth.[31] Conservative media outlets (which are owned by the above-mentioned corporate conglomerates) then broadcast this ideology to millions of viewers, readers, and listeners.

Since corporate interests control the media and push a conservative ideology while hiding the harmful effects of conservative policies from their viewers, conservative politicians are free to enact blatantly anti-democratic and pro-corporate policies and lose no support among their conservative constituents. Recall, for example, when Texas froze over in early 2021 (largely due to conservative political incompetence). During this crisis, conservative media outlets chose to report on Hasbro's decision to remove Mr. Potato Head's gender instead of reporting on the crisis in Texas. Conversative politicians are given free rein to serve the interests of the elites because they know their supporters will never even hear about their actions.

---

[31] Lakoff, G. *Don't Think of an Elephant* (2004). 19.

Corporations consolidate largely because they have a vested economic interest in keeping the American public ignorant about certain policy matters. As John Light, a writer for Billmoyers.com, explains, "When corporations control media coverage, they can keep the public in the dark about legislation that hurts the public interest but helps their bottom line."[32] In other words, consolidating in the media industry enables corporations to create ignorance among the public, which is essential to preserving the risk of economic and political policies that benefit the wealthiest corporations and people.

CORPORATE INVOLVEMENT IN POLITICS

Just as corporations leverage their monetary power to consolidate the media industry and create ignorance, they also use their money to directly influence elections, legislation, and public opinion. Money permeates the American political structure through campaign financing, lobbying, outside spending by special interest non-profit groups, and direct contributions from the ultra-wealthy.

The best example of monied interests corrupting democracy can be found in the ignorance creating actions of the fossil fuel industry. Over the last decade, the Republican Party has made efforts to oppose just about every policy regarding action on climate change. Many members of the Republican Party, including former President Trump, deny that climate change is even real; they call it a "hoax". This was not always the case, however. In 2008, Republican Presidential Candidate John McCain proposed action on climate change as a main part of his platform.[33]

---

[32] Light, J. *How Media Consolidation Threatens Democracy: 857 Channels (and Nothing On)* (BillMoyers.com, 2017).

[33] Davenport C., Lipton E. *How G.O.P. Leaders Came to View Climate Change as Fake Science* (New York Times, 2017).

So, how did the Republican Party flip from one that believed in climate change and proposed solutions to one that vehemently denies it and opposes all political action to halt the crisis? The influence of money, of course, was behind this drastic change. Big Oil believed that they would be destroyed financially if the government took action to limit the burning and mining of fossil fuels. So, these companies, as well as individual donors who have stake in the industry, started using their money to influence legislators.

In 2008, Charles and David Koch (better known as "the Koch brothers"), two billionaire oil tycoons and Republican donors, decided to fight the initiatives of climate activists by creating the "No Climate Tax" pledge. Politicians who signed the pledge agreed to abide by the following statement, "I will oppose any legislation relating to climate change that includes a net increase in government revenue."[34] In return for their loyalty, the Koch brothers promised to financially support the re-election campaigns of all signees. By 2010, they had already persuaded 165 members of Congress into signing the pledge. For all the Republicans who didn't sign the pledge or who spoke out in favor of climate change reform policies, the Koch brothers spent massive amounts of money to make sure they did not get re-elected. As you might imagine, their efforts have been very successful.[35]

The more moderate Republicans, who don't completely deny the existence of climate change, are faced with a paradoxical dilemma. They understand the serious threat climate change poses to our country and our planet, yet they are extremely hesitant to speak out or vote for any climate reform measures because they are afraid that big Republican donors will use their money to make sure they don't get re-elected.[36] For those Republicans, talking about or acting to mitigate climate change is political suicide.

The money peddled by members of the elite like the Koch Brothers does more than turn people into climate change deniers,

---

[34] Ibid.

[35] Ibid.

[36] Ibid.

however. This money also influences actual legislation. One way that fossil fuel giants influence policymaking is through making direct contributions to campaigns. As *The Guardian* reports, "BP donated $13m to a campaign, also supported by Chevron, that successfully stopped a carbon tax in Washington state—$1m of which was spent on social media ads, the research shows."[37]

Additionally, the fossil fuel industry has spent exorbitant amounts on lobbying, which allows them to write the legislation concerning climate change (something we will explore further later). In 2019, it was reported that the five largest companies in the fossil fuel industry spend upwards of $200 million annually in lobbying efforts.[38] While this seems like an enormous amount of money for companies to be spending, it's not. When considering that these lobbying efforts are essential to keep their businesses profitable, the money they spend on lobbying efforts to delay, limit, and prevent climate reform policies is a relatively small amount. Those millions of dollars are easily made back in the profits made possible by the lobbied-for-polices.

Corporate money is also strategically spent to directly shape the minds of the electorate through outside advertising efforts. In our fossil fuel industry example, that means that those same firms who spend large sums of money on lobbying efforts also spend substantial amounts of money on general outside advertising. To offer some context of just how much money we are talking about, in the run-up to the 2018 congressional mid-terms, global oil firms spent $2 million on Facebook and Instagram ads in efforts to influence voters of the benefits of fossil fuel production.[39]

Meanwhile, as these Big Oil companies flex their muscle to block climate reform policies, the way they act publicly hypocritically

---

[37] Ibid.

[38] Laville, S. *Top oil firms spending millions lobbying to block climate change policies, says report* (The Guardian, 2019). https://www.theguardian.com/business/2019/mar/22/top-oil-firms-spending-millions-lobbying-to-block-climate-change-policies-says-report .

[39] Ibid.

suggests they are committed to halting climate change. Edward Collins, a researcher for Influence Map, elaborates on this issue, writing, "They publicly support climate action while lobbying against binding policy. They advocate low-carbon solutions, but such investments are dwarfed by spending on expanding their fossil fuel business."[40] Ignorance is thus created; the public comes to believe companies like Exxon Mobil are working to stop climate change, but, in reality, they are doing everything in their power to block any and all climate-change-halting regulations.

The influence of money has essentially turned the dismissal of clear evidence of climate change into a Republican value.[41] Today, not only do Republican politicians dismiss the threat of climate change, but a large proportion of Republican voters in the country do too. In a poll conducted by the Pew Research Center in 2019, only 27 percent of registered Republican voters said that they view climate change as a serious threat.[42] This is where we see the real danger of the enormous influence money has in politics. In just over a decade, we have gone from a country where both Republicans and Democrats believed in the existence of climate change to a country where believing in climate change is an overwhelmingly partisan issue. Money has turned the climate change debate away from creating solutions. Now, the debate is reduced to whether climate change even exists.

The money spent on lobbying, social media ads, direct contributions, and campaign finance unquestionably contributes to the creation of public ignorance. Politicians "sell-out" to the fossil fuel industry, agreeing to spread the false narrative that climate change is a hoax, or at least not a serious problem. By hiding behind a façade of environmental awareness, claiming to be committed to tackling climate change, Big Oil companies distract the public

---

[40] Ibid.

[41] Ibid.

[42] *Climate Change and Russia Are Partisan Flashpoints in Public's Views of Global Threats* (Pew Research Center, 2019). https://www.people-press.org/2019/07/30/climate-change-and-russia-are-partisan-flashpoints-in-publics-views-of-global-threats/.

of their nefarious actions of: 1) lobbying, 2) outside spending on political ads, and 3) direct campaign contributions. Inevitably, many voters become ignorant of the facts and fall victim to misleading rhetoric.

The example of how money permeates politics in the fossil fuel industry is just that–an example. Ignorance creation via media and political outlets occurs for every risk we will discuss in this book. Money has enormous influence in the political world, and this influence creates public ignorance that leads to the delaying and blocking of action to mitigate the risks we face today.

THE POWER ELITE

To review so far, corporations consolidate to increase their profits and to shape what is reported in the media. The control they establish in the media sphere allows them to create public ignorance, which is essential to the preservation and enhancement of the economic and political systems in place that benefit the wealthiest citizens and corporations. Shielded from public exposure by the created public ignorance, corporations, non-profit organizations, and ultra-wealthy citizens spend large sums of money to influence legislation, elections, and public opinion. Their money is used to create more ignorance about the facts of risks and to create, preserve, and lobby for legislation that increases their profits by exacerbating risks. Yet, to fully understand why ignorance is created, we must understand more about *who* holds power and how they create this ignorance.

To be blunt, even though they are a small group, ultra-wealthy Americans and large corporations have the most power in the United States by a landslide.[43] Without the presence of one big church, an overwhelmingly big government, or a powerful military that can overthrow the government, economic "powerhouse" families have

---

[43] Domhoff, G. *The Class-Domination Theory of Power* (2012) https://whorulesamerica.ucsc.edu/power/class_domination.html.

ruled this country with virtually no opposition since its origin.[44] Yes, I said *ruled*.

Now, you may be confused. *Don't we live in a democracy? How can a small wealthy class be "ruling" the country if we have elections, the freedom of speech and assembly, and the opportunity for social mobility?* Ironically, it is precisely because of the presence of democratic institutions that the wealthy have been able to accumulate and maintain such enormous power. The existence of democratic institutions leads the public to generally believe that the system is fair and that everyone has roughly an equal chance of being successful. In reality, the wealthy have created political and economic structures that overwhelming benefit them, they have weakened the working class by dividing its members against each other, and they have controlled the flow of information, thereby creating the ignorance necessary to preserve their positions at the top and amplify the risks from which they profit.

Within the wealthy population in America, there is a smaller, more powerful group that sociologist G. William Domhoff refers to as the "power elite" (a term originally coined by C Wright Mills). According to Domhoff, this group "consists of active-working members of the upper class and high-level employees in profit and nonprofit institutions controlled by members of the upper class through stock ownership, financial support, or involvement on the board of directors".[45] In other words, the power elite consists of the people who run the most powerful organizations and corporations in the nation and whose wealth and power afford them tremendous authority in politics. The power elite influence politics through lobbying, policymaking, and their enormous influence in candidate selection.

The political spending by the power elite has a significant impact on political representation, which further inhibits action on the issues the public wants addressed. The corrosive power of money is

---
[44] Ibid.
[45] Ibid.

so instrumental in the political world that 90 percent of Americans have virtually no say on whether policies are implemented.

The system basically works like this: if 0 percent of Americans at the bottom 90 percent of the income ladder support a specific policy, it has a 30 percent chance of being passed. Conversely, if 100 percent of Americans at the bottom 90 percent of the income ladder support a policy, that policy still only has a 30 percent chance of being passed.[46] Meanwhile, when there is 0 percent support for a policy among Americans at the top 10 percent of the income ladder, this demographic can completely block legislation, regardless of how much support there is for the policy among the other 90 percent. And when there is 100 percent support for a policy among the economic top 10 percent, the chance that the policy becomes law is nearly 60 percent.[47]

This means that the economic top 10 percent has insurmountably more influence than any other demographic. Unsurprisingly, statistics show that, in relative terms, the top 5 percent have more power than the top 10 percent and the top 1 percent more power than the top 5 percent. That is not how a democratic republic is intended to function. Yet, by creating an ignorant public, the ultra-wealthy have had little opposition in establishing this political system. Thus, they have created a system that is rigged to favor them at the expense of others. The involvement of money in politics acts to practically silence the voices of average Americans and amplify the voices of the super wealthy; it undermines our democracy and enables the continued amplification of risks.[48]

Even more significantly, elite non-profit organizations, like the American Legislative Exchange Council (ALEC), help the power elite realize their political interests through lobbying. ALEC partners

---

[46] Bartels, L. *"Rich People Rule!"* (Washington Post, 2014). https://www.washingtonpost.com/news/monkey-cage/wp/2014/04/08/rich-people-rule/?arc404=true; *Corruption Is Legal in America*. https://youtu.be/5tu32CCA_Ig.

[47] Ibid.

[48] *Corruption Is Legal in America* https://youtu.be/5tu32CCA_Ig.

with powerful corporations to write regulations and laws to benefit those corporations. Those laws are then marketed to lawmakers who are persuaded by ALEC lobbyists into passing them. ALEC, *not politicians*, writes many of our laws. These laws benefit large corporations and ultra-wealthy Americans at the expense of the public.

Doug Clopp, Deputy Director of Programs at Common Cause, illustrates just how influential ALEC is in writing our laws:

> If it's voter ID, it's ALEC. If it's anti-immigration bills written hand-in-glove with private prison corporations, it's ALEC. If it's working with the N.R.A. on 'Shoot to Kill' laws, it's ALEC. When you start peeling back state efforts to opt out of the regional greenhouse gas initiative, it's ALEC.[49]

Essentially, a tiny proportion of the population directly creates (writes) legislation without even being elected to a congressional legislative seat.

The public, of course, is kept in the dark about the role of ALEC in policymaking. None of ALEC's action are covered by mainstream news outlets. *Why would it be?* The airwaves, news shows, internet sites, newspapers, and radio stations that broadcast the ideological discussions and information we are bombarded with are owned by the power elite, who, let's not forget, fully intend to keep us ignorant of any facts, figures, or discussions that may contradict their worldview—or, more accurately, their monetary and power interests. Covering truthful, important information, such as the consequences of the legislation being written by ALEC, would endanger profits for this elite group, so it isn't covered.

The power elite also dominate candidate selection, largely through the financing of political election campaigns. The wealthy have always dominated this aspect of the political world, but their

---

[49] Scola, N. *Exposing ALEC: How Conservative-Backed State Laws Are All Connected* (The Atlantic, 2012). https://www.alecexposed.org/wiki/ALEC_Exposed.

power to do so has increased substantially over the past decade. After the monumental ruling of the *Citizens United* Supreme Court case in 2010, it was determined that corporations and other special interest groups could not be restricted in the amount of money they spend on election campaign finance.

The court ruled that limiting their spending would be an infringement of their First Amendment right to free speech.[50] Daniel Weiner, at The Brennan Center for Justice, has pointed out just how damaging this Supreme Court decision has been for our democracy. He says, "The decision has helped reinforce the growing sense that our democracy primarily serves the interests of the wealthy few, and that democratic participation for the vast majority of citizens is of relatively little value."[51] This Supreme Court decision has given corporations the ability to spend so much money that they can effectively shape public opinion and distract voters from the corruption taking place. By creating this ignorance, our "pay-to-play" democracy remains intact.

Special interest groups and organizations also influence politics indirectly. For example, let's look at the political ads produced by the NRA. While the NRA spends less on directly funding political campaigns compared to other corporations, they do spend an exorbitant amount on TV and online ads. The amount they spend on ads is ten times greater than what they spend on direct contributions to political campaigns.[52] These ads, of course, are intended to persuade people to support their agenda. The NRA also uses their money to tarnish political campaigns of those who support gun control, which dissuades many politicians from including gun control

---

[50] Lau, T. *Citizens United Explained* (Brennan Center for Justice, 2019). https://www.brennancenter.org/our-work/research-reports/citizens-united-explained.

[51] Weiner, D. *Citizens United Five Years Later* (Brennan Center for Justice, 2015).

[52] Hill, C. *The real reason the NRA's money matters in elections Direct contributions to candidates aren't the only way to wield clout* (Vox, 2018). https://www.vox.com/the-big-idea/2018/2/27/17051560/money-nra-guns-contributions-donations-parkland-march

in their platform.[53] Outside spending by special interest groups is a way that these organizations can push a political agenda while simultaneously claiming their money does not influence those who support their mission.

Elite citizens, corporations, and non-profit organizations accumulate and wield so much power in the political world because of the existence of public ignorance. This is primarily because an ignorant public can be easily divided and manipulated to act against their own self-interests.[54] Since the country's origin, the wealthiest Americans have methodically found ways to weaken the working class. From classifications of free versus slave, to White versus Black, to skilled worker versus unskilled worker, the public has always been divided amongst itself. Consequently, a strong united middle and working class that can challenge the power of the wealthy has never been established.

One significant way in which the wealthy stay in power today is by weakening the power of unions. Domhoff elaborates on the difference in union power between the United States and other developed nations:

> There are many democratic countries where the working class—defined as all those white-collar and blue-collar workers who earn a salary or a wage—has more power than it does in the United States. This power is achieved primarily through labor unions and political parties. It is

---

[53] Ibid.

[54] The public is often so heavily influenced by the rhetorical framing they are constantly exposed to, that they come to believe they are acting according to their self-interest even when others would suggest they are not. For example, when a low-income registered Republican votes to preserve the system that allows billionaires to pay less taxes than themselves, one may claim they are voting against their self-interest. However, that voter's worldview (which has been formed by conservative frames) may suggest that this system is fair because billionaires "deserve" to pay less in taxes. And if they vote in line with their world view, are they really voting against their self-interest?

reflected in more egalitarian wealth and income distributions, a more equitable tax structure, better public health services, subsidized housing, and higher old-age and unemployment benefits.[55]

Compared to other wealthy nations, workers in the United States have significantly less union power. In other countries, labor unions have members on the board of directors at companies, and therefore they have more of a say in determining wages and working conditions within those companies. Meanwhile, in the United States, the working class has always struggled to unite in their fight for higher wages and better social benefits largely because it is so divided along racial, ethnic, and gender lines. Our country faces the consequences of this inability of the working class to unite. Of course, the risk of weak unions is a product of the creation of ignorance as well.

Ignorance is, and always has been, the key to the generational reproduction of the elite class in the U.S. By keeping Americans in the dark about their methods to create legislation, frame arguments, and divide the working class, the power elite go unchallenged and maintain their power and wealth. The political and economic systems that benefit them stay in place, and the risks for us all are amplified as a result.

HOW CONSERVATIVE FRAMING CREATES IGNORANCE

Now that we understand who has power, how and why they have that power, and why they are motivated use their power to create ignorance, let's further explore how exactly ignorance is created. To influence the American populace, conservatives have developed methods to rhetorically frame policy issues in ways that serve the monetary and power interests of the elite.

---

[55] Domhoff, 2012.

For example, when George W. Bush became president, he, along with the rest of the Republican Party, began to use the phrase "tax relief" to frame the national discourse regarding tax cuts. In his book *Don't Think of an Elephant*, Professor of Cognitive Science and Linguistics George Lakoff explains how this subtle method of framing creates ignorance around the issue. He writes, "When the word *tax* is added to *relief* the result is a metaphor: Taxation is an affliction. And the person who takes it away is a hero, and anyone who tries to stop him is a bad guy. This is a frame."[56] By framing taxes in this light, the public is manipulated into dismissing the positives that come from paying taxes. By only thinking of taxes in a negative manner, the public becomes ignorant of what taxes really are and what their purpose is. Taxes are less of an affliction and more of an investment in the country and its people.[57] After all, taxes are the source of the funding for public education, public infrastructure, the military, and countless other services that our society depends on (not to mention that taxes pay the salaries of 24 million public servants in our nation).[58]

The "tax relief frame" was first pushed by conservative media, and "tax relief" was catchy. Before long *all* media outlets, whether liberal or conservative, reproduced this frame and espoused a negative view of taxation. The liberal media's inadvertent reproduction of the frame "tax relief" constantly reasserted in everyone's subconscious the idea that tax cuts for the wealthy were good for everyone. Even when the liberal media was criticizing tax cuts and their consequences, by calling it tax relief, the metaphor of taxes being an affliction was triggered in the minds of their viewers. Despite conservative politicians' claim that tax cuts grow the economy and incentivize business investments, tax cuts for the

---

[56] Lakoff, 2004. 4.

[57] Ibid.

[58] Hill, F. *Public service and the federal government* (Brookings, 2020). https://www.brookings.edu/policy2020/votervital/public-service-and-the-federal-government/.

wealthy are not good for the nation as a whole.[59] Tax cuts benefit the wealthy at the expense of the majority of Americans. They save wealthy corporations and citizens money while they deplete the federal budget of funds that could be used to launch and maintain progressive social programs.[60]

Similarly, framing also occurs in the naming of legislation. For example, by assigning positive names to environmental legislation, i.e., the Clear Skies Act, conservative politicians were able to deceive the public into thinking this Act "clears the skies" of pollution.[61] In truth, the Clear Skies Act was a contradiction; it led to increased pollution.[62] But because framing works to keep the public generally ignorant of facts like these, conservative politicians receive no strong electoral pushback and very little criticism for their deceptive framing mechanisms.

Framing a narrative, an issue, and/or legislation is often conducted through strategic word choice, as seen in the examples above. However, framing can also be conducted through visual rhetoric, such as videos and images. A fitting example of this can be found in the Reagan Administration's framing of the crack cocaine epidemic as they attempted to garner support for the War on Drugs. As you will read in Chapter 4, the War on Drugs was launched at a time when drug use was declining.[63] The crack cocaine crisis did not become a "crisis" until a few years after the official beginning of the War on Drugs.[64] Given these facts, the Reagan administration knew that framing this issue would be necessary to garner support for the War on Drugs. Therefore, Reagan's White House hired staff to publicize the new crack cocaine crisis in the belief that this would

---

[59] Thompson, D. *The GOP Tax Cuts Didn't Work* (The Atlantic, 2019).
[60] Lakoff, 2004. 29.
[61] Ibid. 23.
[62] Ibid. 23.
[63] Beckett, K., Sasson, T. *The Politics of Injustice: Crime and Punishment in America* (Thousand Oaks, CA: Sage Publications, 2004). 163.
[64] Alexander, M. *The New Jim Crow: Colorblindness in the Age of Mass Incarceration.* (The New Press, 2012). 5.

build both public and congressional support for the War. Michelle Alexander, author of *The New Jim Crow*, elaborates:

> The Reagan administration hired staff to publicize the emergence of crack cocaine in 1985 as part of a strategic effort to build public and legislative support for the war. The media campaign was an extraordinary success. Almost overnight, the media was saturated with images of black "crack whores", "crack dealers", and "crack babies"—images that seemed to confirm the worst negative racial stereotypes about impoverished inner-city residents. The media bonanza surrounding the "new demon drug" helped to catapult the War on Drugs from an ambitious federal policy to an actual war. [65]

These examples show us how risks are created and amplified through the rhetorical manipulation of a public who doesn't know or completely understand the facts.

Framing is most destructive when facts and evidence are withheld from the public. In his book *Talking to Strangers*, Malcolm Gladwell explains that as humans, our evolution has equipped us with a "default to truth" trait. This means we naturally assume, more often than not, that people don't lie; we believe that people are almost always telling us the truth.[66] So, when we are presented with information about an issue that we know little about, we tend to believe that information is accurate.

We are especially eager to default to truth when the speaker is someone we like, or the speaker is saying something we want to be true. Similarly, we are extra trustworthy when we receive information from a speaker of authority. In other words, the coining of the term "tax relief" by President Bush was effective precisely

---

[65] Ibid.

[66] Gladwell, M. *Talking to Strangers: What We Should Know About The People We Don't Know* (Little Brown, 2019). 73.

because he was the president. If, instead, John/Jane Doe created and used that phrase, it would have been far less impactful.[67]

These attributes of human nature, unfortunately, leave us especially vulnerable to manipulation through framing. Since we trust strangers and tend to believe that people in positions of authority always tell us the truth, particularly those authority figures for whom we have an affinity, we often do not bother to read below the headlines or listen past the soundbites; we feel it is unnecessary to search for the truth about specific issues ourselves. We accept our own ignorance and expect and trust that our politicians and the media will tell us what we need to know.

Politicians and corporations, however, often betray our trust and take advantage of our default to truth disposition. By framing discourse, they keep us ignorant about political issues. Then, by capitalizing on our default to truth disposition, they weaponize this ignorance to enrich and empower themselves. Let's look more closely at how this is done within the media, and why it's dangerous.

HOW CONSERVATIVE MEDIA CREATES IGNORANCE

Conservative media outlets, most notably *Fox News*, take the ignorance creating and weaponizing capabilities of rhetorical framing a step further. They do this by promoting conservative ideology through opinion talk shows that they label as news shows.

Fox News's tagline claim of being "Fair and Balanced" is misleading and their claim that they are primarily a news network is false.[68] Since *Fox* unapologetically picks an ideological side, they can present information to viewers in a "good versus evil" format. This format coaxes viewers into believing that a conservative

---

[67] Fish, S. *Winning Arguments: What Works and Doesn't Work in Politics, The Bedroom, The Courtroom, and The Classroom* (Harper, 2016).

[68] Jones, J. *Fox News and the Performance of Ideology* (Cinema Journal, 2016).

ideology is moral whereas a liberal ideology is evil and threatens to destroy the moral society that conservatives are trying to protect.[69]

The abundance of conflict in their shows makes viewers feel as if they must take a side in this moral fight against the liberal threats to society. As a result, viewers become committed to the brand that is *Fox News*. Researcher Jefferey Jones explains that many people commit to *Fox News* and watch diligently because, "*Fox* thus emerges as the place where viewers can trust that such threats will be exposed and fought against."[70] To exacerbate matters, former President Trump's explicit labeling of liberal-leaning news networks as "fake news" along with his consistent endorsement of *Fox News* (and at the end of his presidency, even further right leaning networks like *Newsmax* and *OANN*) reaffirmed the propagandized beliefs held by many viewers of conservative media.

Perhaps the most significant (and startling) consequence of conservative framing in media and political rhetoric is the fact that the concept of truth has essentially become meaningless.[71] *Fox News* has created a platform where their talk show hosts are able to "produce reality" through their language. This is known as performativity.[72] Essentially, *Fox News* has been able to convince their viewers to believe in false information by branding themselves as news while misleadingly or outright falsely rhetorically framing the issues they discuss. Jones explains how this is possible:

> Performativity points our attention to political speech not for its referentiality or relationship to truth or falsehood but for its potential to bring reality into being by the act of being spoken… [regarding] the success of such utterances in establishing reality, context is everything. And this is where the genre of news is vitally important in making such

---

[69] Ibid.
[70] Ibid.
[71] Ibid.
[72] Ibid.

statements real, believable, accessible, knowable, provable, and repeatable. Without news, such statements are little more than opinions. Within news, they become "facts".[73]

Further, various findings support the claims that conservative media influences the rhetoric of politicians and the voting tendencies of the electorate. A study for the Center of Law and Economics found that conservative media and political rhetoric are intimately connected, reporting:

> Our analysis shows that in response to exogenous variation in viewership, the language of Congressmen is more likely to echo the language of *Fox News*. The effect is driven by framing of topics and consists of durable changes in rhetorical style.[74]

Moreover, a study conducted by the Pew Research Center found that *Fox* has much greater influence on political rhetoric than *CNN* or *MSNBC*. They also found that congressmen and congresswomen utilize more *Fox News* talking points in districts where *Fox* ratings are higher.[75]

We already know that corporations consolidated the media industry and control what is reported and how it is rhetorically framed on media outlets. What these studies show us is that the rhetoric used on those media outlets has a direct influence on the rhetoric used by politicians who are being influenced by those same corporations.

We know that the misleading rhetoric broadcasted on *Fox* has created public ignorance because it been found to have significant

---

[73] Ibid.

[74] Ash, E., Labzina, E. *Does Politicized Media Distort Political Discourse? Evidence from U.S. Cable News Channels* (Center of Law and Economics, 2009-11). (2009-11, Center of Law and Economics).

[75] Ibid.

impacts on public opinion. In April 2020, the Pew Research Center found that among *Fox* viewers, 63 percent of adults believed that President Trump was doing an excellent job in his handling of the COVID-19 pandemic.[76] This statistic is, of course, surprising, considering the state of the nation at this time. Not only was COVID-19 still ravaging the country, but the unemployment rate jumped to a level not seen since the Great Depression and millions of households that were financially stable pre-pandemic found themselves with not enough food or behind on their rent payments.[77] Additionally, only 23 percent of all Americans and only 47 percent of non-*Fox*-viewing Republicans believed President Trump was doing an excellent job handling the pandemic at that time.[78] Fox News viewers, however, were convinced to believe otherwise.

Further, studies have shown that the voting tendencies of Americans are heavily influenced by watching *Fox News*. A study by Emory University political scientist Gregory Martin and Stanford economist Ali Yurukoglu found that watching *Fox News* "increases the probability of voting Republican in presidential elections".[79] They found that the use of manipulative rhetorical framing on *Fox News* has a monumental impact on the voting tendencies of the electorate. Journalist for *Vox*, Matthew Yglesias summarizes their report:

> Specifically, by exploiting semi-random variation in *Fox* viewership driven by changes in the assignment of channel numbers, they find that if *Fox* News hadn't existed, the Republican presidential candidate's share of the two-party vote would have been 3.59 points lower in 2004 and 6.34

---

[76] Holcomb, J. *5 facts about Fox News* (Pew Research Center, 2020).

[77] *Tracking the COVID-19 Recession's Effects on Food, Housing, and Employment Hardships* (Center on Budget and Policy Prioirties, 2021). https://www.cbpp.org/research/poverty-and-inequality/tracking-the-covid-19-recessions-effects-on-food-housing-and.

[78] Ibid.

[79] Martin, G. Yurukoglu, A. *Bias in Cable News: Persuasion and Polarization* (American Economic Review, 2017).

points lower in 2008. Without *Fox*, in other words, the GOP's only popular vote win since the 1980s would have been reversed and the 2008 election would have been an extinction-level landslide.[80]

It may strike you as unsurprising and unimportant that a right-wing news network influences the way one votes. Yet, we should keep in mind that news networks are supposed to simply provide you with news, not influence the way you vote. Furthermore, left-wing news networks do not have a remotely similar effect on voting tendencies as *Fox News* does; this is not an issue where both sides are to blame.[81]

What this evidence shows us is that *Fox News* is not primarily a news network, but it is certainly a propaganda network. Now you might be thinking, *"Woah, woah, woah, I understand how* Fox News *presents misleading information, but is it really a propaganda network?"* The evidence shows us, *yes, it really is*. Let's look at what exactly propaganda is. The Government Accountability Office (GAO) legally categorizes propaganda into the following three types of "inappropriate activity":

1) "self-aggrandizement", 2) "purely partisan purposes", and 3) "covert propaganda". Self-aggrandizement (also known as "puffery") refers to an agency's efforts to overstate its own importance. Purely partisan purposes include efforts solely dedicated to the electoral success of a political party or candidates. Covert propaganda refers to media materials prepared by a government agency and then disseminated by a non-government outlet with the source undisclosed.[82]

---

[80] Yglesias, M. *Fox News's propaganda isn't just unethical—research shows it's enormously influential* (Vox, 2019).

[81] Matthews, D. *A Stunning New Study Shows That Fox News is More Powerful Than We Ever Imagined* (Vox, 2017).

[82] *Publicity or Propaganda* (Cornell Legal Information Institute) https://www.law.cornell.edu/wex/publicity_or_propaganda.

For decades, but certainly under President Trump, many segments on *Fox News* fit this description of propaganda. Tom Rosenstiel, a media scholar and executive director at the American Press Institute, points out that the extremely close relationships that existed between President Trump and the hosts of *Fox News* shows like *Fox and Friends* and *Hannity* are not simply based on ideological similarities, rather they were signs of an active working relationship. Rosenstiel explains how these close working relationships have turned *Fox News* from partisan to propaganda:

> The relationship goes far beyond ideological affinity, to a kind of collaboration that has tilted the scales from *Fox News* doing opinion journalism with grounding in the principles of news to it being an extension of the administration whose purpose, while always commercial, has become focused on supporting the president—a political outcome—rather than covering him. That is when you tilt from journalism to becoming propaganda: when your goal is no longer informing the public but promoting a particular political outcome.[83]

Vast amounts of evidence have been gathered to prove that *Fox News* indoctrinates its viewers with propaganda.

The actions of politicians do not "drive" the media. The media—which is owned by the power elite—drives the actions of politicians. The far-reaching influence of the rhetorical frames produced in conservative news media can be directly linked to the rhetoric of politicians and the voting tendencies of the electorate. In other words, corporate interests have influenced public discourse by controlling what is reported on conservative media and what is espoused by conservative politicians.

Their reach in these spheres has enabled them to vicariously guide public opinion into alignment with conservative ideology.

---

[83] Illing, S. *How Fox News evolved into a propaganda operation: A media scholar on the dangerous evolution of Fox News* (Vox, 2019).

Subsequently, millions of people vote to preserve an economic and political structure that favors the wealthy. Only by understanding these dynamics and mechanisms of ignorance creation can we comprehend the continued election of conservative politicians, whose policies, as we will discuss throughout this book, serve the interests of no one but the wealthy. Because when you think about, there is no logical reason for why over 70 million people should consistently be voting for politicians whose policies favor no more than 33 million (the top 10 percent).

The creation of ignorance by wealthy citizens, corporations, politicians, and non-profit organizations has created risks that have had devastating consequences. These risks, like those of climate change, are amplified exponentially because corporations create the ignorance that leads to inaction. Similarly, all the risks we will cover in this book have been created and amplified thanks to the existence of an ignorant public that is susceptible to manipulation.

SOLUTIONS

Money's influence in politics has been corrupting our society for what seems like forever. Since the dawn of civilization, people with wealth have risen to positions of authority and wielded their power to create public ignorance, influence political systems, and further enrich themselves and others in powerful social positions. *So, what can we do? How can we finally put our foot down and put an end to the historical constant of the corrupting influence of money?*

First and foremost, to start purging our politics and media of monetary influence, we must become more aware of this problem in the first place. Just like every risk we face, it is imperative for society to clearly understand this problem of ignorance creation before we try to fix it. Trying to solve an issue you don't understand is always an unsuccessful strategy. Increasing public awareness regarding the influence money has on politics is a necessary step to creating widespread support for new legislation that would outlaw this legalized corruption. We must acknowledge and reverse the ignorance of how ignorance is created.

THE ANTI-CORRUPTION ACT

The next step after raising awareness is to create and enact new progressive legislation. Fortunately, a bill that would "stop political bribery, end secret money, and fix our broken elections", has already been drafted. As you might deduce after reading this chapter, the reason almost nobody knows about this bill, or bills like it, is that it doesn't receive mainstream media attention. The drafted bill is called the American Anti-Corruption Act, and, if passed, it would rid the influence of money from our politics and empower voters, restoring their political representation.[84] The Act would end gerrymandering, forbid politicians from taking money from lobbyists, prevent politicians from fundraising during working hours, and enact automatic voter registration, just to name a few of its features. The implementation of this Act is crucial to the mission to end corruption in politics and to restore a fair democracy. As you will see when I mention this Act in later chapters, the Anti-Corruption Act just might be the single most important piece of legislation mentioned throughout this book.

TIGHTENING FCC REGULATIONS

We also must tighten the FCC regulations that have been loosened under Republican administrations and not sufficiently strengthened under Democrat administrations. When running for president in 2007, Barack Obama explained why this is so important to our democracy and what we need to do:

---

[84] The Anti-Corruption Act. https://anticorruptionact.org.

I believe the FCC media-ownership rules remain necessary and are critical to the public interest… We should be doing more to encourage diversity in ownership in broadcast media, promote the development of new media outlets and the expression of diverse viewpoints", as well as provide "greater clarity" of broadcasters' public-interest obligations.[85]

To stop the creation of ignorance via the media, we must act to tighten FCC regulations. When corporations consolidate, weak FCC rules and regulations enable them to gain overarching control over what is reported in the media. Logically, the way to reverse the ignorance corporate interests are creating via the media is to bolster these regulations.

Additionally, we must increase funding for public broadcasting. Public broadcasting is a great solution to improving the quality of our news because it is inherently not subject to private monetary interests. Public broadcasting will lead to truthful reporting on important issues, a crucial quality that cannot be overlooked.

A RETURN TO TRUTHFUL NEWS

Next, it is time to stop tolerating what Senator Al Franken dubbed the "lies and liars of *Fox News"*, and other ignorance creating media outlets. We must not sit idle and continue to stomach the blatant lies that spew from the panelists on these talk shows. *Fox News* has been called a propaganda network by former *Fox News* analysts, scholars, and even President Obama because, well, it *is* a propaganda network! We must use the evidence that has been gathered to prove that *Fox News* is a propaganda network, and we must then move to radically reform and regulate all media networks that intentionally create ignorance.

---

[85] Eggerton, J. *Obama Calls for Tighter FCC Regulation of Broadcasting* (Broadcasting and Cable, 2007).

Those who diligently tune into media like *Fox News* are not at blame. Rather, those who use their wealth and influence to weaken FCC regulations and spread misinformation via the media are at fault. Thus, our solutions to this problem should not be focused on strengthening the public's resistance to accepting falsehoods as truth, but instead on preventing the elite from creating ignorance in the first place. When we examine how much damage *Fox News* and other untruthful news outlets have done to our country, it becomes clear just how dangerous it is to allow these networks to freely continue their mission to create ignorance and manipulate the public. There is no place for misinformation media in our democracy.

STRUCTURAL DEMOCRATIC REFORMS

There are also various structural reforms that must be made to our political system to create a fair democracy. From Supreme Court reform to the elimination of the filibuster, our democracy has a lot of improving to do. Luckily, some Democrats have developed plans and drafted legislation to achieve some of these reforms, most notably, the For the People Act. Debates about how to best reform our democracy must become mainstream. Fixing and continuously strengthening our democracy is an extremely important step towards achieving all the other risk-reducing goals we want to accomplish.

EDUCATION REFORMS

Finally, we need to improve our education system and teach and have open discussion with students about the history of ignorance creation and the role of money in politics and media throughout our country's history. Currently, students are not taught the history and consequences of the weakening of FCC regulations, the far-reaching influence of the power elite, and the rhetorical performativity utilized on networks like *Fox News*, but they should be. Our history has been influenced greatly by the ignorance created by the wealthy—any history course that doesn't cover this material is incomplete.

IN SUM

Corporate interests create ignorance, which in turn creates and amplifies risks that benefit the wealthy. The involvement of money in politics and media is the main inhibitor of change and the main contributor to unwanted, corrupt legislation. The power elite have gained enormous power and influence over political rhetoric, news media, and public policy. They have been able to use this power to their benefit. As a result, risks persist and are amplified.

We can fix this broken system. We can halt the rapid creation of ignorance that amplifies risks facing our country. We know what we must do. The solutions have been developed. We must reverse the ignorance of the influence of money in politics and media. We must implement the Anti-Corruption Act to prevent future monetary corruption. We must tighten FCC regulations, enact structural governmental reforms, and improve our education system. Perhaps most importantly, we must act to unite the public by appealing to the "good" in all of us, instead of condemning the "evil" in those who do not share the same worldview.

It is important that we do not seek to create division by appealing to latent prejudices and implicit biases, something that has become all too common in our politics and in the rhetoric of our media. Instead of exposing what makes us different, we must point to what makes us similar. Instead of a "cancel culture", we should promote a "forgiveness culture". Instead of tearing each other down, we must lift each other up. We do this by electing leaders who inspire Americans to think of how they can help others, not just themselves. And we do this by holding our politicians responsible for acting in a way that serves the interests of the public, not the pockets of the wealthy. It's time to restore honesty and integrity in our country's politics and media. It's time to put an end to the creation of ignorance by the elite that harms us all tremendously.

2

The Risk Of Climate Change

The climate crisis has already been solved. We already have all the facts and solutions. All we have to do is to wake up and change.
– Greta Thunberg

Our species best understands the world yet has the worst relationship with it.
– Carl Safina

The most far-reaching risk that faces society today is that of climate change. Before we dive into how ignorance amplifies this risk of climate change, I want to start off by asserting that climate change is *undoubtedly* occurring. The science is clear, and the consensus among the scientific community is strong; the world is getting warmer. NASA, 18 different American scientific societies, and other international and national organizations have provided copious amounts of data and research to back up their position that climate change is real and being caused by human activity.[86] Thankfully, according to polls conducted by the Pew Research Center, the majority of Americans believe that human activity is contributing to climate change, with only about 20 percent of people (mostly very conservative Republicans) believing that climate change is not caused by humans.[87] Of course, 20 percent of people not believing in scientific evidence is problematic, but the point is that climate deniers are in the minority.

Despite this overwhelming belief in the existence of climate change, the question of what we should do about it has remained a heated political issue. Undeterred by most Americans believing in climate change, there were 130 congressmen and congresswomen who had doubted or flat out denied the existence of climate change in 2019; 129 of them are Republicans.[88] This is where we see ignorance creating and amplifying a risk.

Before we get deeper into this chapter it is important to clarify what I mean by, "the risk of climate change". Remember, our definition of "risk" is any social, economic, environmental, or biological condition or institution that produces harm to a large group of relatively powerless people but reaps enormous benefits for a small group of powerful people. As you will read, intentionally created ignorance causes the public to doubt the efficacy of climate reform policies. This leads to the public's reluctancy to support said policies, and this enables corporations with large carbon footprints to continue profiting immensely as they endanger our existence, as well as the existence of many other life forms, on this planet. Thus, the public ignorance that justifies politicians' skepticism and hesitation to enact climate reform policies, creates the "risk of climate change". The risk of climate change can be seen in the

---

[86] *Scientific Consensus: Earth's Climate is Warming* (NASA). https://climate.nasa.gov/scientific-consensus/.

[87] Funk, C., Hefferon, M. *U.S. Public Views on Climate and Energy* (Pew Research Center, 2019).

[88] Cranley, E. *These are the 130 current members of Congress who have doubted or denied climate change* (Business Insider, 2019).

increased frequency of severe weather patterns, the rise in sea levels and ocean temperature, and the wildfires that are running rampant while the elite are benefitting from the international and domestic environmental policies that generate their tremendous profits.

Last chapter, I highlighted the issue of climate change to illustrate how the involvement of money in politics creates perverse incentives for legislators to support the interests of big corporations over the interests of the people (or in this case, the planet). Specifically, I mentioned the No Climate Tax pledge that has been signed by hundreds of politicians (who were almost exclusively Republicans). By signing the pledge these politicians agreed to "oppose any legislation relating to climate change that includes a net increase in government revenue".[89] This commitment to protect the fossil fuel industry, particularly among conservatives, has led many politicians to publicly deny or doubt the existence and severity of climate change and these denials create ignorance among the public. Those denials are in bad faith.

What results from this creation of ignorance is a vicious cycle of ignorance begetting more ignorance. That may have been confusing, so let me explain. While most Americans do believe in climate change, the denial and doubting of climate change by politicians and conservative media figures has contributed to many Americans' questionings of how effective or necessary any policies aimed at solving or mitigating climate change really are. The Pew Research Center captured this fact in a 2019 poll; they found that only 54 percent of Americans agree with the statement that "policies aimed at reducing the effects of climate change do more good than harm".[90] This number drops to 29 percent among more conservative Republicans.[91]

---

[89] Davenport C., Lipton E. *How G.O.P. Leaders Came to View Climate Change as Fake Science* (New York Times, 2017).
[90] Funk, Hefferon, 2019.
[91] Ibid.

By denying or doubting climate change, politicians create doubt in the efficacy of climate policy. The resulting lack of trust in such policies leads many voters to continue to support the conservatives who oppose action on climate change. And for the conservative voters who do believe climate policy would be effective, they are not convinced that climate change is so urgent that they must vote against climate-change-denying-conservatives who agree with them on other issues. The climate denying politicians are re-elected, they continue to spread doubt about climate change, and the cycle repeats. All the while, the risk is amplified by the resulting legislative inaction in Congress.

Meanwhile, as conservatives have been creating ignorance to drive down public support for action on climate change, liberals have done a very poor job at capitalizing on what should be a home-run issue for them. When attempting to pass climate change legislation, many liberals have opted for an "all or nothing" approach. This has, in large part, contributed to the inaction we have seen in congress. What these politicians fail to consider, however, is that when dealing with risks as dangerous as climate change, any action is better than no action! Liberals' refusal to compromise has hindered attempts to implement effective solutions. Significantly, the left's insistence on including substantial amounts of "pork" in their climate legislation (something we will discuss later in this chapter) has made it nearly impossible for them to build a coalition necessary to overwhelmingly demand action on climate change.

Overt ignorance creation by conservatives and an unwillingness of progressive and moderate liberals to compromise with each other has made the issue of climate change increasingly polarizing. This polarization has led to even more inaction and consequently, it has amplified the risk.

Despite all that depressing information, there is hope for our planet. Climate change has been gaining more and more recognition over the last few decades, and, as a result, an abundance of research has been conducted. While the science on climate change isn't complete (no science ever is), we now know more about the nature of climate change than we ever have. Research has pointed us in the right direction, providing thousands of potential solutions to mitigate this risk and save our existence on Earth. We must heed the warnings given by science.

The solutions to save our planet have already been developed and are now ready to be enacted. Climate change is an existential threat to our existence on this planet, but it is not an insurmountable threat. By: 1) reversing the ignorance that prevents Americans from supporting the necessary climate change mitigation policies and by voting for the politicians who will enact these policies, 2) reversing the ignorance that has foiled the liberals' efforts to implement such policies, and 3) by raising public awareness and implementing the effective solutions that ignorance has largely hid from the public, we can mitigate the risk of climate change.

THE CREATION OF IGNORANCE

As we discussed in Chapter 1, money drives the creation of ignorance regarding climate change. Politicians who have ties to the fossil fuel industry cast doubt on climate science and the effectiveness of environmental policy because they have pledged to protect the fossil fuel industry from efforts to turn the country towards clean energy. The media furthers this creation of ignorance by airing the misleading rhetoric spewed by conservative politicians.

One of the main ways in which politicians and media figures create ignorance about climate change is through using the phrase, "I'm not a scientist, but…". Dave Levitan, author of *Not a Scientist*, explains that this phrase originated with Ronald Reagan and has become a staple of conservative rhetoric regarding science ever since. Using this phrase, "I'm not a scientist, but…" and then proceeding to talk about science in a completely misleading manner creates ignorance among the public.

When authority figures speak, their words tend to carry more weight and people are more likely to believe them. So, when politicians cite an uncredible blog post or discredited study to cast doubt on climate change, many take their word as truth. In the age of the internet, politicians' allusions to uncredible sources go viral, and because the public is largely ignorant of which "facts" are legitimately true, it seems to many that there are credible arguments on both sides.

There are not credible arguments on both sides and there are not an equal number of credible sources on both sides. A fair debate between climate scientists and climate deniers would not be a 1 versus 1 debate, it would be a 97 versus 3 debate. Let me clarify. Since 97 percent of climate scientists agree climate change is occurring and being caused by human activity, a fair debate would have to include 97 proponents of climate change being real versus 3 deniers of climate change.[92] Yet, by spreading this false notion that there are two equal, credible sides in the climate change debate, conservatives successfully diminish public support for environmental policies.

Perhaps more damaging to public support of climate legislation is that the debate regarding the existence of climate change has been dominated by media figures who have no expertise in the field and non-climate scientists who also have no experience in the field. The science of climate change is clear and indisputable. Yet, media outlets and politicians have continued to debate the existence of, and threat posed by climate change, instead of having a more useful debate on what should be done about it.

This debate is sensationalist journalism, so unsurprisingly it attracts many viewers. This meaningless debate boosts profits for media conglomerates and creates ignorance among the public. A win-win for the elites. Influenced by what they hear and see on the news, many Americans come to deny or at least become skeptical of the information espoused by the community of climate scientists. Joseph Nightingdale, writer for *The Medium*, elaborates on how

---

[92] *Scientific Consensus: Earth's Climate is Warming* (NASA). https://climate.nasa.gov/scientific-consensus/.

this foolish debate contributes to the creation of public ignorance. He remarks:

> Everyone likes to debate. Right? It seems fair. Equitable. But are all issues up for debate? Are we to question the circulatory system? The theory of gravity? Or the existence of cells?
>
> No. Some things are settled science.
>
> Even if we were to debate gravity, who are the debaters? A physicist and.... Sean Hannity? Tucker Carlson? Or a grad-school quack with a masters in electrical engineering? I mean, it's all science, right?
>
> ...Yet as easy as it is to parody this ludicrous fictional debate, where are the prominent climate scientists to defend their subject. Bill Nye 'The Science Guy', Neil DeGrasse Tyson? Neither are climatologists. They're barely even scientists.
>
> It's no wonder the American public doesn't trust climate scientists. They've barely even heard from them.[93]

Unsurprisingly, this phony debate has manifested itself in widespread ignorance among the American public. In 2016, the Pew Research Center found that only 33 percent of U.S. adults believed that climate scientists knew whether climate change was occurring, only 19 percent believed climate scientists knew the best ways to address climate change, and only 39 percent believed that climate scientists gave trustworthy information about the causes and effects of climate change.[94] These numbers are shockingly low and are a

---

[93] Nightingdale, J. *Why Don't Conservatives Believe in Climate Change?* (The Medium, 2020).

[94] *The Politics of Climate* (Pew Research Center, 2016). https://www.pewresearch.org/science/2016/10/04/the-politics-of-climate/.

direct result of the irresponsible debate regarding the existence of climate change constantly being aired on media outlets.

Over the last few decades, politicians and media figures have distorted and misrepresented science in too many ways to count. They have cast doubt on whether humans are really contributing to climate change. They have pointed to nonsense conspiracy theories about climate scientists colluding with each other and lying to the public. They have created confusion over what is weather and what is climate, and they have downplayed the danger posed by climate change. Former President Donald Trump called climate change a hoax invented by the Chinese to tank American businesses—and people believed him. Perhaps the most damaging misinformation that has been spread, however, is that it is too expensive to act on climate change and thus not worth the effort.

As mentioned earlier, only 20 percent of Americans deny the existence of climate change. To garner public support for climate change, liberals do not need their support. The real challenge is convincing conservative voters who believe in climate change, but who are skeptical of the costs of mitigating action, that their fears are unfounded. Ignorance created this narrative. In reality, not acting on climate change will be much more expensive in the future than acting now. Dave Levitan explains the difference between these two options:

> Keeping global warming to a reasonable level—1.5°C—would cost money, and a lot of it. In fact, it would cost about 1 percent of the entire world's GDP annually by 2050. But without such actions? The costs would be absolutely devasting, falling somewhere between 5 and 20 percent of the global GDP each year.[95]

---

[95] Levitan, D. *Not a Scientist: How Politicians Mistake, Misrepresent, and Utterly Mangle Science* (Norton W.W. & Company, Inc., 2017). 147.

The Risk Of Climate Change

Now, to make that picture a little clearer, let's turn those figures into concrete numbers. Effectively acting to mitigate climate change would cost the world approximately $190 trillion over 25 years. On the other hand, failing to act on climate change would cost us at least $192 trillion over the same period. Why, "at least"? Well, that $192 trillion does not include the damages that will be caused by the global warming we fail to address. If the planet warms by 2.5°C, then the consequences of climate change will cost us an extra $44 trillion, and if matters get really bad and the world warms by 4.5°C, then the costs will rise to an additional $72 trillion.[96]

Let's also not forget that climate change will have negative consequences that cannot be represented fully by monetary values, such as the increased frequency of extreme weather and forest fires, and the rising of sea levels that will lead to many coastal areas becoming completely uninhabitable and result in the loss of life and the displacement of millions of refugees. These predictions are not science-fiction, but fact.

The scientific evidence of human caused climate change is clear, and the economics of why we must deal with the crisis is also indisputable. Unfortunately, for many conservative politicians, accumulating money and power takes priority over the safety of our home on this planet. These politicians have "sold their souls" to the industries invested in the risk of climate change and have chosen to create ignorance among the public to protect the industry giants that are ensuring they remain in power.

Public ignorance does more than stall action, however. It has also led to the reversal and repeal of many important environmental policies. For example, while in office, President Trump reversed over 100 climate regulations enacted by the Obama Administration.[97] Listening to the people who preface their misleading claims with "I'm not a scientist, but…" has had devasting consequences for life on our planet.

---

[96] Ibid. 147-149.

[97] Popovich, N., et. al. *The Trump Administration Rolled Back More Than 100 Environmental Rules. Here's the Full List.* (New York Times, 2021).

By using misleading rhetorical phrases, such as, "I'm not a scientist, but…", conservative politicians have been able to distract people from what scientists are saying. In doing so, politicians gain the opportunity to insert just enough doubt into the minds of the public to cause them to dismiss widely held scientific truths as falsehoods.[98] And that's all they need to do: *plant a seed of doubt.* Conservatives do not need to convince everyone climate change is a hoax. All they must do is convince enough people that we don't have all the facts yet and that it would be a mistake to act on climate change before we know for certain it's occurring.

Think about it. *Why would the public support the major changes proposed in environmental policy if they aren't sure it's necessary and when the politicians they trust tell them it would be a mistake to act on climate change? Why would workers in the fossil fuel industry risk their jobs if they didn't think change was absolutely necessary?* By spreading misinformation and sowing doubt into the minds of the public, conservatives have been able to successfully block action on climate change. Thus, when 130 politicians in Congress blatantly disregard science by casting doubt on or outright denying climate change, a large swath of the public is not surprised or concerned. *There are credible arguments on both sides, of course all politicians don't agree.*

There are numerous methods in which politicians utterly mangle science and create ignorance among the public. Whether it's Republican Senator James Inhofe of Oklahoma confusing weather with climate and bringing a snowball to the floor of Congress as "proof" that climate change is a hoax, or Senator Ted Cruz of Texas using an extremely unreliable data set to claim global warming hasn't occurred in 17 years, the public has been heavily influenced by misleading rhetoric. As a result, the risk of climate change has been amplified. As Dave Levitan writes:

---

[98] Fish, S. *Winning Arguments: What Works and Doesn't Work in Politics, The Bedroom, The Courtroom, and The Classroom.* (Harper, 2016). 26.

Spreading misinformation about climate change has helped delay any global movement to stop it for decades, meaning that scientific ignorance or obfuscation on the part of our leaders could quite literally destroy the world as we know it.[99]

The spread of misinformation is not the only part of the equation regarding the amplification of this risk, however. The concealment and confusion of pertinent information regarding the risk has caused damage as well. The resulting public ignorance of what causes climate change and how to slow it, coupled with increasing political polarization regarding this issue has led to the inaction and misguided action that has exacerbated the threat.

CONFUSION, MISGUIDED ACTION, AND POLARIZATION

The science of climate change is complicated. Unsurprisingly, there is widespread confusion about what really causes climate change and how we must act to mitigate this crisis. The way in which climate change is discussed by politicians often adds to the confusion that already exists. The use of abstract rhetoric when speaking on this issue leads to a misunderstanding, or more accurately, an *incomplete* understanding, of what climate change really is, how it's affecting people, and how it will continue to wreak havoc on our planet. Additionally, political polarization leads many to dismiss facts and evidence as they blindly take the side of their party. The combination of an incomplete comprehension of climate science and increasing political polarization has hindered the implementation of effective climate policies.

First, let's discuss the ignorance that has developed as to the causes of climate change. In recent years, the battle to mitigate climate change has overwhelmingly been focused on controlling

---

[99] Levitan, 2017. 6.

the negative impact of the burning of fossil fuels. Fossil fuel usage has indeed contributed greatly to the acceleration of climate change, but this narrow focus creates confusion about the issue; it has led to the public's ignorance of other causes of climate change, most notably food waste.

Researchers at Project Drawdown (an organization we will highlight later) have found that of all the possible solutions to mitigate climate change, reducing food waste is the most impactful.[100] This is because when food decomposes in a landfill, it is deprived of oxygen; consequently, it propels methane into the atmosphere as opposed to carbon dioxide. Methane, like carbon dioxide, is a greenhouse gas, but it is much more dangerous. In fact, over 20 years, methane contributes to global warming at an 86 times greater level than CO2.[101] Citing research conducted by environmental organizations, the UN, and the EPA, Extrafood.org listed a few startling facts about food waste:

- Every 100 pounds of food waste in our landfills sends 8.3 pounds of methane into the atmosphere.
- If global food waste were a country, it would rank 3rd in greenhouse gas emissions after China and the U.S.
- The contribution of food waste emissions to global warming is almost equivalent (87 percent) to global road transport emissions.[102]

These facts have largely been neglected by the politicians and media figures who inform the public about climate change. As a result, policies to reduce food waste have not been effectively advocated for by the public. The example of food waste is just one of many. There are many major contributors to climate

---

[100] *Food Waste and the Climate Crisis* https://extrafood.org/the-need/food-waste/.
[101] Ibid.
[102] Ibid.

change that are not discussed at length by politicians, such as the clothing waste generated by the "fast fashion" industry. Food waste is not discussed in the media or politics because it confers benefits upon the elite. Corporations that handle food intentionally dispose of it in unsafe manners because it saves them money (in economics this is known as an externality). For this same reason, corporations illegally dump waste and use dangerous pesticides to increase their food supply.

The confusion of what drives climate change creates ignorance in the form of misguided action. When the public is ignorant about what is necessary to mitigate a risk, they often act in unhelpful or even detrimental ways. Regarding the issue of climate change, many have come to mistakenly believe that climate change is a problem that can be solved if everyone becomes more environmentally conscious and takes individual responsibility. It is true that re-using refillable water bottles, carpooling, and avoiding the use of plastic straws can have great effects, and we all should strive to do these things. However, focusing solely on individual responsibility is an approach that dismisses what is truly necessary to mitigate climate change. The approach neglects the fundamental fact that no amount of personal sacrifice will ever be enough to reverse climate change.

Furthermore, focusing primarily on individual responsibility often leads to feelings of hopelessness. Once one come to terms with that reality that no amount of personal sacrifice will ever be sufficient, it becomes very hard for many to continue rationalizing their sacrifices. Professor at the Potsdam Institute for Climate Impact Research, Anders Levermann elaborates on the pitfalls of this individualized approach to climate change:

> Personal sacrifice alone cannot be the solution to tackling the climate crisis. There's no other area in which the individual is held so responsible for what's going wrong. And it's true: people drive too much, eat too much meat, and fly too often. But reaching zero emissions requires very fundamental

changes. Individual sacrifice alone will not bring us to zero. It can be achieved only by real structural change.[103]

This fact that an increase in personal responsibility and sacrifice alone cannot solve the climate crisis should not come as a surprise. Yet, our society has decided to call individuals to task to solve this risk. Again, dismissing this as a coincidence would be naïve. The public does not come to hold beliefs by their own accords. Campaigns that encourage people to take personal responsibility serve as a mechanism for the elite to distract the public from what is truly necessary to mitigate the climate crisis. And they have been successful. Individuals have been distracted from seeing the big picture of climate change, they have been made to feel hopeless, and the required policies have not been implemented.[104]

In the same vein, the lauding of charities and our insistence on trusting them to solve the climate crisis has also stalled the realization of effective change. Charities like 4ocean tout the amazing feats they have accomplished, such as removing over 11 million pounds of trash from our oceans, while asking individuals to donate so they can continue and expand their work. The work being undertaken by charities is noble and should be commended, but it must also be acknowledged that reliance on charities is never a permanent solution.

Instead of asking organizations like 4ocean to clean up our oceans, we should be asking our government and governments around the world why there is so much trash in the ocean to begin with. Charities simply offer a pain reliever for deeper-rooted symptoms. While their role is necessary to minimize suffering in the present moment, transformative policy and structural change is required to mitigate risks and reverse inequities in the long-term. Our love for charities and the idea that their work can solve

---

[103] Levermann, A. *Individuals can't solve the climate crisis. Governments need to step up* (The Guardian, 2019).
[104] Ibid.

the climate crisis is rooted in ignorance and amplifies the risk of climate change by distracting the public from the real changes that are needed.

Political polarization is another form of ignorance that has amplified the risk of climate change. I am labeling polarization as a form of ignorance because it often blinds us from seeing the facts. Polarization leads to the dismissal of logic, reason, and evidence, which creates and amplifies risks. The pressure of political party loyalty has been one of the major roadblocks to the implementation of climate legislation. Republicans in Congress refuse to cross the aisle to vote for the proposed climate change solutions, and progressive and moderate Democrats have refused to budge on their positions. Moreover, voters have also become increasingly divided by party affiliation in their stance on climate change.

In a *Social Psychological and Personality Science* study called "Partisan Barriers to Bipartisanship: Understanding Climate Policy Polarization", researchers found that political affiliation has a large influence over whether a voter will support a policy regarding climate change. The researchers found that while self-identifying Republican voters are less likely to support climate policies in general, they are more likely to support the policy if they are told it has Republican support. Similarly, Democrat voters are more likely to support a policy when they are told it has Democrat support. Those facts probably aren't surprising.

What is interesting, however, is that Democrat voters (who claim to support action on climate change) are less likely to support that same policy when it is said to have Republican support, and Republican voters are less likely to support that same policy when it is said to have Democrat support.[105] This is a clear dismissal of the facts and evidence, caused by political polarization. It is very difficult to bring any voter over to the side of supporting action on

---

[105] Ehret, P., Van Boven, L., Sherman, D. *Partisan Barriers to Bipartisanship: Understanding Climate Policy Polarization* (Social Psychological and Personality Science, 2018).

climate change when they care more deeply about party affiliation than they do about policies themselves.

Party affiliation has a significant impact on how voters feel about climate policy, and this polarization hinders our ability to build a broad coalition advocating for climate change legislation.

IGNORANCE, PERFECTIONSIM, AND COALITIONS

In the beginning of this chapter, I told you that 80 percent of Americans believe climate change is real and that human activity is causing it. Additionally, many Americans are willing to go one step further; the same Pew Research Center poll found that 67 percent of Americans believe the U.S. government is doing too little to reduce the effects of climate change.[106] While one can argue that those percentages should be higher, the fact is that a clear majority of Americans believe we need to act on climate change. Very few political issues exhibit such widespread support on one side. The will of the people is clear: they want action. So, *why is this even a topic for debate?* Action on climate change should be a clear winning issue for liberals, but it isn't. This is largely because liberals have taken misguided approaches to building coalitions that strongly support and demand action on climate change.

While climate change should be a winning issue for liberals, many people who support action on climate change continue to vote for conservative politicians who do not. Therefore, most of the support that exists is effectively neutralized and our government is pretty much evenly split on this issue. Almost all conservative voters who agree action needs to be taken on climate change clearly don't feel the issue is important enough to make them vote for a liberal candidate who supports climate change policies instead of a conservative who does not. This disconnect between agreeing that

---

[106] Funk, Hefferon, 2019.

action is needed, while simultaneously voting to block action on climate change, can be partially attributed to the liberals' ignorant approach to building a coalition.

There are two major failings in the approach taken by liberals in advocating for climate change policies: 1) they haven't attempted to connect with the moral values of conservative audiences, and 2) they have refused to compromise to pass less bold, but still significant climate reform policies.

In his book, *The Righteous Mind*, Jonathan Haidt identifies six major concepts that form the basis of our moral values. They are: care, fairness, loyalty, authority, sanctity, and liberty.[107] Whereas conservatives endorse all six of these concepts to some degree, liberals only subscribe to two: care and fairness.[108] This disconnect of values makes it extremely hard for liberals to reach conservatives with their message. Joseph Nightingdale sums up this problem saying, "The two sides are speaking separate languages. They're talking past each other, causing a growing mistrust… Liberals are selling a message that conservatives cannot buy."[109]

Furthermore, liberals' insistence on embedding other issues into climate legislation and climate change talking points (a political practice known as "pork-barrel politics") has only fueled ignorant suspicion of climate change reform policies that exists among conservatives. As we have discussed, conservative politicians and media figures have created public ignorance by casting doubt on climate science and the *true* intentions of liberals who push for climate change reform policies. Conservatives often claim that liberals are simply advocating for climate change reform policy to enact other progressive policies. When liberals weave other risks into their rhetoric on climate change, it only strengthens the suspicion held by conservatives. Nightingdale explains this by commenting on a quote by Greta Thunberg in

---

[107] Nightingdale, 2020.
[108] Ibid.
[109] Ibid.

which she connected the issues of colonialism, racism, and the patriarchy to climate change:

> Greta and her acolytes are embracing divisive politics; confirming all of the Republicans' worst fears. She may loath Donald Trump or Rush Limbaugh; but with every argument she advances, she loads a bullet in their gun. Contrary to Greta's proclamation, the climate crisis is only about the environment; smuggling progressive talking points under the cloak of scientific enlightenment will further cast the movement in shadow and suspicion. We need to get back to basics.[110]

While Greta is correct in that climate change is connected to racism, colonialism, and patriarchy, it is also an issue that has become deeply entrenched in the political world. As Nightingdale explained, weaving other progressive political matters into the political issue of climate change is playing right into the hands of ignorance creators. Rhetorically connecting climate change with other issues gives conservative voters a reason to be opposed to climate legislation, and this drives them to vote for conservative politicians who don't support those policies.

Including progressive "pork" occurs in policymaking, too. Representative Alexandria Ocasio-Cortez lobbied to include universal free higher-education, among other progressive stipulations, in the Green New Deal. While a debate about free college tuition is an important debate to have, including funding for such a proposal in the Green New Deal only helps to fuel conservative suspicion. Most importantly, it creates more public ignorance as people come to believe that liberals have other agendas and ulterior motives when they push for climate policy.

Finally, Congresspeople on the far-left have hindered our ability to pass climate change reform policies by refusing to compromise

---

[110] Ibid.

The Risk Of Climate Change

with moderates. As we will discuss in the solutions section when we review the lessons to be learned from the Montreal Protocol, some action (indeed any action) is better than no action when confronting a risk as dangerous as climate change. By refusing to compromise with moderate Democrats to develop a climate policy solely about climate, progressives have prevented any action on climate change. Yes, we must be bold in this moment, but being bold in theory does nothing to stop the climate crisis in reality.

As time goes on and we continue to see inaction, the risk of climate change intensifies. Refusing to change the way we talk about climate change to conservative audiences, insisting on tackling every problem at once when drafting legislation to reduce the effects of climate change, and failing to reach compromises are all examples of ignorance. They are the result of some liberals ignorantly believing that every policy they propose must be perfect, solve every issue, and that we cannot compromise because incremental change does nothing. This perfectionism is preventing us from doing *anything* to tackle climate change. Consequently, this ignorant approach is amplifying the risk of climate change.

If liberals can start to recognize the pitfalls of their perfectionist approach, they can start to build a broad coalition eager to tackle climate change. Only with this coalition, will they be able to go bold. As I keep alluding to, most people already agree that more action is needed to confront the climate crisis. What we must do now is demonstrate: 1) climate change is an issue of such paramount importance that people who consider themselves conservatives should cross party lines to vote for politicians who support action on climate change, 2) acting on climate change is in the best interest of the planet and the economy, and 3) there is not a hidden non-climate related agenda behind climate policy. I know that sounds like a tall order, but the solutions for how to do this have already been developed. Let's discuss them.

SOLUTIONS

As the quote by Greta Thunberg at the beginning of this chapter asserts, the climate crisis has already been solved. However, the creation and manipulation of an ignorant public has effectively blocked all serious attempts to implement these solutions. Hence, the risk of climate change. This section is focused on reversing that ignorance and removing the barriers to much needed climate change legislation.

Before we dive into solutions specific to climate change, I want to remind you of a solution we discussed in Chapter 1: the Anti-Corruption Act. For any progress to be made on climate change, we need to solve the problems facing our democracy. The passage of the Anti-Corruption Act is the most important individual solution in this book because creating a fairer democracy is paramount to implementing all policy solutions. As we discussed in this chapter, there is no evidence or legitimate argument for the opposition of action on climate change. Because of this, the debate on climate change has aptly been called a "fictional debate" by some. However, this fictional debate will continue unless we pass the Anti-Corruption Act and free politicians from their ties to the industries with an active interest in the preservation and amplification of the risk of climate change.

LISTENING TO SCIENTISTS

One of the most important actions we must take is listening to climate scientists. Although there is an overwhelming consensus among climate scientists that human activity greatly contributes to climate change, the American people remain divided about whether we must act as a country. Much of this division comes from the simple fact that most of us get our information regarding climate change from bad faith politicians and media figures. We must no longer allow bad faith conservative politicians to malign science under the protection of using the phrase "I'm not a scientist, but...". We must call these politicians out for spreading misinformation and point out the science that refutes their false claims.

We must allow the American people to hear from climate scientists directly. This means putting *real* scientists on media networks, not just select personalities like Bill Nye the Science Guy. If we want Americans to trust climate scientists and their messages, they must see and hear from them. Politicians must also lead by example by following their advice. If our leaders make it clear that they trust and listen to scientists, the Americans public will follow their example and listen as well.

CHANGING OUR RHETORIC

The United States is a large country, filled with people from all different backgrounds, cultures, and values. When we talk about any issue, we must be sure to frame it in a way that the specific audience we are addressing can comprehend and understand it. If we do not do this, it will be impossible to persuade them to join our side. As we discussed earlier, when we ignorantly forget to do this "audience analysis", our message completely fails to resonate with the audience. This concept is not radical, in fact it is literally a concept in "Public Speaking 101". The textbook *The Public Speaking Playbook* elaborates on this idea of audience analysis:

> Would you be wise to deliver the exact same speech to two or more different audiences? The answer is, "Probably not." ... In fact, successful speakers view the audience as central to their speech...Your success depends on how well you partner with or reach your audience—building your relationship and sharing your message. That's why we focus on audience analysis, the process of gathering and interpreting information about receivers, and putting yourself in their shoes, so you can empathize with them,

and adapt your message to meet and reflect their needs and interests.[111]

To build a broad coalition of voters who support climate change legislation and the politicians who will enact said legislation, we must adopt this essential concept of audience analysis in our rhetoric. This means that when we speak to conservatives about climate change, we must frame our persuasive speeches to appeal to conservative moral values. We can talk about how it is our duty to protect and preserve God's creation of Earth (sanctity), how we must act on climate change to ensure our children have a safe planet to live on (loyalty), how the United States must lead the world in this charge (authority), or how positive action on mitigating climate change will also have a positive economic impact for all people (fairness).

We also must amplify the few conservative voices that are calling for action on climate change. Showing conservative voters that not everyone in the Republican party is a climate change denier can help us persuade them of the urgency of the issue. Similarly, we should take some conservative proposals for fighting climate change seriously, such as Pigouvian taxes that include the cost of environmental damage in product prices (we will return to this idea shortly).[112]

Liberals and climate change activists also must make more consistent appearances on conservative media networks to meet voters where they are. If conservative voters never hear directly from the politicians who want to act on climate change, or the climate scientists, we cannot expect the message to resonate with them.

---

[111] Gamble, M. *The Public Speaking Playbook* (Sage, 2020).
[112] Nightingdale, 2020.

AN OPPORTUNITY TO BUILD NATIONAL COMMUNITY

Our domestic response to the climate crisis will include a massive transition away from the fossil fuel industry and towards green energy. According to climate scientists and energy experts, this transition is necessary,[113] so I will not spend time substantiating why we should do this. What I do want to discuss is how we can make this transition as smooth as possible. If we are ignorant in how we approach this decision, the upheaval of our energy industry will have disastrous consequences.

While the economy has changed dramatically in recent decades and it is no longer the norm to have one job for your entire career, for many people, their job is still at the heart of their identity. As we transition to green energy, we must keep this idea of identity in mind. Secretary of Transportation, Pete Buttigieg, recognized this important concept of identity and made it central to his plan for climate change when he was running for president in 2020. At the Climate Crisis Forum in 2019, Buttigieg pointed out two central ideas we must not forget in our transition to green energy: 1) many of the new jobs we create will not be all that different from traditional union jobs we see in factories today, and 2) we must recruit people to be part of climate change solutions in ways in which they can be proud.[114]

Therefore, Buttigieg's plan for climate change called for local and state investment as well as federal investment. It is also why Buttigieg called for a U.S. Climate Corps that would be open to high school graduates dedicated to fighting climate change through education and rebuilding infrastructure.[115] Reminding voters who

---

[113] *Climate and Energy Experts Debate How to Respond to a Warming World* (New York Times, 2019). https://www.nytimes.com/2019/10/07/business/energy-environment/climate-energy-experts-debate.html.

[114] *Pete Buttigieg: Fighting Climate Change Could Also Create Traditional, Union Jobs* | MSNBC (MSNBC, 2019). https://www.youtube.com/watch?v=iJc86k5xU7k.

[115] Mcdonald, J. *Pete Buttigieg unveils climate change plan that would cost more than $1 trillion and aim to create 3 million clean energy jobs* (CNBC, 2019).

fear losing their job and identity that they can have similar jobs in a green energy industry is a very effective way to dispel fears that prevent people from supporting this transition. Our response to the climate crisis must take advantage of the unique opportunity we have to build strong community at the local, state, and national levels.

We also can build community by launching a national campaign for individuals to go green in our daily lives. Calling on individuals to do little things like recycling, turning off the lights when they leave a room, and being conscious of reducing their food waste won't solve the problem of climate change completely, but if done correctly, it can create the energy and commitment we need to implement large scale changes to solve the climate crisis. Calls for individual responsibility, when done effectively, should not be disregarded as useless. There is strength in numbers. A strong call for individual responsibility can lead to strong community and collective commitment that will strengthen the movement for action on climate change on a global level.

CORPORATE RESPONSIBILITY

This idea of building community by inviting people and organizations of all levels to be part of the climate solution must be applied to the corporate world. Big corporations, driven by profit, have exacerbated the risk of climate change. For example, many corporations, in a variety of sectors, have found that it serves them better financially to dispose of waste illegally than to dispose of waste safely and legally. This, of course, causes damage to the environment. Moreover, as we've discussed, the fossil fuel industry has accumulated enormous profits and has engaged in extensive lobbying to ensure the economic protection of their industry. To solve the climate crisis, we need to reign in capitalism and give these corporations incentives to go green. This idea is the thesis of economist Rebecca Henderson's Ted Talk, "To Save the Climate, We Have to Reimagine Capitalism".

In her speech, Henderson explains that our markets are offering us prices that do not reflect "real costs":

> We're letting the firms who sell fossil fuels, and indeed anyone who emits greenhouse gases, cause enormous damage for which they do not have to pay. And that is hardly fair. Imagine for a moment that my hands are filled with a cloud of electrons, 10 dollars' worth of coal-fired electricity that could power your cell phone for more than 10 years. That probably sounds like a pretty good deal. But it's only so cheap because you're not paying for the harm that it causes. Burning coal sends poisons like mercury and lead into the air, increasing healthcare costs by billions of dollars and causing the death of hundreds of thousands of people every year. It also emits huge quantities of carbon dioxide. So, another part of the real cost of coal is the climate damage it will cause and is already causing… generating 10 dollars' worth of coal-fired electricity causes at least eight dollars' worth of harm to human health and at least another eight dollars' worth of climate damage and probably much more. So, the true cost of this handful of electrons? It's not 10 dollars. It's something more like 26.[116]

This policy of requiring corporations to pay for the damage they cause is known as a Pigouvian tax. We must implement these taxes to ensure that corporations pay for the damage they are causing our environment. Henderson believes that our approach must not be one in which we attack corporations, rather it should be an approach that invites corporations to join "the green side". As Henderson correctly reminds us, it is in the best interest of the private sector to solve the climate crisis. The economist explains, "The truth is business is screwed if we don't fix climate change.

---

[116] Henderson, R. *To save the climate, we have to reimagine capitalism* (TED, 2020).

It's going to be hard to make money when the great coastal cities are under water and millions of angry people are migrating north as the harvests fail."[117]

To get businesses and large corporations to be environmentally responsible, our political leaders must make contact with them and persuade them to run environmentally friendly businesses. Basically, we should encourage a philosophy of being allies not enemies of corporations. The approach many liberals have been taking, the one in which we demonize the wealthiest most powerful corporations in the world, is clearly a losing strategy. When we attack, they attack back, and they "win" just about every time.

Instead, we must show corporations how working together to solve risks like climate change is in the best interests of both sides. This is something we must remember when confronting every risk. Mitigating risks is in the best interest of everyone, the elites included. However, the elite class is too concerned with short-term profit that they lose sight of what's truly important. This ignorance of the elite results largely because it is so easy for them to enrich and empower themselves by amplifying risks.

As we discussed briefly earlier, many companies dispose of waste illegally or damage the environment through other cost-saving actions. While this is illegal and corrupt, the businesses can "get away with it", because they all do it and no one "snitches", for lack of a better term. They amplify risks because it's an easy way to profit. As Henderson puts it, "Corruption works best when it's hidden."

To fix this corruption, Henderson identifies what she calls the four pillars of change. First, she calls on corporations to build business models that can set the right price (that is a price that accounts for the human health and environmental damage). Second, she calls on corporations to persuade other corporations to follow suit, as she believes this is the most effective strategy of persuasion. Third, she calls on companies to encourage investment by reminding

---

[117] Ibid.

investors of the big picture. In other words, she calls on businesses to remind investors that there is money to be made by going green and that profits will plummet if they do not. Finally, Henderson says the government must "put the right price into law" (through Pigouvian taxes and a tax on carbon emissions) so that businesses that do not comply with green initiatives cannot survive.

In this fight against climate change, we do not have time to make enemies. We cannot ostracize all conservatives by calling them "stupid" when they don't understand how serious climate change is. We must instead appeal to their value system and win them over to the "green side". We must not disregard the concerns of workers in the fossil fuel and nonrenewable energy industries. We must instead ensure those workers that they will have a comfortable life and a good job in the business of green energy. We cannot declare war on the fossil fuel industry and corporations who commit environmental crime. We must instead persuade them to join the fight by showing them that fighting climate change is in their best interest.

LEARNING FROM THE MONTREAL PROTOCOL

When looking for the solutions to any social problem, examining history is always a good place to start. Fortunately, history provides us with lessons for how to approach the issue of climate change.

In the 1980s, we had the ozone crisis. The production and consumption of over 100 man-made chemicals was depleting the ozone at an alarming rate. The ozone layer, which functions as a protective layer against harmful ultraviolet rays from the sun, was in desperate need of global corrective action. The world answered this call to action with the signing of the Montreal Protocol in 1987.

It has been estimated that the Protocol has prevented what would have been two million deaths per year to skin cancer by 2030, copious damage to crops, a sizeable increase in eye damage, and a similarly large increase in damaged immune systems.[118] Today, the Montreal Protocol, which has been amended and improved over time, is regarded as one of the most successful international climate agreements of all time. It can teach us many lessons.[119]

Reversing our ignorance by learning from the lessons of the Montreal Protocol was the topic of climate scientist Sean Davis's Ted Talk. Davis believes there are three main lessons to be learned from this rare environmental success story. The first lesson is that we should not wait until we are absolutely certain about everything regarding climate change before we decide to act. Davis reminds his audience of two points when discussing this lesson: 1) we were less certain about the science regarding the ozone depletion than we are about climate change today, and 2) we make decisions in the face of uncertainty all the time.

As we discussed earlier in this chapter, the case that "we shouldn't act until we are certain" is often made by those who oppose action to climate change, particularly bad faith politicians and media figures seeking to create ignorance. It is not a sound argument, and it amplifies the risk of climate change.

In life, many of our decisions are made when we are less than 100 percent certain of an outcome. Davis explains this fact in his Ted Talk by alluding to our decision to wear seatbelts:

> We make decisions in the face of uncertainty all the time, literally all the time. You know, I'll bet those of you who drove here tonight, you probably wore your seat belt. And so, ask yourself, did you wear your seat belt because someone told you with a hundred percent [certainty] that you would get in a car crash on the way here? Probably not. So that's the first lesson. Risk management and decision making

---

[118] *About Montreal Protocol* (United Nations Environment Programme). https://www.unenvironment.org/ozonaction/who-we-are/about-montreal-protocol.
[119] Ibid.

always have uncertainty. Ignoring risk and focusing only on uncertainty is a distraction.[120]

As we confront the crisis of climate change, we cannot afford to wait for "absolute certainty". The risks of not acting on climate change now far outweigh the uncertainty.

The second lesson we can learn from the Montreal Protocol is that to successfully reduce the effects of climate change we must build a broad alliance of people, groups, and governments. The Montreal Protocol featured environmental organizations, government agencies, corporations, and climate scientists, among other groups. All these people and groups had "a seat at the table and played an important role in the solution", and this is a large reason why the Montreal Protocol was successful. [121] We must take a similar approach to addressing climate change. Climate change is a global crisis. To solve it we will need action at all levels—individual, organizational, state-wide, national, and international.

Finally, Davis implores us to not "let the perfect be the enemy of the good".[122] In his speech, Davis explains that while the Montreal Protocol is viewed as extremely successful today, the initial agreement did very little to save the ozone layer. Instead, it was the later amendments to the agreement that have resulted in the success of the Protocol. However, if we decided to not sign the initial agreement because we felt it did not go far enough, we may not have solved the ozone crisis. Davis urges the audience to not make the mistake of refusing to compromise for less than perfect climate change policies. Specifically, Davis believes it would be a mistake to abandon the Paris Climate Accord because it is not perfect. We can build on the Paris Climate Accord, or, for that matter, a domestic climate policy perhaps less bold than the Green

---

[120] Davis, S. *Can We Solve Global Warming? Lessons from How We Protected the Ozone Layer* (TED, 2017).
[121] Ibid.
[122] Ibid.

New Deal, but we cannot afford to let our obsession for perfection lead to inaction.

We must take these lessons to heart and keep them at the forefront in our struggle against climate change.

INTERNATIONAL ACTION

We must build on the Paris Climate Accord and further extend our international action. The United States has for decades claimed to be "the leader of the free world". It is time for our country to live up to that moniker once again and lead the world in the fight against climate change. We cannot ethically call on other countries to curb their carbon emissions or act against climate change if we do not do the same. We must lead by example.

It is imperative that we lead the charge and cross borders to call for wide-scale international action on climate change. This is an idea that is championed by the organization "NOW!". The only way to solve the biggest crises facing our planet is to launch a global movement. The organization believes we must follow a three-step process to launch this global movement: 1) craft global solutions for climate change, 2) create a common consciousness around transnational progressive solutions, and 3) campaign to implement these solutions into law across the globe.[123]

Finally, we must call on the United Nations to declare a climate emergency to signify the seriousness of this risk, which should galvanize and inspire countries across the globe to spring into action. Climate change is too vast a problem for any one nation to handle alone. That is why it is so important for the United States to lead the global movement that will give us the transnational solutions necessary to effectively confront this crisis.

---

[123] NOW! *Methodology.* https://www.now.world/methodology_full.

PROJECT DRAWDOWN SOLUTIONS

The solutions to climate change have been devised. While there has been much opposition to action on climate change, there has also been sustained effort on the part of multiple organizations and non-profits to craft solutions to the crisis. The organization Project Drawdown has devised extremely detailed, empirically tested solutions to the climate crisis in a wide array of sectors. The extensive list of these solutions can be found on the website of Project Drawdown.[124] The solutions range from the sectors of agriculture to electricity, buildings, land sinks, food waste, and transportation, among numerous other sectors. This organization has done a remarkable job compiling an extensive list of solutions (and they are continuously adding more). We must make sure their work does not go to waste. We must demand that our government and governments around the world consider, and ultimately implement, these and similar solutions.

AVOIDING DISASTER

Saving our species and biodiversity from climate change seems to be a daunting task, but it is not an impossible task. Luckily for us, the heavy lifting has already been done; we have the solutions to combat climate change. The risks of climate change are the consequence of public ignorance. Our mission is to dispel and reverse this ignorance. That means reversing ignorance about how serious climate change is and what it takes to solve it, but it also means moving away from the ignorant, ineffective rhetorical approach we have been utilizing to attempt to persuade people to vote for politicians committed to tackling climate change.

We must recognize the existence of ignorant and/or bad faith politicians who are destroying our home on this planet and we must

---

[124] Project Drawdown. *Table of Solutions.* https://www.drawdown.org/solutions/table-of-solutions.

build the coalitions necessary to vote them out of office at all levels—replacing them with "pro-fighting-climate-change" politicians. We can build a strong community and a collective commitment to tackle this risk only if we reverse the ignorance that has prevented us from doing so. This is feasible; there is always hope when we reverse ignorance. Our actions today will determine whether we can tell our grandchildren that we saved our home on this planet. It is imperative that we act in accordance with the evidence, not the ignorance, if we want to protect our habitat on this beautiful Earth.

3

The Risk Of Racism

They are in effect still trapped in a history which they do not understand and until they understand it, they cannot be released from it.
– James Baldwin

Racism has plagued the United States of America since its inception. While the days of chattel slavery and Jim Crow are behind us, racism is still ingrained in the structure of all our institutions as well as deep in all our psyches in the form of unconscious, implicit bias. Consequently, the risks of racism also amplify just about every other societal risk. The risk of racism was created, is maintained, and is amplified by ignorance.

For many of us today, the topic of racism is avoided in our social circles because it is deemed too uncomfortable to talk about. On the rare occasions that we do engage in conversations about racism, our discussions are often misguided and inaccurate. Our ignorance about the biological nature and social meaning of race, the origin of racist ideas, the strategic creation and perpetuation of racism, the development of unconscious racial bias, the potential benefits of racial equity, and the steps we must take to end systemic and individual racism all combine to exponentially increase racism's destruction to the social fabric. I know that was a lot; feel free to re-read that sentence.

One's acceptance of the validity of racist ideas always stems from ignorance. Racist ideas have absolutely no biological backing. All ideas that suggest the biological or cultural inferiority of the Black population can be dismantled through informed scientific discussion and historical analysis. Since its founding, our country has made no serious effort to reverse the widespread public ignorance that leads people to accept false ideas about race. Consequently, there have been no serious, sustained attempts to eliminate and replace racist ideas and policies with antiracist ideas and policies.

To the contrary, history has shown that ignorance about race and racism has been intentionally perpetuated among the public. This is because those in power—the elite class of Americans—have always displayed an active interest in preserving and amplifying the risk of racism. The indoctrination of racist ideas into the minds of Americans has always served as a way for the elite to create ignorance among the public. The ignorance they create exacerbates the racial exploitation and inequities that enriches them at the expense of the Black population and the public as a whole. And since the ignorance they create leaves the public vulnerable to political manipulation, the power elite can quite easily maintain this structural racism that only benefits their class.

This imposed ignorance enables conservative elites to maintain power and preserve the systems of oppression from which they profit. To name a few throughout history, these systems have included slavery, convict leasing, sharecropping, and mass incarceration. Racist ideas and policies serve as a mechanism for reproducing the socioeconomic structures that serve the interests of the elite. From justifying slavery by labeling Blacks as innately inferior to claiming Whites are "losing the country" and that racial barriers no longer

The Risk Of Racism

exist for Black Americans, racist ideas have been weaponized to convince non-elite Americans—who identify as conservative—to vote against their economic self-interests and accept a system that benefits the elites at the expense of everyone else. This is the primary "risk of racism".

On the other side, self-identifying liberals and progressives are typically more conscious of the existence of systemic racism.[125] Oftentimes, however, liberal and progressive activists lead "antiracist" campaigns that ultimately fail to dismantle the deep-rooted social injustices that disproportionately disadvantage people of color.

These campaigns fail because they focus on "changing the hearts" of racists. *If only we can reverse conservatives' ignorance. If only we could make people kinder and more loving. If only we could make everyone treat others with respect.* While all these aspirations are noble, they do very little to bring about the fundamental changes needed to end systemic racism. Systemic racism is about policy—not just attitudes—and it is exceptionally difficult to determine accurately or objectively who is racist and whose heart "needs changing". We all harbor racist biases to some degree, and we can act on these biases even if we have a conscious desire to not be racist.[126] Inherent in the definition of systemic racism is the truth that even if everyone did not harbor racist beliefs, racial inequities would still exist due to the racism that is embedded in the workings of society.

Furthermore, any approach to end racism that does not acknowledge why people accept racist ideas in the first place will inevitably be misguided—and doomed. People accept racist ideas because they are manipulated by intentionally created ignorance. The sad truth is that many people who vote for conservative leaders (leaders who have an underlying agenda to preserve systemic racism and deny others of equal rights) do so because they *mistakenly*

---

[125] *Race in America 2019* (Pew Research Center, 2019). https://www.pewsocialtrends.org/2019/04/09/race-in-america-2019/.

[126] Eberhardt, J. *Biased* (Viking, 2019).

believe that helping one group—people of color—results in hurting another—White people. This is called a "zero-sum game".

However, the idea of a racial zero-sum game is a myth that has intentionally been spread by the elite. Multiple studies and historical evidence have proven that aiding society's most vulnerable and attempting to end systemic oppression is beneficial for everyone. [127] Until people who rally behind conservative leaders out of fear of "losing" the racial zero-sum game understand that they (and society as a whole) do not stand to lose—but instead stand to benefit—from eradicating systemic racism, any attempt to achieve racial justice will prove futile.

The public's ignorance of racism is complicated. From top to bottom, there are many layers of ignorance that allow racism to exist, cause harm, and misguide us in our mission to end the oppression of people of color, particularly Black Americans. However, these layers of ignorance can, and must, be stripped away.

Although the presence of systemic racism and prevalence of misguided "antiracist" campaigns make the prospects of racial progress seem dismal, we should not lose hope. Fortunately, many effective solutions and plans to lead us into an antiracist world have been developed and are being enacted successfully on local levels across the country. Our mission now is to scale these local solutions and sufficiently educate all Americans about the true racist history of our country, how to be actively antiracist, and how to dismantle and replace the current racist systems in place with antiracist ones that will benefit all Americans.

If you vote for conservative politicians who promote racist ideas and oppose action to eradicate systemic racism, it does not matter whether you consciously harbor racist beliefs or if you consider

---

[127] Systems that discriminate have historically hurt all demographics except for the elite, while systems that are inclusive have historically helped all demographics. For example, all white people who weren't slaveowners suffered immensely economically during slavery. On the other hand, White people thrived during the 1930s through the early 70s because antiracist policies were being enacted. See Kendi, I. *Stamped from the Beginning.* (Bold Type Books, 2017), 504.

yourself to be "colorblind". The only way to dismantle systemic racism and achieve racial justice is to enact transformative antiracist policies, and the only way those policies will be enacted is if we elect antiracist politicians who vow to do so.

THE ORIGIN OF RACE AS WE KNOW IT

Despite the popularity of Ancestry.com tests and other tests that claim they can identify your race and ethnicity, race is not biologically identifiable, nor is it biologically significant in any way. Race does not determine behaviors, intelligence, performance, or athletic ability. PhD researcher Vivian Chou explains this simple fact in her paper about race, writing:

> If separate racial or ethnic groups actually existed, we would expect to find "trademark" alleles and other genetic features that are characteristic of a single group but not present in any others. However, the 2002 Stanford study found that only 7.4% of over 4000 alleles were specific to one geographical region. Furthermore, even when region-specific alleles did appear, they only occurred in about 1% of the people from that region—hardly enough to be any kind of trademark. Thus, there is no evidence that the groups we commonly call "races" have distinct, unifying genetic identities… In the biological and social sciences, the consensus is clear, race is a social construct, not a biological attribute.[128]

In simpler terms, race merely refers to superficial physical differences. Phenotypical variations between humans can be explained through the geographical origins and genes of one's ancestors.

---

[128] Chou, V. *How Science and Genetics are Reshaping the Race Debate of the 21st Century* (Harvard University Science in the News, 2017). http://sitn.hms.harvard.edu/flash/2017/science-genetics-reshaping-race-debate-21st-century/.

Nevertheless, each society constructs its own system of labeling people by "race". What defines a race is not consistent across different societies and cultures. In the United States, for example, our concept of race is constantly changing, as evidenced by the "race question" on the census, which many Americans struggle to answer.[129] However, as Dr. Chou so eloquently states, "Even if most scientists reject the concept of 'race' as a biological concept, race exists, undeniably, as a social and political concept... race remains an incendiary issue in today's society." Dr. Chou is right. As you will read, false ideas of the biological determinism of race have been weaponized for political gain by politicians and elite members of society throughout history, and this makes race "real".

Elites and conservative politicians have created ignorance so effectively that despite the clear consensus among natural scientists, historians, and social scientists proving race is not biologically identifiable or significant, a large swath of the American population still holds the belief that race, in some way or another, *is* biologically significant and determines traits in humans. Many express the belief that being Black makes you a better athlete or being Asian makes you a better student. More devastatingly, many people believe that Black individuals are more likely to commit crimes, exhibit violence, and suffer from poverty due to a biological or cultural aversion to "personal responsibility and hard work". In reality, there is no single behavioral or physical attribute that is shared by every individual within a racial group (or among humans in general, for that matter).

To gain a deeper understanding of race, it is crucial to examine the origins of race and racist ideas. Historically, the concept of race as we know it today was not part of the European/Mediterranean understanding of the world until the 15th or 16th centuries. However, the idea of categorizing people and labeling certain groups as inferior has been present at least since the time of the Greek philosopher

---

[129] Demby, G. *What Is Your Race? For Millions of Americans, A Shifting Answer* (NPR, 2014). https://www.npr.org/sections/codeswitch/2014/06/09/319584793/what-is-your-race-for-millions-of-americans-a-shifting-answer.

Aristotle; the philosopher believed non-Greeks were barbarians and that some people were "natural slaves".[130] From this example alone, we can begin to understand how and why race has become significant in societies around the world.

As mentioned in Chapters 1 and 2, humans tend to put greater trust in and give greater significance to speakers of authority. The racist ideas of Aristotle were widely accepted by the Greek population precisely because the ideas came from Aristotle; the fact that his ideas contradicted the logic of human biology proved rather irrelevant, for his name trumped the flaws of his philosophy. This theme of the public believing fallacious claims made by powerful or influential people has remained consistent throughout history, enabling those in power to strategically create and maintain widespread ignorance.

Preceding the introduction of the concept of race around Aristotle's time, the desire to classify and "dehumanize" specific groups of people that appear different from one's own group can be traced back to humans' earliest existence. In the *Science Magazine* article "Roots of Racism," journalist Elizabeth Culotta attests that through studying humans and our primate relatives, scientists have discovered that evolution has equipped humans with a tendency to classify those who share similar characteristics as members of "in-groups"—who are favored, trusted, and believed to be superior—and those with different characteristics as members of "out-groups"—who are vilified, feared, and regarded as inferior

This age-old tendency to group others that differ from us as "less than", however, is not based on sound biological theory, but on trivial differences.[131] Aristotle's classification of non-Greeks as barbaric, for instance, was not based on evidence that non-Greeks were genetically barbaric; rather, his classification was derived from a delusional idea based on the insignificant difference that non-Greeks were simply not from Greece.

---

[130] *In Theory Aristotle (Part II)* (2011). https://ceasefiremagazine.co.uk/in-theory-aristotle-2/.

[131] Culotta, E. *Roots of Racism*. (Sciencemag.org, 2012).

If Only We Knew

Perhaps you can understand why people accepted racist ideas during Aristotle's time, considering they were not informed of the true science regarding race. But, if race is truly biologically insignificant, why did the scientific revolution fail to create a post-racial society? The ignorance creating faculties of the power elite are to blame. Despite proof that race is not biological, the power elite still attempted to explain phenotypic differences through employing science—or, more accurately, pseudoscience.

Beginning in the 17th and 18th centuries, scientists began to publish essays and books containing so-called empirical evidence of the existence of a natural racial hierarchy. From German anatomist Johann Friedrich Blumenbach, who studied human skulls and categorized them into five races, to Charles White, who similarly categorized the races based on various physical attributes, to Carl Linnaeus, who created a human hierarchy that resembled the hierarchy he created for the animal kingdom, prominent scientists preached that the African race was "naturally inferior" to the "supreme" White race.[132]

While it is easy for us to look back on these ideas and dismiss the claims of those scientists as absurd and comical, it's important to try to put ourselves in the shoes of the average American during this time. Take a moment to consider how we feel about today's accepted science and qualified scientists. *Do we not trust in the accuracy of the claims of the scientists who discovered DNA? How about the scientists who discovered the elements that compose the periodic table? Or the scientists who discovered quantum mechanics?* While we may not completely understand scientific concepts, we trust that scientists do. We trust that they are telling us the truth about their findings.

Naturally, when the prominent, well-respected scientists of the 17th, 18th, 19th, and 20th centuries told the public that they discovered indisputable evidence of the biological existence of a racial hierarchy, what reason did the public have not to trust them?

---

[132] Kendi, 2016. 45-46.

Through their misleading work, scientists assisted the elite members of society in creating public ignorance and the risk of racism by perpetuating the power construct of a racial hierarchy.

Yet, we don't always listen to science. In 2000, when scientists definitively discovered that race is biologically insignificant, racist ideas did not disappear. Now, you may be wondering how this is possible. *If there was proof that racial categories had been socially constructed and were not a natural reality, why do people continue to categorize and make assumptions about humans based on race?* Racism did not originate from science, it originated from the greed of the elite class. Therefore, scientific discoveries alone will never eradicate racism.

Let's dive into the question of *why? Why were racist ideas created? Why did we listen to scientists when they made claims of a racial hierarchy and White superiority? Why did we ignore them when they disproved such claims?* Well, if you've been paying attention so far, you may be able to guess that the answer has everything to do with the elite's desire to rake in enormous profits and their willingness to create ignorance to fulfill this desire.

WHY RACIST IDEAS WERE CREATED

When the first Africans were brought to American colonies in 1619, many of them came as indentured servants, not slaves. This was because the concept of race, as we know it today in the United States (one largely based on physical attributes, namely skin color and hair texture), did not exist 400 years ago. Lerone Bennet Jr., author of *The Shaping of Black America*, explains this seemingly alien world as follows:

> Back there, before Jim Crow, before the invention of the Negro or the White man or the words and concepts to describe them, the Colonial population consisted largely of a great mass of White and Black bondsmen, who occupied

roughly the same economic category and were treated with equal contempt by the lords of the plantations and legislatures. Curiously unconcerned about their color, these people worked together and relaxed together. [133]

This racial harmony, obviously, did not last forever.

As the population in the colonies continued to grow, the demand for land and cheap labor among plantation owners skyrocketed. Unsurprisingly, plantation owners salivated at the opportunity to institute the exploitative system of slavery, the cheapest form of labor available. Since Native Americans were able to fight back against forced enslavement, and because enslaving European immigrants would bring a halt to European emmigration, enslaving Africans was the ideal economic choice for plantation owners.[134] So, slowly but surely, plantation owners moved away from the forced indentured servitude of Africans and instead began enslaving them.

The transition from the system of bond labor to chattel African slavery was expedited by the uprising known as Bacon's rebellion in 1676. The rebellion was led by a multiracial alliance of bond workers who attacked the planter elites, demanding compensation and an end to their servitude. Although the rebellion was staved off, a deep-seated fear of a potential revolution was instilled in the minds of elites.[135] Michelle Alexander, author of *The New Jim Crow*, elaborates, writing, "In an effort to protect their superior status and economic position, the planters shifted their strategy for maintaining dominance. They abandoned their heavy reliance on indentured servants in favor of the importation of more Black slaves."[136] The present-day concept of race emerged to justify this new system of chattel slavery.[137]

---

[133] Bennet Jr., L. *The Shaping of Black America* (Penguin Books, 1975). 62.
[134] Alexander, 2012. 24.
[135] Ibid.
[136] Ibid.
[137] Ibid. 22.

The Risk Of Racism

For elites with enslaving interests, the dark complexion of Africans served as the key differentiator that enabled them to brand Africans with the mark of inferiority. Soon afterward, as we previously discussed, scientists began to publish literature confirming the supposed inferiority of the Black race. The consensus among the scientific and elite communities further confirmed the idea of a White supremacist racial hierarchy in the minds of almost every White American, as well as in the minds of many Black Americans.

The notion of White superiority and Black inferiority appealed heavily to elite plantation owners who became extremely wealthy thanks to cheap labor in the form of slavery. But this notion of White superiority especially struck a chord with impoverished White Americans. While they could not own slaves, they were afforded the privilege of not being seen as the outcasts of society.[138] As the elite reaped the economic benefits of slavery, the concept of race was coincidingly created to justify among poor Whites the socioeconomic hierarchy that pigeonholed Black Americans as the pariahs of society.

Wealthy Southern plantation owners quickly grew dependent on the immense profits of slavery. They created and spread racist ideas that enabled them to garner public support for their new lucrative industry from the rest of White America, especially poor White people who came to believe that upholding their superior status was paramount to maintaining their livelihood. The profits generated from slavery and the fabricated racial hierarchy that justified the system became so lucrative and beneficial to the elites in America that the Founding Fathers structured the Constitution accordingly.

As historian Charles Beard explained in his influential book *An Economic Interpretation of the Constitution of the United States* published in 1913, the Founding Fathers, with almost no exceptions, drafted the constitution with their own economic interests in mind.[139]

---

[138] Ibid. 25.

[139] Beard, C. *An Economic Interpretation of the Constitution of the United States* (1913).

These "economic interests" had everything to do with maintaining slavery and dividing the masses along racial lines so that they could not unite and challenge the power of the elites. Michelle Alexander makes this connection, writing:

> The structure and content of the original Constitution was based largely on the effort to preserve a racial caste system—slavery—while at the same time affording political and economic rights to Whites, especially propertied Whites.[140]

The Founders included multiple clauses in the Constitution that directly benefitted slave owners and enabled the perpetuation of slavery. From the Fugitive Slave Act to postponing the ban of the Atlantic slave trade, framers consistently accommodated the demands of elite slave owners. Perhaps most significantly, the authors of the Constitution determined that slaves would only count as three-fifths of a person, specifically stating "Three-fifths of the number of slaves in any particular state would be added to the total number of free White persons, including bond servants, but not Indians, to the estimated number of congressmen each state would send to the House of Representatives." The infamous "three-fifths compromise" rendered slaves legally less than human. This rationale thwarted public shame of slaveholders, which gave them the leeway to keep profiting from slave labor.

The three-fifths compromise strengthened the idea of a racial hierarchy in the public consciousness. Further, ignorance creation was not restricted to the legal realm; it became entangled in religion as well. Americans who favored abolition were discouraged from speaking out against slavery by politicians and scientists who deemed slavery as a "necessary evil," but also by churches that, for centuries, used the Bible to justify slavery.[141]

---

[140] Alexander, 2012. 25.
[141] Kendi, 2016. 183.

While scientists published literature on nature's racial hierarchy and the Founding Fathers drafted a racist Constitution based on these "truths", ethnographers, poets, and Enlightenment thinkers purposely created false stereotypes about Africans and those with African heritage.[142] They spread false racist stereotypes claiming Africans "walked around naked like animals".[143] They asserted that Africans were better off as slaves in the United States than they were in Africa, regardless of how bad slavery was.

Additionally, they created contradictory stereotypes, claiming African slaves were docile and therefore fit to be slaves, yet when they revolted, all Africans were labeled as brutes, aggressive, and criminals. Ideas of Black criminality were created way back when Africans first illegally resisted their enslavement upon arrival in 1619. Any act of illegal resistance was labeled as "violent crime" in newspapers, and the "evil nature" of Africans was compared to that of the Devil. The stereotyping applied to all Black Americans, including those who were not slaves. Property was regularly stolen from free Blacks, yet the poverty of the Black community was always attributed to their alleged inferior nature. Their inherent laziness, sexual promiscuity, and stupidity.

These baseless stereotypes and ignorant claims were not spread innocently. They were used as tools of manipulation by the elite class: by spreading them, the public was led to rationalize and support slavery, as well as racial inequities, in general. Racism, however, is not a relic of a past era. The elite's manipulation of an ignorant public through the spreading of false ideas has survived well past the era of slavery. Public ignorance has given the elites the ability to employ racist ideas to justify and perpetuate many other systems of oppression throughout history.

---

[142] Ibid. 81.
[143] Ibid.

If Only We Knew

HOW RACIST IDEAS HAVE BEEN PRESERVED

When slavery was abolished after the Civil War, the southern economy and social structure were in shambles. Powerful White people were desperate for a new system of exploitation from which they could profit, and poor White people desired to maintain superior social status over newly freed Black Americans.[144] Their desires were soon satisfied when President Andrew Johnson's administration effectively pardoned all Confederate leaders and destroyed any hope of an effective reconstruction.

Racist elites in the South lobbied to have laws passed that allowed them to arrest Black Americans for just about *any reason*. These laws made vagrancy and loitering illegal for Black people specifically—they could be arrested for not having a job, for being homeless, or even for simply being in a town they were not from or could not prove they were from.[145] Black people were even arrested for "crimes" such as speaking too loudly to White women.[146] In an era that preceded the existence of pay stubs and drivers licenses, it was impossible to prove where you work or where you live. Unsurprisingly, Black Americans were arrested in droves simply because of the color of their skin.

With Black Americans being arrested at alarming rates, a large population of prisoners was soon established.[147] The elite publicized the higher arrest rates of Blacks to indicate that Black Americans committed more crimes.[148] Once again, the elite created ignorance by reaffirming the age-old racist idea that Blacks are dangerous criminals who needed to be locked up. Once the public had been convinced arresting Black Americans en masse was not only

---

[144] Alexander, 2012. 26-27.

[145] Ibid. 28.

[146] *Slavery by Another Name* (PBS). http://www.pbs.org/tpt/slavery-by-another-name/watch/.

[147] Ibid.

[148] Kendi, 2016. 282.

The Risk Of Racism

morally acceptable, but also socially necessary, the elite class had the green light to establish the next profitable system of oppression and exploitation. This time, a revamped form of slavery.

Those in power in the South soon realized they could re-enact a system of oppression and exploitation by utilizing a clause in the Thirteenth Amendment, the clause that outlaws slavery "except as punishment for a crime". Through a system known as "convict leasing", prisons began "leasing" inmates to plantations, mines, and railroads that needed workers.[149] Additionally, plantation owners forced many Black laborers into servitude through the system of peonage and sharecropping, which placed Black workers in inescapable debt. Black workers with debt that was deemed unpayable were forced to sign contracts in which they conceded to continue their work without compensation. These contracts subjected them to be whipped and confined. Essentially, they were forced to sign themselves up for slavery.[150]

By manipulating the ignorant public with untrue racist ideas, the elites re-established the profitable industry of slave labor in the form of new oppressive systems, convict leasing and peonage. The convict labor industry even proved to be more profitable than slavery itself.[151] *How?* Well, in the era of slavery, enslaved Africans were sold as a commodity and had a high market price. Most did not own enslaved people, and the plantation owners who did usually only owned a few.[152] Therefore, slave owners had an economic incentive to keep those they enslaved alive. In the new system of convict leasing, however, these laborers were *not* in short supply. As such, there was no economic reason for those using prison labor to keep prisoners alive. So, prisoners were literally worked to death.

---

[149] *Slavery by Another Name* (PBS). http://www.pbs.org/tpt/slavery-by-another-name/watch/.

[150] Ibid.

[151] Ibid.

[152] *Conditions of antebellum slavery* (PBS). https://www.pbs.org/wgbh/aia/part4/4p2956.html

According to the PBS documentary, *Slavery by Another Name*, the system of prison labor was 50–80 percent cheaper than slavery.[153]

During this era of convict leasing, those in power employed subtle changes in the rhetoric, rules, and laws of the country, which was essential in replacing the old system of control with the new one. By taking advantage of the highly adaptable nature of racism and racist institutions, Southern elites ensured Jim Crow segregation juxtaposed the exploitative systems of peonage and convict leasing. Legal segregation became the new law of the land.[154]

Once again, this was possible because of the intentional creation of ignorance. Black men were labeled as aggressive, dangerous, lazy, and stupid. It was insisted by those in power that Black people needed a system of rules and codes to follow so that White people could live safely among them. Fear, hatred, and a sense of superiority towards the Black race persisted in the White community as a result.[155] The racist rhetoric, codes, and laws that called for explicit segregation in seemingly every institution (e.g., schools, public transportation, restaurants, and public facilities including bathrooms and water fountains)[156] were implemented to prevent upward social mobility of the Black community. The resulting absence of social advancements within the Black community was then used to reinforce the negative racist stereotypes that labeled Black people as inferior. The systems of control in place were rationalized by created ignorance. Then, ignorance was weaponized, and this amplified the risks posed by legalized racism.

In addition to racist legal codes, the systems of convict leasing and peonage were supported by White supremacist terror organizations, which were abundant during this period. These organizations fulfilled the desire of White people to remind Black

---

[153] *Slavery by Another Name* (PBS). http://www.pbs.org/tpt/slavery-by-another-name/watch/.

[154] Alexander, 2012. 21.

[155] Ibid. 27.

[156] Ibid. 35.

people of their inferior and subordinate position in society.[157] Terror groups bolstered the existence of the racist institutions and systems through the lynching of Black Americans and by using scare tactics and brutal violence to deter Black people from voting in elections. Black Americans lived in constant fear of terror organizations and of a justice system that made no effort to protect them. When I say, "no effort", I mean it: from 1889–1929 it is estimated that a Black man was lynched *every four days*, yet from 1876–1966 only *one* White man was convicted of first-degree murder of a Black man.[158] Lynchings served as a public reminder that Black lives were inferior and expendable in America.

Discrimination and terror against the Black community enabled powerful White people—the elite—to maintain public support for their extremely profitable industries built on the exploitation of Black people. Elite Americans were able to create and weaponize ignorance so effectively that they manipulated the non-elite White community into believing the lies of racist ideas so whole-heartedly, that non-elite White people started terror organizations to bring their racist beliefs into violent fruition. Meanwhile, these non-elite White people were acting against their self-interests, considering that antiracist policies would have benefitted them far more than the racist ones they helped maintain (more on this later). This is perhaps the greatest sleight of hand in history. Intentionally created ignorance blinded these non-elite White Americans from the truth, and the elites profited immensely from this ignorance.

The Civil Rights movement of the 1960s led to the removal of explicitly racist policies in legislation and laws. However, it did not dismantle the racist systems of oppression and exploitation. Today, the business of exploiting the Black community for virtually free labor has been upheld by the system of mass incarceration, which, due to generations of "practice" with other systems, has been

---

[157] Ibid. 27.

[158] *Slavery by Another Name (*PBS). http://www.pbs.org/tpt/slavery-by-another-name/watch/.; Kendi. (2016), 259.

constructed in such a way that it is extremely resistant to change and reform.[159]

One aspect of mass incarceration's durability ironically emanates from the absence of blatantly racist laws and regulations standing in the way of success for Black people. Despite the façade of equality under today's laws, there is still an undeniable presence of racial barriers ingrained in the structure of our society. Yet, without explicitly racist laws, the economic and social hardships endured by Black people have been largely, and falsely, attributed to their own behaviors and perceived personal shortcomings or failings.

The White elite seized the opportunity to transform racist ideas in the "age of colorblindness" by shifting the concept of Black inferiority from biology to culture. By calling on the Black community to take on more "personal responsibility" and to get off welfare, the elites could preserve public ignorance while abandoning the old racist ideas that claimed Blacks' biological stupidity and laziness.[160] They successfully preserved widespread ignorance among the public claiming that the Black community caused their own hardships and was therefore undeserving of assistance.[161] Perhaps most significantly to the established of mass incarceration, the rhetoric of calling for "law and order" (which we will discuss further in the next chapter) reasserted the idea of Black criminality and spawned the perceived need to create a "tough-on-crime" mentality in legal codes across the country.

Now, almost 50 years later, this misleading notion continues to surround the issue of economic and legal injustice within the Black community. The current insistence that we have achieved a post-racial society is false and perpetuates already existing ignorance.[162] The removal of explicitly racist language, combined with the success of some Black citizens, celebrities, and politicians (most notably the

---

[159] Alexander, 2012. 4, 22.
[160] Ibid. 48.
[161] Ibid. 45.
[162] Ibid. 11.

election of Barack Obama),[163] has led many to believe members of the Black community are now afforded the same opportunities as members of the White community. As a result, many White people incorrectly believe there are no longer racist obstacles preventing Black people from achieving success. The widespread belief in a post-racial society makes it exponentially more difficult to eradicate racist ideas and root out systemic racism. But, of course, that was the point.

HOW OUR EDUCATION SYSTEM PERPETUATES IGNORANCE

Public ignorance of the risk of racism is largely maintained through our K-12 education system. By examining the shortcomings apparent in the elementary and secondary education systems, we can begin to understand why young adults leave high school without a factual, firm grasp of what slavery truly entailed, its lasting consequences, and the extent of racial injustices seen throughout American history. What we learn in history classes is almost always a "whitewashed" history of our country. It should be noted that history is not merely a record of facts; how those facts were recorded and by whom they were recorded are also components of "history". Typically, the history we are taught is based on accounts of White people with White experiences and White nationalist biases.

For example, let's look at the book *American Negro Slavery* written in 1918 by Ulrich Bonnell Phillips. The book disregarded all the facts about what slavery really was, opting instead to promote ignorance by claiming that slavery was, "An unprofitable commerce dominated by benevolent paternalistic planters civilizing and caring for a 'robust, amiable, obedient and content' barbaric people."[164] While that may sound like an outrageous, obvious lie

---

[163] Ibid. 11.
[164] Kendi, 2016. 287.

today, it was widely accepted during the early 20th century, and the author, Ulrich Bonnell Phillips, was one of the most respected academics of his time. In a society where the public is kept ignorant of the many layers of racism, blatant lies such as Phillips' are often passed as truth.

The revising and neglecting of Black history, however, is not a practice of a past era. It still happens today. A perfect example of Black history that has been excluded from our history textbooks is the 1921 Tulsa race massacre, which was an extreme act of racial violence in which White mobs attacked and murdered Black people, their homes, and their businesses. Today, because of the intentional shortcomings of our education system, our society remains ignorant of the true history of racism.

While this revisionist practice of history is commonplace in education textbooks across the country, the state you live in determines the material you learn regarding racial history. So-called "conservative states" simply do not do anywhere near an appropriate job of teaching the topic slavery and racial injustice to students. In North Carolina, for example, students learn that African slaves came to the United States as immigrants.[165] Frequently, "conservative" educators are very skeptical of, and sometimes strongly opposed to, any curriculum that includes lessons centered on the *1619 Project*, a project developed by the *New York Times* that re-assesses the impact slavery has had on the shaping of the United States.[166] The Trump Administration's 1776 commission, which blatantly disregards historical evidence to the point where the slave-owning Founding Fathers are portrayed as abolitionists, is another example of conservatives rewriting history to preserve ignorance. To wipe lessons of slavery, the civil rights movement, and other Black history

---

[165] Duncan, J., Zawistowski, C., Luibrand, S. *50 States, 50 Different Ways of Teaching America's Past* (CBS News, 2020). www.cbsnews.com/news/us-history-how-teaching-americas-past-varies-across-the-country/.

[166] *Where Left and Right Agree on Civics Education, and Where They Don't* (Education Next, 2020). www.educationnext.org/where-left-right-agree-civics-education-where-they-dont/.

from elementary and high school curriculums, conservatives across the country have also called into question Critical Race Theory—a graduate level academic theory. The refusal to accurately teach the history of slavery directly affects how young adults come to see the world around them.

Our education system offers our children an incomplete education of our history. The years of legalized slavery and Jim Crow are critical to understanding the history of America, but they are far from the only hardships that have plagued—and continue to plague—the Black community. Yet, vague lessons about slavery and Jim Crow are often the full extent to which we teach our children about the history of racism. The oversimplified selection of what we are taught regarding the plight of the Black community points to the intentional creation of ignorance in our education system.

For example, the average person typically knows more about slavery than convict leasing, which, as previously discussed, rivaled slavery in its horrendous treatment of Black Americans. This is precisely because most young adults never learn about convict leasing. It is worth asking why the era of convict leasing is given little importance in the history books.

Those who construct school curriculums choose to neglect significant historical facts in the post-civil rights era when covering the history of race relations in the United States. We are taught to believe Martin Luther King Jr.'s "dream" has been fulfilled, and that we are now an equal society for all races. *How can we possibly expect the public to be knowledgeable about systemic racism and the risks it poses to society if we don't even bother to teach our kids comprehensively about race and inequality?* The answer is simple: we cannot.

Of course, the inadequate education of our history that we currently provide did not develop by accident. Racist ideas have always played an instrumental role in preserving racist, exploitative institutions and laws. Historian and antiracist activist Ibram X. Kendi sums up this relationship perfectly in his book, *Stamped from the Beginning*. He writes about the Virginia slave codes put in place after Turner's rebellion, noting that, "Racist ideas, clearly, did not generate these slave codes. Enslaving interests generated these slave codes. Racist ideas were produced to preserve the enslaving interests."[167]

An ignorant public has always been essential to the preservation of oppressive, exploitative systems. By keeping the public ignorant of basic human biology, the elites who profited from slavery were able to convince the public of racist pseudoscience and anti-Black stereotypes. Similarly, the elites who currently profit from mass incarceration and the exploitation and oppression of Black people have preserved such stereotypes, in large part by keeping the public ignorant of historical facts.

By perpetuating racist ideas, elites have successfully persuaded a large proportion of White America to consistently vote to preserve racist socioeconomic systems. While these systems benefit the rich, they disadvantage everyone else, those of color and those non-elite White people. When we see conservatives pushing to purge the teaching of Black history from school curriculums, we must not be fooled into thinking they are acting in good faith. They do not believe removing Black history from curriculums is beneficial for the education of children. They are motivated by profits. By implementing legislation that will create deep-rooted ignorance for decades, they will maintain the public ignorance that is essential to the preservation of the exploitative systemic racism from which they and the power elite profit.

Let's think back to a question we contemplated earlier in this chapter: *If the concept of race is not backed by biological evidence, why did the United States construct a racist society that believes in the inferiority of certain races?* To unearth the answer to this question, all we must do is follow the money trail.

Over centuries, financial greed has been the engine driving the generation and preservation of the racist myths that exist in the public consciousness. The institution of slavery was established

---

[167] Kendi, 2016. 174.

because it was more cost effective than the system of indentured servitude. The creation of the false idea of a natural racial hierarchy was a direct attempt to justify this new economic system. After slavery was outlawed, Southerners lost their source of free labor, but through convict leasing and peonage they found ways to enslave African Americans legally. These systems solidified the stereotype of Black criminality. Starting in the mid-20th century, racist ideas shifted from biology to culture. By espousing the racist rhetoric associated with the War on Drugs, the calls for "law and order", and the insistence on personal responsibility, the elites in America have found new ways to profit from the discrimination of African Americans, primarily through mass incarceration.

There is no such thing as a fact-based racial hierarchy. The ignorant ideas our society holds about race can be attributed to the ruling class's pursuit of maximizing profit, as outlined by the notion of a racial hierarchy that justified slavery in the 17th, 18th, and 19th centuries, convict leasing and peonage in the 19th and early 20th centuries, and mass incarceration in the 20th and 21st centuries. Similarly, the racist policies of redlining, predatory lending, and segregation can all be traced back to elite White Americans' and corporations' pursuit to maximize profits and maintain power. These ideas were born out of the pursuit of power and profit, the risk of racism was established via the creation of an ignorant public, and this risk has been amplified through the manipulation of the ignorant public.

AN INGRAINED IMPLICIT BIAS

As we move forward and examine how racism affects us today, we must not forget that race is merely a social creation. As mentioned in the sections above, the concept of race emerged as powerful men searched for ways to justify profitable systems of oppression. This is a very important distinction to make, so I will say it again. Race does not exist on its own. *Racist ideas create race*. This notion that racism creates the "illusion of race" is what Karen and Barbara Fields call "racecraft".[168] The authors assert that racism has become the dangerous risk that it is because we have built our country upon a foundation of racist ideas.

Consequently, we have created an environment in which we all adopt and harbor racial biases, and we are all at risk of "entering the twilight zone of America's racecraft".[169] Growing up in an environment saturated with racial stereotypes and subtle (yet powerful) social reminders of a racial hierarchy (e.g., the color of Band-Aids matching the skin color of White people) causes everyone to develop unconscious racial biases. Inevitably, racist societies produce citizens who act racist.

Fields and Fields essentially argue that we have built a racist culture in this nation, and this culture prompts people to act in racist ways. Our culture has been influenced by our centuries-long history of promoting racist ideas. Unsurprisingly, this cultivation of a racist culture has negative consequences because our culture exerts significant influence over our actions and behaviors. In his book *Becoming Wild*, ecologist Carl Safina elaborates on how our culture plays a large role in who we become, writing:

> We become who we are not by genes alone… Culture stores important information not in gene pools but in minds. An individual receives genes only from their parents but can receive culture from anyone and everyone in their social group.[170]

Put simply, our environment greatly influences how we perceive the world.

---

[168] Fields, B., Fields, K. *Racecraft: The Soul of Inequality in American Life* (Verso, 2012).
[169] Ibid. 27.
[170] Safina, C. *Becoming Wild How Animal Cultures Raise Families, Create Beauty, and Achieve Peace.* (Henry Holt and Company, 2020).

The Risk Of Racism

The influence our culture has on our actions has been studied in the field of psychology. Jennifer L. Eberhardt, a Stanford social psychologist and author of *Biased*, explains in her book that all humans think in stereotypes, which vary from culture to culture. For Americans, grouping and stereotyping has been heavily influenced by deep-rooted racist stereotypes in our culture. Dr. Eberhardt, alongside others in her discipline, has found that an unconscious racial bias exists in the minds of every individual. She defines unconscious bias as the following:

> The beliefs and feelings we have about social groups that can be triggered without our awareness and can influence how we make decisions and take action... it is not limited to a few bad apples with evil intentions. Instead, anyone can be vulnerable to unconscious bias. It can affect us in ways that we are unaware of and despite our conscious desire not to be biased.[171]

Dr. Eberhardt explains that our unconscious, also known as implicit, racial biases are not merely our beliefs in stereotypes about particular groups. Rather, they are the product of the wiring of our brain and the racist disparities present in our society. Through implicit bias, racist beliefs and stereotypes literally change the way our brain functions. Eberhardt offers the following example:

> Because we associate Blacks with criminality, the mere presence of a Black face can facilitate our ability to recognize a blurry image of a gun or a knife. It can lead us to see Black neighborhoods as crime ridden and filled with disorder—regardless of the actual crime level and the amount of debris on the streets.[172]

---

[171] *A Conversation with Jennifer Eberhardt: Author of Biased: Uncovering the Hidden Prejudice that Shapes what we See, Think, and Do.*
[172] Ibid.

In other words, racist stereotypes can physically alter your brain's perception of reality.

That fact alone is indicative of the damaging effects the elite's creation of ignorance has on everyone. As Americans, we have grown up in a country that has been regurgitating racist stereotypes since its origin. Again, this is because the spread of racist ideas serves as a way for the elite to create conscious ignorance among the public. Yet, this ignorance has become so pervasive and deeply rooted that it has had a direct effect on the inner workings of our brains. In his autobiography, Malcolm X explained the impact of our racist culture perfectly: "The American political, economic, and social *atmosphere* ... automatically nourishes a racist psychology in the White man."[173]

THE EVOLUTION OF RACISM

The concepts of racecraft and unconscious bias are crucial to our understanding of the racism in our society that greatly disadvantages communities of color, especially the Black community. The problem of racism in our country today is threefold: 1) racist policies, laws, and institutions still remain in our society, 2) as individuals, we are woefully incompetent when it comes to understanding antiracism, recognizing when we, someone else, or a law is racist, managing our biases, and understanding the situations that may trigger our biases, and 3) we have collectively failed to recognize that racism hurts each and every one of us economically, socially, and spiritually.

We are not adequately educated in school. The core issues of the risk of racism are rarely talked about in the media and are largely neglected by politicians and activists who campaign for the eradication of systemic racism. As politicians, activists, and everyday Americans debate the best solutions to eradicate racism,

---

[173] X, M., Haley, A. *The Autobiography of Malcolm X: with the Assistance of Alex Haley.* (Ballantine Books, 1973). 308.

they consistently fail to consider a very important piece of the puzzle. *Racism doesn't require a racist and having a conscious desire to act without bias does not always prevent one from doing so.* Ignorance, however, distracts us from this truth.

Conservatives often deny the existence of racism in modern society by rhetorically framing it in comparison to past eras. They say the eras of slavery and Jim Crow were racist, and today is nothing like those eras. Therefore, today we are not racist. Progressives respond to this frame by claiming that today, in many ways, is quite similar to those eras. Conservatives respond back calling progressives crazy and accuse them of playing victim or making a big deal out of nothing.

The truth is that while "old-fashioned racism"—a form of racism in which people are openly racist and act on their prejudices—does still exist (as evidenced by hate crimes seen on the news), it is not as prevalent as it once was. There is no longer a lynching every four days. But that does not mean racism no longer exists. Far from it. While racism has become less "old-fashioned", it is highly adaptable and has taken on new, more implicit forms. Ibram X. Kendi describes this phenomenon as a "dueling duality" where antiracist progress has been mirrored by the evolution of racist ideas.[174]

For example, when segregation was condemned and outlawed during the civil rights movement (an antiracist policy and idea), we enacted racist legislation with "colorblind language" to maintain segregation (a racist policy and idea). As a result, while we do not have explicitly racist laws in place to segregate schools today, we have covertly racist laws and regulations that have made the schools of today more segregated than those of 40 years ago.[175]

Additionally, as mentioned previously, centuries of both implicit and explicit promotion of racist ideas have created an environment in which every American harbors various unconscious racial

---

[174] Kendi, 2016.

[175] Strauss, V. *Report: Public schools more segregated now than 40 years ago* (Washington Post, 2013).

biases. Such biases manifest themselves as racist actions that disproportionately affect Black Americans in myriad ways (e.g., Black Americans disproportionately face economic and healthcare hardships, experience microaggressions and hate crimes by fellow Americans, and, most notably, fall victim to police brutality and an unjust criminal justice system at higher rates). Progressives' ignorance about the evolution of racism has hindered their ability to enlighten those who have fallen victim to the idea that racism died during the civil rights movement of the 1960s. More damaging, however, is the manipulation of the ignorance held by the population who denies racism's contemporary existence.

THE MANIPULATION OF PUBLIC IGNORANCE

As explained earlier, racist ideas have been created and maintained primarily because they enable the elite class to make money—lots of it. Manipulating the public to believe in racist ideas weakens the solidarity of the working class.[176] It drives working class Whites to vote against their economic self-interests in favor of policies that almost exclusively help the wealthy. After the Civil Rights movement, conservatives realized that their appeal to voters who hold racist ideas would have to be delivered in a race-neutral language. Make no mistake, however: racism and racist fearmongering was, and still is, at the center of their political strategies. Michelle Alexander elaborates:

> Some conservative political strategists admitted that appealing to racial fears and antagonisms was central to this strategy, though it had to be done surreptitiously. H.R.

---

[176] Reich, M. *Who Benefits from Racism? The Distribution among Whites of Gains and Losses from Racial Inequality* (The Journal of Human Resources, 1978). 525.

Haldeman, one of Nixon's key advisers, recalls that Nixon himself deliberately pursued a Southern, racial strategy: "He [President Nixon] emphasized that you have to face the fact that the whole problem is really the Blacks. The key is to devise a system that recognizes this while not appearing to." Similarly, John Ehrlichman, special counsel to the president, explained the Nixon administration's campaign strategy of 1968 in this way: "We'll go after the racists." In Ehrlichman's view, "that subliminal appeal to the anti-Black voter was always present in Nixon's statements and speeches." [177]

How have conservatives been so successful at maintaining racist ideas and manipulating the voting tendencies of those who hold them? To answer this question, we must understand why people hold racist ideas and have an interest in preserving systemic racism in the first place.

Typically, those who oppose racial equality (i.e., those who deny systemic racism and oppose policy proposals aimed to uplift and invest in the Black community) falsely believe that achieving racial equality is a zero-sum game. They believe that helping one group—the Black community—will hurt another group—the White community. This has led many White Americans to believe that in recent years anti-White discrimination has increased while anti-Black discrimination has decreased. University of Denver professor of law, Rebecca Aviel, explains:

> White Americans are increasingly expressing anxiety about anti-White discrimination, with more than half of the respondents in a recent survey embracing the view that it is "as big a problem" as discrimination against people of color. This startling and inaccurate assessment is perhaps best explained by research revealing that many Americans

---

[177] Alexander, 2012. 43, 44.

view rights as a zero-sum game, in which advances for some necessarily bring losses for others. This attitude toward rights has enormously troubling implications... the zero-sum premise is particularly corrosive to our aspirations for racial justice.[178]

The widespread belief in a racial zero-sum game is grounded in the ignorance spread by the elites. There is no evidence to support it. In contrast, there is an abundance of evidence proving that the zero-sum game theory does not apply to racial justice. Professor Gordon Hodson of Brock University's department of psychology and his PhD student, Megan Earle, found evidence suggesting that anti-Black and anti-White discrimination have both decreased over time and that "a rising tide of tolerance lifts all boats".[179]

Yet, despite the overwhelming body of evidence debunking the idea of racial justice as a zero-sum game, Hodson and Earle concluded the following:

> Such themes of White loss and perceived anti-White discrimination are also central in the emerging far-right populism and (White) nationalist movements in the United States and Europe in recent years, and reverse discrimination is believed to have played a role in the presidential election of Donald Trump.[180]

Hodsen and Earle found that the same ignorance exploiting strategy Nixon once used to secure the Southern racist vote was applied by Donald Trump in his 2016 presidential campaign. *The difference?* Trump, ever aware of the shifting demographics in our nation, decided to primarily attack immigrants instead of narrowly

---

[178] Aviel, R. *Rights as a Zero Sum Game* (Arizona Law Review, 2018).
[179] Gander, K. *Republicans Tend to Think Blacks and Whites Face Similar Levels of Racism, Study Suggests* (Newsweek, 2019).
[180] Ibid.

focusing on the Black community. He labeled Mexican immigrants as rapists, murderers, and drug dealers. He called for a ban on all Muslim immigrants. He even went as far as to call on our nation to stop welcoming immigrants from "shithole" countries. Creating ignorance that predisposes the public to accept racist ideas, and then appealing to these racist, hateful attitudes has always been, and still is, at the center of most conservative political campaigns.

But, *how exactly have Republicans convinced a large proportion of the United States population to believe in an idea that is completely grounded in ignorance?* To understand, we must study history. The idea of a zero-sum game for racial equity has its origin with President Andrew Johnson. When Johnson vetoed the very moderate Civil Rights Act of 1866, he and his constituents spread the zero-sum game and reverse discrimination myths to support their position. As Ibram X. Kendi explains, "If there was any semblance of equal opportunity, these racists argued, then Blacks would become the dominators and Whites would suffer. This was—and still is—the racist folklore of reverse discrimination."[181] Today, by evolving and rephrasing racist ideas, and by continuously inciting the fear of a zero-sum game regarding racial equity in many generations of White Americans, the modern-Republican Party has been able to galvanize voters around a racist platform.

We can identify careful, strategic rhetoric in the following conservative refrains, all of which are racist: *"If Black people didn't commit so many crimes they wouldn't be in prison", "If they listened to the officer and didn't resist, they wouldn't have been shot", "If their fathers didn't abandon their families Black children would be more successful", "If they just worked harder they could be successful; look at Barack Obama and Lebron James."* The list goes on.

Statements like these dismiss the systemic reasons behind the plight of the Black community, as well as the data and statistics that dispel such racist notions. They blame the struggles of the

---

[181] Kendi, 2016. 239.

Black community on Black Americans and Black culture, not once considering the historical and sociological evidence of the systems of oppression that target the Black community and have ultimately relegated them to second-class citizen status in America.

Of course, these racist ideas of today are nothing new. Black people were blamed for causing their own problems when they were slaves, once they were freed, and during Jim Crow.[182] Black people have been labeled as criminals, lazy, dangerous, stupid, and sexually promiscuous from the moment they arrived in the colonies of America.[183] Do not be fooled into thinking that the racist ideas of today are not the same as the racist ideas of the past. If you could see how these stereotypes were based on untrue, ignorant, racist ideas in 1857 (the year "separate but equal" was declared the law of the land), in 1963 (the year of the Birmingham church bombing and the subsequent civil rights movement), or even in 1992 (the year Rodney King was infamously brutalized by police officers) you should be able to see that they are still racist ideas today.

The conservative elites in America have been evolving and re-wording racist ideas because they need ways to convince poor White America to vote against their economic interests. The existence of systemic racism, and racist ideas that aim to justify it, is vitally important for conservatives' ability to maintain power and preserve economic policies that benefit them and the wealthiest Americans.

Systemic racism works to oppress the Black community. This oppression deprives the Black community of wealth, quality education, good health and healthcare, equal treatment under law, and representation in media, politics, and executive leadership positions. Then, racist ideas are consistently promoted in politics, the media, and our history books, leading White America (especially poor White America) to believe that Black Americans cause their own problems. And with the removal of explicit racism from law, alongside the fact that racism doesn't always require an explicitly

---

[182] Ibid.
[183] Ibid.

racist person, institutional racism is made invisible, as there is no one person or no one policy at blame. Furthermore, conservative media platforms and politicians (including former President Trump) repeatedly affirm that systemic racism is a myth while engaging in aggressive fearmongering about the zero-sum game. Consequently, racist beliefs are firmly established in the minds of many, whether they realize it or not.

After people come to accept these racist ideas, their psychology equips them with a confirmation bias that predisposes them to readily accept any information that confirms their racist beliefs. Dr. Eberhardt elaborates this point:

> People tend to seek out and attend to information that already confirms their beliefs. We find such information more trustworthy and are less critical of it, even when we are presented with credible, seemingly unassailable facts that suggest otherwise. Once we develop theories about how things operate, that framework is hard to dislodge. Confirmation bias is the mechanism that allows these inaccurate beliefs to spread and persist. And these days there is no shortage of venues offering confirmation for whatever you believe.[184]

The vicious cycle repeats when people are successfully driven to vote for conservatives who continue to operate with this racist agenda.

This is how conservative elites have been able to manipulate the public. Their agenda is entirely dependent on creating, maintaining, weaponizing, and manipulating public ignorance. Only with this in mind is it explainable that 78 percent of Americans live from paycheck to paycheck and still elect a conservative President and Congress, whose economic policies overwhelmingly help the elite at their

---

[184] *A Conversation with Jennifer Eberhardt: Author of Biased: Uncovering the Hidden Prejudice that Shapes what we See, Think, and Do.*

expense. They vote for conservatives because conservatives promise to protect them from losing the zero-sum game of racial equity.

Let me repeat: *Conservatives depend on racism to persuade people to vote for politicians who will preserve economic systems that allow the wealthy to profit immensely at the expense of everyone else.* For this reason, conservatives actively perpetuate ignorance of systemic racism and intentionally fail to solve issues of racial inequality.

Please do not misinterpret the information above. By no means am I suggesting that every conservative voter is aware of, or actively participating in, the financial motivation that drives and preserves racist ideas and oppressive institutions. Most conservatives, both poor and wealthy, have indeed fallen victim to believing in racist ideas and stereotypes and vote conservatively in accordance with their ignorant beliefs. However, conservative elites, and the conservatives who build party platforms and create campaign strategies, have always been (and still are) aware of the monetary motivations to preserve systemic racism, oppressive racist policies, and racist ideas.

We must no longer avoid calling out their problematic, malicious intentions. It is not enough to condemn their actions; we must recognize and condemn their intentions as well. Racism was never an accident, and racism is still not an accident. Racist systems and policies were intentionally created, and racist campaign strategies are still utilized. Just as the elite antebellum plantation owners viewed slavery as a "necessary evil", the conservative elites of today view the preservation of public ignorance of racism as the "necessary evil" of our era.

SOLUTIONS FOR CREATING AN ANTIRACIST SOCIETY

The mission to dismantle the risks posed by racism in the United States will undoubtedly be a monumental task. While racism may seem like an abstract idea that exists only in one's mind, it manifests itself in real, material ways. We must recognize the connection between racism and unjust social phenomena, such as the housing policies and employment discrimination that has in large part led to the significant wealth disparity between Black and White Americans. We must openly acknowledge and discuss the real existence of the racial inequities present in the economy, education, the justice system, law enforcement, healthcare, and the electoral voting system.

Only by reversing the ignorance that obscures the roots of these inequities can our society begin to acknowledge and confront racial inequities as systemic issues, rather than dismiss them as isolated incidents. Indisputably, this country was founded with White supremacist institutions. Virtually every university in the nation has an African American History Department whose research confirms this fact.

Since our country's beginning, the elite have been successfully propagating racist ideologies among the public. This has created an environment in which we all unconsciously develop a racial bias grounded in ignorant stereotyping. Undoubtedly, these racial inequities and ideas were purposely created. Modern-day racism and racial inequities are therefore completely predictable and expected. It is no accident that we are where we are today. For this reason, attempting to solve the risk of racism through reactive policies that don't address the roots of racial inequities or by supporting "colorblind" initiatives will be ineffective. Intentional racist action brought us to this point, so intentional antiracist action is required to get us out of this mess.

CABINET OFFICE FOR RACE RELATIONS

To build a nation that treats all its citizens equally in every regard, we must be proactively antiracist. For this reason, I believe the creation of a cabinet office at the federal level of government that specifically addresses race relations is imperative. Currently, antiracist research centers are being established on college campuses across the nation. If universities can recognize that having an office devoted to antiracism is necessary, our government should recognize this, too. The appointed official for this position should rely on the research, studies, and solutions developed by scholars in Black studies, sociology, psychology, history, and civil rights law, among various other disciplines that provide insight on how to achieve antiracist progress.

As always, the most effective way to reduce the risks posed by racism is to reverse our ignorance. We must honestly educate the public, especially young people, so they understand and recognize that the plight of people of color is due to discrimination and a lack of opportunities, resources, and wealth—not inferiority. In a 2006 interview with esteemed journalist Bill Moyers, the late advocate of Black Liberation Theology, James Cone, had this to say regarding the need for Americans to confront our ugly history of racism: "[W]hen America can see itself historically… then we can figure out how we can start to overcome that legacy. You can't overcome something if you never acknowledge its presence."[185] When we honestly confront our history, we will be able to garner the public support necessary to enact the bold solutions I lay out in this section.

Although many solutions to eradicate racism have been developed and implemented on a local level in several institutions, very few people are aware of them. That said, there are countless solutions that have yet to be discovered, ones that only a commitment to proactive antiracism will reveal.

Now, our job is to spread awareness of the available solutions (so they may be scaled to a national level) and inspire passion for antiracist research (so we can work toward a more equitable society). So, let's talk about some of these solutions.

---

[185] Moyers, B. *Bill Moyers Journal: The Conversation Continues* (The New Press, 2011). 324.

The Risk Of Racism

DISPELLING THE ZERO-SUM GAME MYTH

First and foremost, to garner support for an antiracist movement, we must dispel the ignorant notion of the racial zero-sum game. As mentioned earlier, the belief in a zero-sum game has driven many White Americans to vote conservatively, and this belief has been the key mechanism in preserving systemic racism and racist ideas. The zero-sum game for racial equity does not exist. In fact, the exact opposite is the case. CEO and founder of PolicyLink, Angela Glover Blackwell, explains this fact:

> There's an ingrained societal suspicion that intentionally supporting one group hurts another. That equity is a zero-sum game. In fact, when the nation targets support where it is needed most—when we create the circumstances that allow those who have been left behind to participate and contribute fully—everyone wins. The corollary is also true: When we ignore the challenges faced by the most vulnerable among us, those challenges, magnified many times over, become a drag on economic growth, prosperity, and national well-being.[186]

The benefit of aiding society's most vulnerable and marginalized groups is known as the "curb-cut effect". Deriving its name from the curb-cuts that were installed in sidewalks to help people with physical challenges navigate the streets more easily, the idea holds that uplifting the most vulnerable communities helps everyone. While curb-cuts were specifically installed to aid people with physical challenges, it turns out that they also help people with no physical challenges as well; with curb-cuts, rolling luggage, riding bikes, and delivering goods and services becomes much easier. Let's dig a little deeper into this example of curb-cuts.

---

[186] Blackwell, A. *The Curb-Cut Effect: Laws and programs designed to benefit vulnerable groups, such as the disabled or people of color, often end up benefiting all of society.* (Stanford Social Innovation Review, 2017).

CURB-CUT EFFECT

You may be wondering, *"I understand how curb-cuts benefit everyone, but how does the curb-cut effect apply to systemic racism?* As you will see, the curb-cut effect *absolutely* applies to racism! Let's look at some examples.

- Reversing voter-suppression, which disproportionally hurts Black and Brown communities, creates a fairer democracy for everyone. [187]
- Reducing economic inequality by closing the racial pay gap would make the United States 14 percent richer overall.[188]
- Preserving and redesigning welfare programs to aid Black and Brown communities, which experience high rates of poverty, would help working class White Americans more than any other demographic as they make up the greatest number of welfare recipients.[189]
- Tackling segregation in our schools (which has extremely negative consequences for minority children) by increasing integration initiatives would decrease prejudice among all students, increase diversity, lead to higher achievement on test scores, and increase the chance of going to college among students of all races.[190]

---

[187] McElwee, S. *Why the Voting Gap Matters.* (Demos, 2014). https://www.demos.org/research/why-voting-gap-matters.

[188] McKay, T. *Why Racial Equality Is Good for the Economy, in One Chart.* (Mic, 2014).

[189] Black. R., et. al. *The 'Welfare Queen' Is a Lie.* (The Atlantic, 2016); Jan. T. *The biggest beneficiaries of the government safety net: Working-class whites* (The Washington Post, 2017).

[190] Kamenetz, A. *The Evidence That White Children Benefit from Integrated Schools.* (NPR, 2015); *The Benefits of Socioeconomically and Racially Integrated Schools and Classrooms* (The Century Foundation, 2019).

Those are just a few examples, but they present clear evidence that the zero-sum game regarding racial equity is a myth. It is crucially important to expose this.

NO SCARE TACTICS

Often, people vote in accordance with their perceived self-interests to protect themselves from danger and things they fear—according to Psychologist Dr. Nigel Barber, this tendency is particularly common amongst conservatives.[191] Conservative politicians and media figures, as we have discussed over these past few chapters, use the tactic of fearmongering to influence voters to vote for conservative politicians. By using the rhetoric of "law and order", depicting the world as filled with "good guys" and "bad guys", suggesting the criminality of Black Americans, and alluding to popular refrains such as "real Americans are losing the country", conservative politicians and media figures manipulate much of the population to vote based on a distorted fear of losing certain advantages that other groups would gain. Taking this scare-tactic tool away can only be done by reversing ignorance. When people become aware that the zero-sum game of racial equity is a myth and realize the existence of a curb-cut reality, they will be far less susceptible to racially charged fearmongering.

TRUSTING SCIENCE AND DATA

We must place trust in the science and data telling us that racism is predictable because when something is predictable, it is solvable. Statistician Nate Silver explains in his TED talk that

---

[191] Barber, N. *Why Do Some Poor People Vote Against their Interests?* (Psychology Today, 2019). https://www.psychologytoday.com/us/blog/the-human-beast/201903/why-do-some-poor-people-vote-against-their-interests.

racism (and its effect on how one votes) is predictable based on one's level of education, the quality of one's education, and one's exposure to people of other races and cultures (which is usually determined by one's neighbors and co-workers).[192] These factors help explain why Midwestern and Southern states tend to be more conservative, given that the "quality" of education is often lower and the segregation of both communities and schools is higher in southern states, comparatively.

Ignorance of the roots of racial inequities often leads to the acceptance of racist ideas as truth. Inadequate education coupled with a lack of exposure to people of various racial backgrounds creates this ignorance. Accordingly, again we see that the best way to mitigate the risk of racism is to reverse ignorance. Aside from improving education, which we will cover in just a moment, we should also look to adopt other solutions offered by Silver, such as smart street grids to increase interaction between pre-dominantly Black neighborhoods and pre-dominantly White neighborhoods, fostering more diverse and sustainable cities, and an intercollegiate exchange program where, for example, college students from NYU can study for a semester at Emory University (and vice versa) to experience different cultures within our country.[193]

ANTIRACIST EDUCATION

We need an educational revolution in the United States. While plenty of people emphasize the importance of improving education to improve social mobility and mitigate racial economic inequities, it's important to recognize that truly investing in educating means we must do more than just throw money at the problem (even though increasing funding is certainly important).

---

[192] Silver, N. *Does Racism Affect the Way You Vote* (TED, 2009). https://www.ted.com/talks/nate_silver_does_racism_affect_how_you_vote?language=en.
[193] Ibid.

We cannot continue to teach children the same material in the same way and expect them to process it differently. We do not provide children with an honest and adequate education of the history of our country. We must start teaching elementary and high-school students about the origin, intentional preservation, and evolution of racist ideas, and we must start teaching them about the perverse motivations behind such ideas. Additionally, we must start teaching students how to be antiracist and how to both recognize and manage their unconscious biases. This step is crucial to creating future generations of antiracist individuals.

Finally, we must adopt education reform policies that directly help disadvantaged communities. I'm talking about reducing the sizes of schools and the classes within them,[194] investing in integration initiatives,[195] and creating a fairer discipline system to eradicate the school to prison pipeline.[196] These are solutions that have been demonstrated to result in better socioeconomic outcomes for all children, but especially for children of color. Public ignorance, however, has prevented us from scaling these initiatives across the nation. We must raise awareness of their effectiveness and necessity, and subsequently pressure state and local politicians to implement these reforms in school districts across the country.

Moreover, we must also shift our focus away from charter schools and other methods of school choice in our effort to offer better education for disadvantaged groups. While some school choice initiatives have proven to be effective, the fact is that while some students benefit from these programs, the vast majority do not get the opportunity to leave their under-resourced, underfunded, low-quality public schools and they suffer the consequences. We

---

[194] Biddle, B., Berliner, D. Small *Class Size and Its Effects* (Educational Leadership: Journal of the Department of Supervision and Curriculum Development, 2002).

[195] Logan, J., et. Al. *The Geography of Inequality: Why Separate Means Unequal in American Public Schools.* (The Journal of Health and Social Behavior, 2012).

[196] *How Can We Stop The School-To-Prison Pipeline?* (MST Services, 2018).

must improve all schools, especially those experiencing the most hardships.

POLICE REFORM

One of the most important racial justice reforms we must tackle comes from within the police system. While we will continue our discussion of the criminal justice system in Chapter 4, this issue is tied so intimately to race that it must be discussed here in this chapter as well. We must demilitarize the police (i.e., take away their tear gas and machine guns, among other unnecessary weapons). Military grade weapons in the hands of police officers are unnecessary and dangerous, especially when considering that de-escalation methods are much more effective for reducing crime than resorting to violence.

We must re-examine police budgets and re-allocate funding by investing in community services that tackle drug addiction, mental illness, and homelessness. For racist reasons, we have decided to underfund and over-police the most vulnerable communities in our country, and this has had fatal consequences for too many people in the Black community. The militarization of the police and the extremely broad discretion we have afforded them in their use of force has left entire generations of communities of color traumatized. It is time to stop traumatizing our own citizens.

We must remove all perverse incentives for the police to fund themselves, such as the practice of civil forfeiture and the requirement to reach a quota for minor traffic tickets. Such incentives inherently target overpoliced marginalized communities at higher rates. These minor stops have immense potential to cause significant economic harm and they prompt unnecessary stops for extremely minor crimes, which far too often have tragic endings. The role of the police must shift from managing a wide array of community issues (e.g., dealing with minor traffic infractions, homelessness, and the mentally ill) to managing serious crimes (e.g., dealing with domestic abuse, murder, and burglary).

We must require training in de-escalation practices, and we must also make the "#8cantwait" policies required in every precinct.[197] We must increase accountability for police officers who are guilty of serious misconduct by abolishing qualified immunity and independent review boards, and by making it impossible for police officers who have been fired for misconduct to be hired in another police precinct. Finally, we must follow the lead of the Center for Policing Equity and make their CompStat for Justice required use within every police department.[198] The Center has seen tremendous success in reducing racist police conduct by measuring racist behaviors and holding police officers accountable to a zero-tolerance metric.

ECONOMICS, HEALTHCARE, AND VOTING

On a broader scale, racism is connected to economic inequality, health inequality, and voting inequality. We must raise the minimum wage so that everyone is paid a living wage. We must guarantee universal health care so that everyone can receive preventative care or a prescription without going broke. And we must pass the Anti-Corruption Act (mentioned in Chapter 1) and the For the People Act to ensure fair voting rights for everyone. These solutions, among others, will be discussed in more detail in later chapters.

REMOVAL OF HISTORICAL RACIST SYMBOLS

We must declare all Confederate and Nazi symbols as hate speech and label any display of such symbols as a hate crime. Display of such symbols is not free speech—it is dangerous speech. Following this logic, we must remove all statues of Confederate

---

[197] 8 Can't Wait. https://8cantwait.org.
[198] Policing Equity. https://policingequity.org.

leaders and we must rename anything and everything named after a Confederate leader. Additionally, all White supremacy groups, such as the Proud Boys, should be labeled and treated as domestic terrorist organizations.

REPARATIONS AND ANTIRACIST INTIATIVES

We must pass HR 40, which is the bill calling for an inquiry into issuing reparations for slavery. Whether we end up deciding to issue reparations, the passing of this bill is necessary if we are serious about combatting our ignorance. We must not fall victim to the ignorant notion that reparations are an outlandish proposal. In the past, we issued reparations for the Japanese whom we held in internments camps. Slavery and its legacy have lasted far longer than the duration for which Japanese were held in these camps. We may find that reparations are necessary, or we may decide to opt for alternative antiracist strategies. Author Ta-Nehisi Coates states the importance of HR 40 so eloquently in his book, *We Were Eight Years in Power*:

> Perhaps after a serious discussion and debate—the kind that HR 40 proposes—we may find that the country can never fully repay African Americans. But we stand to discover much about ourselves in such a discussion—and that is perhaps what scares us. The idea of reparations is frightening not simply because we might lack the ability to pay. The idea of reparations threatens something much deeper—America's heritage, history, and standing in the world.[199]

In the 2020 Democrat Party primaries, progressive leaders put forth plans to combat the racial inequity in our country. We should follow and implement these plans. From Pete Buttigieg's Douglass

---

[199] Coates, T. *We Were Eight Years in Power: An American Tragedy* (One World, 2017).

Plan to the Biden Plan for Black America to Bernie Sanders's plan for racial justice, progressives have done their research and have presented legitimate plans that need to be enacted. Additionally, we must listen to the Black activists of our time: Bryan Stevenson, Ibram X. Kendi, Michelle Alexander, Dr. Bernice King, Dr. Phillip Atiba Goff, and Dr. Michael McAfee, to name a few. We must amplify both their voices and proposed solutions.

VOTE

Finally, we must persuade people to *vote against* the conservative candidates who have an active interest in preserving systemic racial oppression, and instead implore them to *vote for* antiracist candidates who vow to enact policies aimed at eradicating systemic racism. To usher in an antiracist society, we cannot ignorantly believe and act as if all we need to do is change the beliefs people hold in their hearts. In theory, changing hearts is great, but it does not come close to what is necessary to eradicate systemic racism. Similarly, inspiring antiracist passion through grassroots movements like marches, protests, and signing petitions is a great first step, but, as Dr. Bernice King (daughter of Martin Luther King Jr.) frequently remarks, it is imperative that we channel that energy and connect it to the agencies that can facilitate change on a large scale. Otherwise, our protests will fail to achieve substantial change. This logic applies to charity as well. Charities of all varieties simply treat the symptom; they fail to address the root cause of the problem.

The thing about systemic racism is that even if every individual was antiracist, the system itself is racist, so it will always produce racist outcomes. The only way to change our society and build a nation that treats all its citizens fairly and equally is to enact transformative policies at all levels of government, organizations, and institutions. And the only way to do that is to vote to elect the right people for that job. Ultimately, if you vote for conservatives who have an active interest in perpetuating systemic racism and racist ideas, whether you believe you yourself are racist or antiracist is irrelevant. As Ibram X. Kendi explains:

> An antiracist America can only be guaranteed if principled antiracists are in power, and then antiracist policies become the law of the land, and then antiracist ideas become the common sense of the people, and then the antiracist common sense of the people holds those antiracist leaders and policies accountable.[200]

We should have hope at this moment. While it is true that we are constantly reminded that we still suffer from a racist culture that has been built over the course of centuries, let us not forget, if we could build racist systems of hate and violence, then we can also tear them down and rebuild the beloved community of which Martin Luther King Jr. dreamed; one with antiracist systems of love, healing, and non-violence.

If we can reverse the widespread ignorance that acts as the host cell of the parasite that is the risk of racism, we can usher in an antiracist society.

---

[200] Kendi, 2016. 510.

4

The Risk Of Mass Incarceration

Many of the forms of discrimination that relegated African Americans to an inferior caste during Jim Crow continue to apply to huge segments of the Black population today—provided they are first labeled felons.
– Michelle Alexander

The United States of America incarcerates the most people of any country in the world. In this country, there are over 2.3 million people in prisons, 4.5 million on parole or probation, and approximately 10.6 million jail admissions each year.[201] No other nation incarcerates nearly as many people, not even the oppressive

---

[201] Sawyer, W., Wagner, P. *Mass Incarceration: The Whole Pie 2020* (Prison Policy Initiative, 2020). https://www.prisonpolicy.org/reports/pie2020.html; *Probation and Parole Systems Marked by High Stakes, Missed Opportunities* (Pew Trusts, 2018). https://www.pewtrusts.org/en/research-and-analysis/issue-briefs/2018/09/probation-and-parole-systems-marked-by-high-stakes-missed-opportunities

authoritarian states of China and Russia. Not only does the United States have the largest population of prisoners, but the country also touts the highest incarceration rate at 698 people per 100,000.[202] Considering the United States has over 330 million people, these numbers may not strike you as problematic. *Is 2.3 million out of 330 million people really that much?* The answer is simply, yes.

When comparing these prison statistics with those of other developed democratic nations and considering the negative ramifications of having millions of people behind bars, the risk of mass incarceration becomes clear. Mass incarceration has led to the widening of the racial health gap and the destruction of the nuclear family in communities across this country, especially Black communities.[203] It costs taxpayers at least $80.7 billion annually,[204] and, by all indications, is making society less safe.[205] Moreover, by subjecting those in prison to a slavery-esque prison labor system in which they are paid an hourly rate of between $.86 and $3.45, the true economic cost of incarceration is effectively shifted to prisoners.[206] Perhaps most damaging, mass incarceration preserves the racial caste system that has been oppressing Black Americans for over 400 years.[207]

So, what is going on here? Why are so many Americans behind bars? Does the U.S. simply have more "bad guys" than any other country in the world? Or, conversely, is the American justice and legal system intentionally set up to incarcerate its citizens at shockingly high rates?

---

[202] Sawyer, W., Wagner, P. *States of Incarceration: The Global Context 2018* (Prison Policy Initiative, 2018). https://www.prisonpolicy.org/global/2018.html.

[203] Wang, E., Wildeman, C. *Mass incarceration, public health, and widening inequality in the USA* (The Lancet, 2017).

[204] Arnold Ventures. https://www.arnoldventures.org/work/criminal-justice.

[205] Kirkpatrick, B. *Deterrence, Tough on Crime, and Links to the Prison Population Rate* (John Carroll University, 2016).

[206] Sawyer, Wagner, 2020.

[207] Alexander, 2012.

The Risk Of Mass Incarceration

The roots and consequences of mass incarceration have been researched by numerous civil rights organizations and scholars across the country. The answers to the aforementioned questions have been determined by scholars who: 1) examine who is being imprisoned and how that coincides with systematic racism, 2) study the graphs and proportions that show prison growth, 3) understand the racial power grab at play, 4) expose the monetary motivations behind the prison system, and 5) recognize how changes to the law (and how it is enforced) have contributed to mass incarceration.

The average American exhibits an incredible lack of knowledge and understanding about mass incarceration. Some don't understand how the factors listed above contribute to mass incarceration. Some don't know what these factors are. Significantly, others don't think to question the "fairness" of the justice system in their country. As we will discuss in this chapter, Americans are ignorant about mass incarceration because of intentionally spread misinformation. This created public ignorance enabled elites to establish the risk of mass incarceration with far-reaching strong support and very little resistance. The preservation of this ignorance has ensured the survival of mass incarceration and the amplification of the risk it poses.

Mass incarceration has presented one of the most threatening risks facing our nation and democracy for the last half-century. Yet, because ignorance has been created, the American people do not understand just how pressing this issue is. Hence, the prevalence of ignorance has made the crisis of mass incarceration practically invisible, amplifying the risk dramatically.

IGNORANCE = INVISIBILITY

Mass incarceration affects the Black community at staggeringly disproportionate rates. Racial inequality in the justice system is so great that Michelle Alexander has likened mass incarceration to a racial caste system, labeling it the "New Jim Crow". As Alexander defines it:

The term mass incarceration refers not only to the criminal justice system but also to the larger web of laws, rules, policies, and customs that control those labeled criminals both in and out of prison. Once released, former prisoners enter a hidden underworld of legalized discrimination and permanent social exclusion.[208]

Today, reminiscent of the slavery and Jim Crow eras, a large proportion of the Black population in the United States is subject to *legal* discrimination. In the current era of mass incarceration, it is legal to discriminate against former convicted felons who are in search of employment, housing, education, and public benefits.[209] This issue has led to myriad negative consequences for our society.

This crisis, however, has largely been misunderstood or unheeded by the American public. Public ignorance regarding the consequences of incarceration has allowed this problem to persist and has stifled the policy reforms necessary to make positive change. A 2016 poll conducted by *Morning Consult* and *Vox* shows just how dangerous this ignorance is.

The poll found that while most Americans say they are "against mass incarceration", they do not support legislation that would reduce the prison population and imprisonment rates.[210] Americans may very well hold progressive ideals in the abstract, such as theoretically being opposed to mass incarceration, but their knowledge of the problems they want to fix is shockingly and severely underwhelming. In other words, public ignorance is preventing actions being taken that are needed to end this injustice, even though most Americans agree that change is needed.

When we don't understand how a risk has been created and what we must do to mitigate it, the problem becomes virtually invisible.

---

[208] Ibid. 12.

[209] Ibid. 2.

[210] Lopez, G. *Want to end mass incarceration? This poll should worry you (Vox, 2016).* https://www.vox.com/2016/9/7/12814504/mass-incarceration-poll.

The Risk Of Mass Incarceration

This invisibility manifests in a public that is generally aware of an issue and wants to solve it, but their ignorance about the issue they want to solve prevents action and change. The invisibility of mass incarceration—like every other risk heightened by ignorance—doesn't just prevent action, it exponentially amplifies the risk.

I call mass incarceration invisible, because while it is an extremely serious crisis, it is not treated as one by most people in our country. *Why is this the case? How has an injustice so great been able to fly under the radar?* Invisibility is the result of intentionally created ignorance. Mass incarceration is given virtually no mainstream media attention and our current lawmakers and politicians are certainly not prioritizing the policies necessary to fix this crisis. As you may have inferred after reading Chapter 1, this lack of coverage is an upshot of the elite class's control over the media and political spheres. There have been no nationwide protests against mass incarceration akin to those against Jim Crow in the 1960s. Only by understanding the elite's control of the media and political spheres can we recognize why.

Aside from the lack of coverage in the media and by our politicians, one of the chief contributors to our ignorance comes from the intentional legislative decision to deprive felons of their right to vote. Since those who are affected most by mass incarceration (felons and ex-felons) are of no electoral value to politicians because they have been disenfranchised, lawmakers have little incentive to push for criminal justice reform. In other words, because they cannot vote, former felons are deprived of their voice to advocate for change and few politicians choose to use their voice to advocate for former felons.[211]

Ironically, as we discussed last chapter, ignorance has also been intentionally created via the removal of explicitly racist language in laws. After the Jim Crow era and the civil rights movement, state and federal legislatures barred virtually all blatant racial discrimination in the text of laws. While seemingly a positive change, replacing

---

[211] Kirkpatrick, 2016.

racist policies with "race-neutral" policies written in colorblind language has had very negative consequences.

The new legal language worked to covertly preserve systemic racism while constructing the façade that systemic racism was a relic of the past. Despite the appearance of legal equality for all, today, systemic racism is still ever-present in our legal codes. What is vital to recognize was that the switch to colorblind language in our laws was written with the intention to create risks. The intentional decision by lawmakers to amend legislation in a so-called "colorblind" fashion created ignorance among the public of the continued existence of racial inequality under law, and thus preserved systemic racial oppression.

Today, many have been duped into believing the law equally applies to White people and people of color. Further, the exalting of the ideal of colorblindness has convinced people racism is a problem of a past era. Ignorant of the racial disparities in the justice system and the elite's intentions behind the switch to colorblind writing in legal codes, many see no sociological reasons why the Black community is incarcerated at higher rates. Unsurprisingly, the public becomes vulnerable to accepting racist ideas that appear to resolve this paradox.

Influenced by the ignorance created through the propagation of racist ideas, many turn to blame the mass incarceration phenomenon on the violence and criminality "inherent" in Black culture.[212] Some even go as far as to claim that Black youth actually take pride in being incarcerated.[213] Yet, according to Donald Braman, author of *Doing Time on the Outside*, and clinical psychologist Diana Baumrind, this claim that Black youth take pride in being incarcerated has been found completely inaccurate. Through four years of extensive interviews with prisoners, ex-prisoners, and their families, Braman found that Black people do not feel pride

---

[212] Heideman, P., Birch, J. *The Poverty of Culture* (Jacobin Magazine, 2014). https://www.jacobinmag.com/2014/09/the-poverty-of-culture/.
[213] Ibid.

in incarceration, rather they feel shame.[214] Furthermore, Baumrind found that Black families place a greater emphasis on rule following and obeying authority than White families.[215] Still, since racist ideas are so deeply rooted in our society, many ignore or flat out deny statistics that disprove racial stereotypes and dismiss the ever-present shortcomings and injustices within our criminal justice system.

Public ignorance of mass incarceration is reproduced in our K-12 education system as well. In the last chapter, we discussed that while most social studies and history curriculums include some instruction on our country's history of racial injustice, the content taught is woefully inadequate. The education system doesn't afford students the ability to form a comprehensive understanding of the reality of the situation, which is that a legal, exploitative, and discriminatory racist industry known as mass incarceration is alive and well today. We have chosen to teach systematic racism and racial subordination as if it is confined to the past instead of teaching it as the living, breathing risk that it truly is.

Significantly, schools contribute to the creation of ignorance by not sufficiently teaching students about the Thirteenth Amendment. The Amendment reads, "Neither slavery nor involuntary servitude, except as a punishment for crime whereof the party shall have been duly convicted, shall exist within the United States, or any place subject to their jurisdiction." Students learn that the Thirteenth Amendment abolished slavery, but what is usually omitted is discussion of the clause in the amendment that permits slavery as "punishment for a crime". This incomplete education on the Thirteenth Amendment and its implications for society leads to widespread public ignorance about the fact that forms of slavery still legally exist for a significant proportion of our population—over two million people at any given time, to be specific.

---

[214] Braman, D. *Doing Time on the Outside: Incarceration and Family Life in Urban America* (University of Michigan Press, 2004).

[215] Baumrind, D. *An Exploratory Study of Socialization Effects on Black Children: Some Black-White Comparisons* (Child Development, 1972).

This clause in the Thirteenth Amendment enabled White people to continue to legally oppress and exploit the Black community after the abolition of slavery through convict leasing and peonage. The sub-minimum wage pay and forced labor of today's prisoners are also a consequence of this clause. The omission of teaching a complete history that includes mass incarceration and the ramifications of the problematic clause in the Thirteenth Amendment is part of the ongoing intention of the elites to create ignorance about our troubled history.

Racism is taught to students as a phenomenon of a past era. Consequently, contemporary issues of racial injustice are barely discussed, if ever, in schools. Students very rarely learn about the consequences of the "tough-on-crime" laws that were enacted during the War on Drugs, such as mandatory minimums and "three strikes" laws. These new laws, which disproportionately target people of color, were, and still are, directly correlated to the dramatic rise in incarceration.

It is a major failure of our education system that mass incarceration, the greatest racial injustice of the last half century, is not taught to students. Yet, of course, it is not really a failure. It is a success of the elite in their mission to create public ignorance. It is crucial to recognize just how instrumental the education system is in the elite's ability to create and perpetuate ignorance.

All these factors mentioned above have combined to produce the ignorance that has enabled the rise of mass incarceration. Systems that oppress and exploit Black Americans have never been eradicated, they have simply adapted to changing social norms and morphed into new systems. Do not be fooled; these new systems of oppression are just as vital to the elite class's existence in our society as past systems of oppression.

Michelle Alexander elaborates further when she writes, "As the systems of control have evolved, they have become perfected, arguably more resilient to challenge, and thus capable of enduring for generations to come."[216] Throughout American history, the racial caste system has

---

[216] Alexander, 2012. 22.

been dismantled and reincarnated over and over again. After slavery, the systems of convict leasing and peonage were established. The era of Jim Crow segregation functioned as a system of social control that juxtaposed those exploitative systems of convict leasing and peonage. When the civil rights movement began to dismantle the era of legal racial discrimination under Jim Crow law, the roots of mass incarceration—a system that sidesteps civil rights progress to re-establish legal racial discrimination—began to take form. Widespread public ignorance has always been created and maintained by the elite because its existence is essential to the reproduction of racially oppressive systems from which they enrich and empower themselves. So, let's look deeper into why and how we got here.

LAW & ORDER

As the Civil Rights movement was gaining serious momentum, conservatives realized that the era of explicit, open racism, i.e., Jim Crow and segregation, was unsustainable. Conservatives and the power elite, however, refused to accept the possibility of a society without a racial caste system. There was too much money being made and too much power being accumulated at the top for the elites to even consider relinquishing control. And because the elites had created ignorance of race so effectively, they had the support of non-elite White people who were determined to maintain their supposed racial superiority.

So, just like their predecessors replaced slavery with convict leasing and Jim Crow, conservatives, and the elites they advocate for, set out to create a new racial order. Living in post-Civil Rights Movement America, they realized that this new system had to be rhetorically race-neutral. Hence, to continue relegating Black Americans to the bottom rung of the totem pole, conservatives decided to shift their rhetorical tagline from "segregation forever" to "law and order".[217]

---

[217] Ibid. 39.

The call for "law and order" came at a time when crime and unemployment for young Black men were both on the rise in America. However, this rise in crime was less of an increase in the number of violent criminals as it was an increase in people in general. Michelle Alexander again provides us with a great explanation of this phenomenon:

> The reasons for the crime wave are complex but can be explained in large part by the rise of the "baby boom" generation—the spike in the number of young men in the fifteen-to-twenty-four age group, which historically has been responsible for most crimes. The surge of young men in the population was occurring at precisely the same time that unemployment rates for Black men were rising sharply, but the economic and demographic factors contributing to rising crime were not explored in the media. Instead, crime reports were sensationalized and offered as further evidence of the breakdown in lawfulness, morality, and social stability in the wake of the Civil Rights Movement.[218]

This framing in the media was instrumental to the conservative strategy of creating public support for "law and order".

Through this framing, ignorance was created among the public. Nearly everyone, including many in the Black community, fell victim to the misleading narrative that the crime rate was spiraling out of control and that no one was safe until the dangerous criminals were behind bars. Many even made the racist claim that the rise in crime was directly connected to the new freedoms gained by African Americans in the civil rights movement. Despite being illogical and negligent of facts, this method of ignorance creation was effective.

Conservatives were able to create a demand for the re-establishment of a racial order without being explicitly racist. Further, as many

---

[218] Ibid. 41.

were claiming that the rise in crime was due to the encouragement of criminality inherent in Black culture, many in the Black community were driven to support "tough-on-crime", "law and order" rhetoric to signal to others they were not "part of the problem". And once the Black community began to support the calls for "law and order", the conservatives had all they needed to "prove" that their "law and order" agenda was not racist, even though it always was.[219]

The Republican party quickly adopted the theme of "law and order" as their new defining characteristic. The slogan was so popular among the public that it practically became political suicide to not be "tough-on-crime". Therefore, after consistently losing political races down the ballot for decades the Democrats, who claimed to be liberal, eventually jumped on the racist "tough-on-crime" bandwagon as well.

THE WAR ON DRUGS

In 1982, President Ronald Reagan declared a War on Drugs in a supposed attempt to rehabilitate drug addicts and prevent further drug abuse. His solution was incarceration. Today, the War on Drugs isn't being waged with the same fervor as when it was first announced, but the "tough-on-crime laws" and negative public opinion of drugs and drug users that were introduced remain intact.[220] While this "war" may have superficially appeared to be a serious effort to reduce drug use, there is a darker truth that lies beneath the surface. Intentionally created public ignorance of the drug epidemic and other circumstances surrounding the War on Drugs allowed powerful people to

---

[219] Ibid. 42.

[220] *Study: Public Feels More Negative Toward People with Drug Addiction Than Those with Mental Illness (John Hopkins Bloomberg School of Public Health, 2014).* https://www.jhsph.edu/news/news-releases/2014/study-public-feels-more-negative-toward-people-with-drug-addiction-than-those-with-mental-illness.html.

manipulate and virtually control how an entire country viewed the issue of drugs and criminality.

The War on Drugs is often associated with the crack cocaine epidemic of the eighties and nineties. While it is certainly true that the emergence of crack cocaine fueled support for the War, it is important to realize that the War on Drugs was not launched as a response to crack abuse. The crack cocaine crisis that began to spread at alarming rates (mostly in inner-city and poor Black neighborhoods) came to the attention of the public a few years after the official beginning of the War on Drugs.

The Reagan Administration, steered by monied interests, saw an opportunity to use the crack epidemic to their benefit. Reagan's White House hired staff to publicize this new crisis of crack cocaine abuse with the belief that this would build both public and congressional support for their War on Drugs. They were right. Soon after they began pushing the crisis of crack cocaine, the media was overflowing with images of Black "crack whores", "crack dealers", and "crack babies".[221]

Still, the government went further. They did not simply galvanize support for their war by calling attention to a problem. They played a large role in creating the problem in the first place. Michelle Alexander explains further:

> The CIA admitted in 1998 that guerrilla armies it actively supported in Nicaragua were smuggling illegal drugs into the United States—drugs that were making their way onto the streets of inner-city Black neighborhoods in the form of crack cocaine. The CIA also admitted that, in the midst of the War on Drugs, it blocked law enforcement efforts to investigate illegal drug networks that were helping to fund its covert war in Nicaragua.[222]

---

[221] Alexander, 2012. 5.
[222] Ibid. 6, 49.

The Risk Of Mass Incarceration

The Reagan Administration intentionally overlooked the smuggling of drugs into the United States. Further, the Administrations' fiscal policies that exacerbated economic hardship in Black communities are largely to blame for the despair that drove many to drugs.[223]

These appalling admissions, along with the fact the War on Drugs was launched at a time when drug use was declining, and when only two percent of people considered drugs a serious problem in the United States, greatly discredit the narrative that the war was a failed, but well-intentioned, effort.[224] If the Reagan Administration had seriously wanted to curb drug abuse, they would have cracked down on drug smugglers and implemented policies that aligned with evidence. But they didn't. The war on drugs was not about drugs. It was about decimating Black communities, re-establishing mechanisms to relegate Black Americans to second class citizenship, exploiting prisoners for profit, and securing the White racially motivated vote by stoking fear of ever-present Black criminals.

As mentioned earlier, the War on Drugs and "tough-on-crime" initiatives became so popular among the public that it became politically detrimental for liberals to oppose the gospel of "law and order". Unsurprisingly, when the Democrats reclaimed the White House with the election of Bill Clinton, "law and order" policies were instrumental to their platform. Eventually, after passing numerous "tough-on-crime" laws that continued to grow the prison population and hand out hasher prison sentences, President Clinton hammered the final nail into the coffin when he passed the 1994 crime bill. While future measures would also contribute to increase the prison population, this bill unequivocally firmly established the era of mass incarceration.

For shielded White America, the War on Drugs and resulting

---

[223] Tolson, A., Hand, Q. *Reaganomics and Black Americans* (The Black Scholar, 1985). 37-49.; Dunlap, E., Johnson, B. D. (1992). *The setting for the crack era: macro forces, micro consequences (1960-1992).* (Journal of Psychoactive Drugs, 1992). 307–321.

[224] Beckett, K., Sasson, T. *The Politics of Injustice: Crime and Punishment in America* (Thousand Oaks, CA: Sage Publications, 2004). 163.

mass incarceration confirmed that the worst stereotypes of the Black community were grounded in truth. Black people were portrayed as criminals, lazy freeloaders, a drain on our society. Public ignorance gave life to these stereotypes in the first place, and ignorance about the War on Drugs and "tough-on-crime" bills justified and amplified them. The negative connotations of the Black community warranted the War on Drugs in the eyes of many.

So, when the U.S. prison population grew from 300,000 to over 2 million people and the United States began to imprison a greater percentage of its Black population than South Africa at the height of Apartheid,[225] the public didn't blink an eye. Once again, ignorance empowered the elite to successfully create a system that oppresses and disenfranchises a large proportion of the Black community.

Before dismissing the idea that oppressive racial motivations were behind the War on Drugs and the 1994 crime bill (The Violent Crime Control and Law Enforcement Act) as mere conspiracy, it is important to understand that this is not an historical anomaly. Throughout history, people occupying powerful social and political positions have used their influence to create wars, conflicts, and laws to stay in power and maximize their socioeconomic interests. This is just one more example of powerful people capitalizing on an uninformed (or better, intentionally ill-informed) public to create a narrative that benefits them. This is how the world has always operated, and until public ignorance of the greatest risks facing our society is significantly reduced, there will not be accountability for powerful organizations and individuals. They will undoubtedly continue to prioritize their own interests at the expense of the less powerful and the marginalized.

---

[225] Alexander, 2012. 6.

FALLING IN LOVE WITH PUNISHMENT

A key factor in the popularity of the War on Drugs was the emergence of an idea in criminology known as "deterrence theory". Deterrence theory revolves around the idea that a potential criminal, just like anyone else, will weigh the pros and cons of their actions before committing a crime. Therefore, it follows that if the negative consequences outweigh the positive outcomes for criminal activity, crime rates will drop. In other words, if the public fears potential punishment, they will be deterred from committing a crime, and if a person who committed a crime is punished severely, they will be deterred from committing another crime in the future.[226] As the theory went: the harsher the punishment, the greater the deterrent and the lower the crime rate.

However, what most experts who purported this theory overlooked (or chose not to convey) was that most criminals don't know the punishment for the crime they committed before they commit the crime. No one plans on going to prison after committing a crime. Most people who commit crime either think they will get away with it or they never have time or the interest to consider the consequences of their actions. Therefore, instituting more severe punishments has a very insignificant deterring effect.

Yet, ignorant to these facts, deterrence theory makes sense to the average American. So, when policymakers started to design and implement "tough-on-crime" laws in the 1970s, there was support, not resistance. Capitalizing on the ignorance that created and amplifies the risk of racism, the elite wielded their influence in the media and political spheres to push sensationalized crime and drug stories. They galvanized support among the public by appealing to their fear and anger. This was the start of the criminal justice system's shift in purpose, from rehabilitation to punishment. Americans became eager to punish criminals and give them what they deserve. In this shift, the public lost sight of the humanity of those who committed crimes.

---

[226] Kirkpatrick, 2016. 4.

Multiple studies, including one conducted by Brennan Kirkpatrick of John Carroll University, have unsurprisingly found a direct and strong correlation between "tough-on-crime" laws and the rapid rise in prison population. Since ignorance was created among the public, the rise in the prison population was viewed as beneficial by many. Yet, the consequences of "tough-on-crime" laws were not beneficial. They were disastrous. Thanks to these laws, millions of Americans have been disenfranchised, America has become less safe, a "revolving door" has been created where former prisoners return to prison at extremely high rates due to a lack of opportunity and high scrutiny and shame after release, and the stereotypes of criminality that have been attributed to Black and poor communities have been cemented in the public subconscious.[227]

THE DUAL LEGAL SYSTEM

The "tough-on-crime" mentality has become widespread in America's criminal justice system, and it has disproportionally affected people of color, specifically Black Americans. Many in the public have fallen victim to the false notion that all citizens are viewed equally in eyes of the law. In reality, America virtually operates under a "dual legal system" that unequally enforces the law and targets Black Americans at a disproportionate rate. In an article for the Economic Policy Institute, Dr. Robynn J.A. Cox elaborates on the unequal enforcement of "tough-on-crime" laws, writing:

> These tough-on-crime laws, which applied to all Americans, could be maintained only because of the dual legal system developed from the legacy of racism in the United States. That is, race allowed for society to avoid the trade-off between society's "demand" to get tough-on-crime and

---

[227] Ibid.

its "demand" to retain civil liberties, through unequal enforcement of the law. In essence, tying crime to observable characteristics (such as race or religious affiliation) allowed the majority in society to pass tough-on-crime policies without having to bear the full burden of these policies, permitting these laws to be sustained over time.[228]

By creating ignorance of this dual legal system among the public, specifically among White Americans, it was possible to create a racial caste system without raising broad suspicion of foul play. In other words, White Americans supported "tough-on-crime" laws because they were almost never subjected to them.

The myth that the law is applied to people of all races equally has led to many White people accepting the racist notions that Black people are incarcerated at higher rates because of their inferior biology or culture. While that may sound like a harsh analysis, if you refuse to acknowledge that systemic racism is to blame for higher incarceration rates among Black people, you are by default attributing the disparity to the faults of the Black race. This ignorant idea, and the refusal to acknowledge its logical shortcomings, has greatly amplified the risk of mass incarceration.

Let's look at some examples of how the dual legal system has operated in the United States since the dawn of the War on Drugs. When the government decided to crack down on drug-related crimes, they made important distinctions in the law. These distinctions negatively affected people of color much more than Whites.

For instance, consider the prison sentencing disparity between convicted crack cocaine abusers and powder cocaine abusers. Crack cocaine and powder cocaine are the exact same substance. However, powder cocaine is very expensive and is predominately used within upper class communities, in which the demographic is typically White.

---

[228] Cox, R. *"Where do we go from here?" Transportation justice and the struggle for equal access* (Southeastern Geographer, 2015). 418.

If Only We Knew

Meanwhile crack cocaine is much cheaper and is predominantly used in poorer communities, in which the demographic is typically Black. Despite crack cocaine and powder cocaine being the same substance, lawmakers decided to charge crack abusers with longer sentences than cocaine abusers. This was made possible by the 100:1 sentencing disparity ratio. In practice, this ratio meant that if a crack cocaine user was facing a five-year mandatory minimum prison sentence for distribution of 5 grams of crack cocaine, a powder cocaine distributer would have to sell 500 grams of powder cocaine to receive the same five-year sentence. Today, this ratio of prison time has been reduced from its previous rate of 100:1, but it is still existent at a rate of 18:1.[229] There is no reason why the ratio should not be 1:1, other than that the ratio was intended to produce racist sentencing outcomes.

The disparity between crack and powder cocaine sentencing illuminates the risks of systemic racism. Intentional policy decisions have set up the Black community for failure. Racist housing and economic policies shuttled and trapped Black Americans into ghettos where they are deprived of economic opportunity. Children attend intentionally underfunded, failing schools. There are few jobs available and the jobs that are available pay poverty wages. Inevitably this environment breeds violent behavior. These circumstances lead to hopelessness and despair, arguably the greatest precipitator of drug use. Yet, instead of addressing these faults in the system, our government decides to disproportionally and excessively punish Black Americans who fall victim to drug use.

Another example of the dual legal system can be found in the implementation of stop-and-frisk policing in New York City where Black people were stopped at 10 times the rate of White people, despite there being zero evidence to suggest that Black people possessed guns or drugs at higher rates than White people. In fact, studies show that people of all colors *use and sell* illegal drugs at

---

[229] *Fair Sentencing Act* (ACLU). https://www.aclu.org/issues/criminal-law-reform/drug-law-reform/fair-sentencing-act.

remarkably similar rates; the differences that do exist suggest white people use drugs at slightly higher rates.[230] Yet, Black men have been sentenced to prison on drug charges at rates 20 to 50 times greater than those of White men.[231]

These statistics suggest that the War on Drugs could, and maybe should, have been waged in suburban White neighborhoods instead of low-income Black neighborhoods. However, this didn't happen because the intent behind the war was never to curb drug use but rather to establish a new racial caste system.

Yet, because ignorance was created so effectively the public strongly believed the drug problem was a problem of the Black community, not of all Americans. By spreading ignorance to create and amplify the risk of racism, the elites have been able to create the risk of mass incarceration. Establishing the existence of unconscious racial bias in every American and the widespread acceptance of racist ideas was a prerequisite for Americans' acceptance of the false ideas regarding the efficacy of punishment, such as deterrence theory.

Deterrence theory has led many to accept the idea that incarceration decreases crime, but incarceration rates usually have no correlation with crime rates. As Michelle Alexander explains:

> Sociologists have frequently observed that governments use punishment primarily as a tool of social control, and thus the extent or severity of punishment is often unrelated to actual crime patterns… Although crime rates in the United States have not been markedly higher than those of other Western countries, the rate of incarceration has soared in the United States while it has remained stable or declined in other countries.[232]

---

[230] Alexander, 2012. 6.
[231] Ibid.
[232] Ibid. 7.

As discussed, "tough-on-crime" laws have been found to be positively correlated to the rise in prison populations.[233] Before legislators introduced these laws, they assured the public that these laws would make them safer. Americans took their word for it. This was not the case. The result of these laws was the addition of millions of people to the prison system. When we "got tough-on-crime", we didn't make streets safer. Instead, we broke families. We decimated communities. We branded millions of people as second-class citizens. A recipe for increasing crime.

The numbers and analyses are clear: "tough-on-crime" attitudes and laws are not an effective way to decrease crime. Today, this evidence is irrefutable, and thanks to the internet, it is widely accessible to the public through ted talks, academic articles, YouTube videos, and the like. Yet, the abundance of evidence has not changed public opinion. Many of the same politicians who originally claimed that harsher laws would deter crime, still actively promote that belief today. They dismiss the evidence and create ignorance among the public, thereby allowing these laws that cause mass incarceration to remain in effect.

PRISON WORK AND PRIVATE PRISONS

Establishing a second-class citizenry and amplifying the risk of racism is the main incentive for the elite to create the system of mass incarceration. Of course, there are monetary incentives of establishing the risk of mass incarceration in itself too. These monetary incentives come in the form of the prison work and the private prison industry.

As mentioned, the loophole in the Thirteenth Amendment that enabled the systems of convict leasing and peonage, remains in the Amendment. Consequently, there remains an exploitative prison labor system that resembles the system of convict leasing. The prison labor

---

[233] Kirkpatrick, 2016.

system today operates in two main ways: 1) a relatively small number of prisoners work for private companies, and 2) a much larger number of prisoners work for the state and within prisons. Private companies exploiting the labor of prisoners experience great profits because labor costs are reduced so drastically. Much more significantly, however, the large number of incarcerated people working within prisons is necessary for the survival of mass incarceration. Today, prisoners are forced to work for virtually nothing. Researcher Vicky Peláez explains:

> For the tycoons who have invested in the prison industry, it has been like finding a pot of gold. They don't have to worry about strikes or paying unemployment insurance, vacations or comp time. All of their workers are full-time, and never arrive late or are absent because of family problems; moreover, if they don't like the pay of 25 cents an hour and refuse to work, they are locked up in isolation cells.[234]

This allows prisons to avoid the true cost of running a prison.[235] This shifting of costs is essential to the survival of the oppressive mass incarceration system. Just as previous elites paid a cheap price to sustain the systems of slavery, convict leasing, and Jim Crow, today mass incarceration is affordable due to the prison labor system.

It is possible for the U.S. to lock up over two million people, relegating them to second-class citizenship and causing irreparable harm to communities across the country, because they can do so at a discount. It costs, on average, between $20,000 and $40,000 to house one inmate for a year.[236] Think about how expensive it would be to pay all the prison laborers state minimum wage on top of all

---

[234] Peláez, V. *The Prison Industry in the United States: Big Business or a New Form of Slavery?* (Global Research, 2019).

[235] Sawyer, Wagner, 2020.

[236] *What is the Average Cost to House Inmates in Prison*. (The Law Dictionary, 2012).

the other expenses of running a prison. It would be impractical to expect taxpayers to provide such funding for millions of people. We spend an exorbitant amount of money on prisons as it is, over $80 billion annually to be specific.[237] Yet, this expense is just small enough that the average American does not notice how much they are being taxed in order to operate these prisons. If the cost of prisons was to balloon, taxpayers may very well catch on and demand that we incarcerate fewer people to lower taxes.

The manipulation of public ignorance played a major role in the creation of this uncompensated labor force. The shift in public opinion of a prison's purpose, from rehabilitative to punitive, is paramount in justifying forcing inmates to work for next to no pay. Basically, this injustice is conveyed to the public as merely a form of punishment that the prisoners deserved.

Along with the existence of a prison labor system, private prisons provide elites with another way to profit off the backs of prisoners. Privately operated prisons emerged coincidingly with the explosion in the prison population. The rationale behind their creation was that the private sector could provide better prison services at lower costs than the government.[238] However, privatizing prisons financially incentivized incarcerating more people for longer periods of time. Private prisons profit from each person they hold behind bars, so their entire business model is to incarcerate as many people as possible for as long as possible. No wonder they spend so much money on lobbying efforts for "tough-on-crime" laws.

Only by creating a general mass ignorance could these institutions be established and sustained. The elite who created these risks in our society have also framed the way we hear about them. They have intentionally created ignorance and encouraged us to support mass incarceration by hiding the truth of its consequences.

---

[237] Lewis, N., Lockwood, B. *The Hidden Cost of Incarceration* (The Marshall Project, 2018).

[238] Lukemeyer, A., McCorkle, R. *Privatization of Prisons: Impact on Prison Conditions* (American Review of Public Administration, 2005).

AN AMPLIFIED RISK: THE SIDE EFFECTS

Mass incarceration has burdened former convicts with devasting penalties. Its consequences, however, affect far more people than just former felons. Mass incarceration negatively affects the families of prisoners, the communities these families and prisoners are from, and the country as a whole. In other words, mass incarceration hurts us all. Our ignorance of mass incarceration has contributed to the amplification of many other risks in society.

The widening racial health inequity gap we are experiencing is a great example of this. According to a series study called *America: Equity and Equality in Health* conducted by Christopher Wildeman (Yale school of medicine) and Emily A. Wang (Bureau of Justice Assistance, Washington, DC, USA), young Americans in prison face a higher risk of poor mental and physical health.[239] More importantly, evidence has shown that former prisoners experience harmful health consequences throughout their lifetimes. Studies have also shown that the children of fathers in prison are significantly more likely to have behavioral and mental health problems.

Harmful health effects also stem from our country's treatment of former prisoners upon their release. Our justice system rarely provides medication for those who have chronic illnesses after they are released. Most ex-convicts are either uninsured upon release or are underinsured and can't afford to pay for medical care. Additionally, many former inmates have mental illnesses that impair their ability to follow through with care.[240]

Wildeman and Wang further elaborate on the health side-effects of mass incarceration, writing:

> Incarceration exacerbates financial hardships beyond what would be expected due just to decreased earnings.

---

[239] Wildeman, Wang, 2017.
[240] Ibid. 1468.

Incarceration also disrupts romantic unions. The resulting decrease in adults' time available for household duties might reduce the time spent on health-related activities. Having an incarcerated family member—and re-incorporating a former inmate—is also stressful. Moreover, if the stigma attached to incarceration pervades families, as research suggests, having a family member incarcerated could reduce the social support available to families.[241]

These consequences are an outgrowth of ignorance. Longitudinal health studies have consistently excluded inmates, and studies of the connection between health disparities and the consequences of incarceration on health have been significantly underfunded. These two factors have severely curtailed research on this risk, which has led to a sustained ignorance in the public consciousness and the minds of the experts. This ignorance largely contributes to why the health gap continues to widen and inmates, ex-inmates, their families, and their communities continue to suffer. Findings from the same cross-international study provide the following analysis: "US life expectancy would have increased 51.1 percent more and infant mortality would have fallen 39.6 percent more from 1983 to 2005 if incarceration had remained at the mid-1980s level."[242] *If only we knew.*

All formerly incarcerated individuals are forever marked with the "felon" label. Thus, formerly incarcerated people almost always struggle to find a job. Despite their predictably grim job prospects, lawmakers decided to prohibit all former felons from receiving safety net services such as food stamps and living in government subsidized housing. Additionally, former felons are released from prison with virtually no money, and, as we discussed, in many states, they are stripped of their right to vote which gives them no say in who is elected to represent them and gives politicians no reason to serve their interests.

---

[241] Ibid. 1468.
[242] Ibid. 1470.

For those on parole or probation, their situation is just as bleak. In many states, ex-felons are required to pay their parole or probation officer and are required to meet with them at the officer's convenience.[243] For many, finding a job is a requirement of parole as well. If they don't meet these requirements, they can be sent back to prison. However, because parole officers' most often work 9 a.m. to 5 p.m., it is challenging for those on parole to find a job with a schedule that permits time for a visit during their workday. These obstacles, frequently prove to be insurmountable barriers for ex-convicts attempting to assimilate back into society.[244]

The convergence of these forms of legal discrimination leads many formerly incarcerated people back down a path of crime, such as selling drugs, to survive and make a living. Of course, this leads them right back into the criminal justice system.[245] Accordingly, the five-year recidivism rate, according to the U.S. Sentencing Commission, is 76.6 percent from state prisons and 44.7 percent from federal prisons.[246] *In light of these facts, who would expect the statistics to be otherwise?* Yet, the public *does* expect different results because we have been made ignorant of the obstacles that create high recidivism.

We have a system that sets up newly released inmates for failure, widens the health gap, and tears apart families and communities. This system was purposely created by those in pursuit of, and those who held, money and power. Only by examining the power grab, profit motivations, and racial prejudices at play can we recognize that mass incarceration isn't a well-intentioned response to the existence of crime but rather a malicious attempt by the elite to create an exploitative, oppressive system that further enriches and empowers them.

---

[243] Bannon, A., Nagrecha, M., Diller, R. *Criminal Justice Debt: A Barrier to Reentry* (Brennan Center for Justice, 2010); Oliver, J. *Prisoner Re-entry* (Last Week Tonight, 2015). https://youtu.be/gJtYRxH5G2k.

[244] Alexander, 2012. 4.

[245] Kirkpatrick, 2016. 8.

[246] *Report Documents U.S. Recidivism Rates for Federal Prisoners* (Prison Legal News). https://www.prisonlegalnews.org/news/2016/may/5/report-documents-us-recidivism-rates-federal-prisoners/.

If Only We Knew

IGNORANCE AS AN OBSTACLE TO REFORM

What we find today is a profound contradictory mindset in our society. As referenced earlier in this chapter, while most Americans claim they want to end mass incarceration, they don't support legislation necessary to decrease the prison population. Cornell Professor, Peter K. Enns, who conducts quantitative research of public opinion and representation, found in a recent study that continued support of "tough-on-crime" laws by the U.S. public is largely why there have been no major moves to reverse these policies.[247] Today, we have a "socially woke" public that has no idea how to make real systemic changes to improve society; in other words, we have a public that knows social problems exist, but doesn't know what causes them or how to fix them.

Ignorance in this case, as you have just read, does not mean the public is completely unaware of the injustice of mass incarceration. In fact, the opposite is true; according to The American Civil Liberties Union Campaign for Smart Justice, 91 percent of Americans support criminal justice reform.[248] Public ignorance, in this case, involves a lack of knowledge or awareness of the steps necessary to eliminate the risk of mass incarceration. Clearly, simply knowing that mass incarceration exists and is "bad" is not enough. It has not resulted in any of the proposed major reforms necessary to mitigate the risk.

Recently, many activists and politicians have been focusing their attacks on "tough-on-crime" laws and the justice system's unfair punishment of non-violent offenders. This movement, however, has created a new ignorance among the public, as many now believe that non-violent criminals are the only ones who have been damaged by the criminal justice system.

---

[247] Enns, P. K. *The Public's Increasing Punitiveness and Its Influence on Mass Incarceration in the United States: Punitive Attitudes and Mass Incarceration* (American Journal of Political Science, 2014). 58(4), 857–872.

[248] *91% of Americans Support Criminal Justice Reform ACLU Polling Finds* (ACLU). https://www.aclu.org/press-releases/91-percent-americans-support-criminal-justice-reform-aclu-polling-finds.

The Risk Of Mass Incarceration

According to a survey conducted by *Vox*, when given the option of true, false, or "don't know", 61 percent of American voters confidently answered that nearly half of all U.S. prisoners are in prison for drug offenses.[249] In reality, the percentage of drug offenders in prison and jail is only 20 percent.[250] This key misconception has resulted in insufficient plans to combat the risk of mass incarceration.

The rise of "tough-on-crime" laws made sure that violent criminals received extremely long sentences as well, and while the public's opinion of the fairness of punishing non-violent criminals has changed, their opinion about violent criminals has not.

Politicians who claim to be pro-reform of our prison system are focused solely on justice for low-level drug offenders when they should be focused on why we created criminogenic social conditions and then punish and incarcerate people for committing crimes. For example, part of 2020 Democratic primary candidate Senator Cory Booker's plan to end mass incarceration included granting clemency to a record number of 17,000 nonviolent drug offenders in federal prison. It must be acknowledged that this policy would barely make a dent in reducing the prison population which sits above two million people. If we are serious about reducing the risk of mass incarceration, we must have an honest conversation about what that means. Ignoring those incarcerated for violent offenses and focusing solely on achieving justice for non-violent offenders will only perpetuate the risk.

---

[249] Lopez, 2016. https://www.vox.com/2016/9/7/12814504/mass-incarceration-poll.
[250] Sawyer, Wagner, 2020.

If Only We Knew

SOLUTIONS

REVERSING IGNORANCE

Mass incarceration creates a racial caste system like that of Jim Crow. This caste system serves to amplify the risk of racism we discussed last chapter as well as the risk of gun violence we will discuss in Chapter 5, the risk of health we will discuss in Chapter 6, and the risk of poverty we will discuss in Chapter 7. Further, through the prison labor and private prison industry, mass incarceration generates huge profits for the elite who are invested in the system. Since mass incarceration has now existed for a half a century, it has become deeply rooted in our economy. Ending mass incarceration would mean closing prisons everywhere and shedding hundreds of thousands of jobs in this industry.[251] The system of mass incarceration is extremely complex and will not be solved through a few pieces of legislation. What is required is a movement that resembles that of the Civil Rights movement of the 1960s. Michelle Alexander elaborates, writing:

> The notion that all of these reforms can be accomplished piecemeal—one at a time, through disconnected advocacy strategies—seems deeply misguided. All of the needed reforms have less to do with failed policies than a deeply flawed public consensus, one that is indifferent, at best, to the experience of poor people of color.[252]

The solutions in this section all align with the goal of creating a movement to change the public consensus Alexander references. It is also worth remembering what we discussed last chapter about legislation and public opinion. Before we can change hearts, we must change laws. People's opinions change as laws change.

---

[251] Alexander, 2012. 230.
[252] Ibid. 233.

If we implement legislation to end discrimination and restore rights for incarcerated and formerly incarcerated individuals, the public will begin to regain their vision of the humanity of this population.

To create a movement to end mass incarceration, the first action we must take is to combat ignorance. Vast amounts of research have been conducted regarding the complex roots of mass incarceration, what purpose it serves for the elites, how it's affecting us all, and the solutions needed to mitigate the crisis. So, since the information is out there, our responsibility as citizens is to acknowledge our ignorance, reverse it, and take action to start the movement.

We must understand that the system we have today was not developed accidently.[253] Mass incarceration functions to create a caste system that relegates the poor and many Black Americans to a second-class citizen status. This system serves to benefit the ruling class. To dismantle a system created to oppress, we must understand how that oppression affects us all. The justice system we have today is not a rehabilitation or correctional system. Our criminal justice system was systematically designed to create more criminals,[254] and that must be acknowledged. Mass incarceration should be treated as the Jim Crow of our era because it *is* that serious. It must be at the forefront of the fight for racial justice.

We must also examine and move to change how crime and incarceration are covered by the media. If the goal is to treat mass incarceration as an injustice similar to Jim Crow, it must be covered more frequently in the media. We cannot expect ignorance to abate if nobody hears about the problem and how serious the consequences really are. Thus, refer to the solutions in chapter 1.

---

[253] Ibid. 238.
[254] Ibid. 236.

If Only We Knew

DISPELLING THE MYTH OF "BAD PEOPLE"

The oversimplified notion that people who commit crimes are inherently bad people is another false generalization that we must put to rest. To understand why people commit crimes, it is imperative that we understand how social deviance is developed. Sociologist Edwin Lemert explains the creation of a "social deviant" in the following way:

> The sequence of interaction leading to secondary deviation is roughly as follows: (1) primary deviation; (2) societal penalties; (3) further primary deviation; (4) stronger penalties and rejections; (5) further deviations, perhaps with hostilities and resentments beginning to focus upon those doing the penalizing; (6) crisis reached in the tolerance quotient, expressed in formal action by the community stigmatizing of the deviant; (7) strengthening of the deviant conduct as a reaction to the stigmatizing and penalties; and (8) ultimate acceptance of deviant social status and efforts at adjustment on the basis of the associated role.[255]

As we will discuss in greater detail in the last chapter, we must seek to understand the reasons people are driven to crime. We must abandon the medieval notion that some people or some cultures are inherently criminal; no one is born with a greater tendency to commit crime than anyone else.

A criminal justice system that does not attempt to address and consider the true development of social deviance is one that attempts to fight crime with one hand tied behind its back. To curb crime, we must stop people from becoming criminals in the first place! Various socioeconomic reforms (which I will also discuss in later chapters) are necessary if we want to stop funneling children through a pipeline to prison.

---

[255] Lemert, E. *Social Pathology* (New York McGraw-Hill, 1951). 77.

The Risk Of Mass Incarceration

It is crucial that we bring attention to the motivations and the circumstances that drive people to commit crimes. Currently, of the 2.3 million people behind bars, 64 percent of inmates have a mental illness and 68 percent have a substance abuse problem.[256] These people are not "bad people", they are sick, traumatized, hopeless, and neglected. Unsurprisingly, incarceration does more harm than good for these people, and society takes on a huge financial burden as a result. The Laura and John Arnold Foundation elaborates:

> Too often, the needs of these vulnerable populations are not only unmet, but inadvertently worsened by emergency response systems. With police having to act as the primary responders to a crisis, individuals often end up in situations that lead to the use of force, arrest, and/or incarceration. These approaches fail to address individuals' underlying health, societal, and financial struggles; are cost-inefficient; and cause significant harm to both the individual and the community.[257]

To tackle this problem, society must do a better job of identifying and connecting at-risk individuals—specifically those who are mentally ill, suffering from substance abuse, and/or homeless—to more effective care providers. Right now, our system is failing these people who are sick, and it is failing the community as well. However, plans and solutions have been developed to effectively treat people suffering from mental illness and drug addiction.

In 2010, the Miami-Dade County, Florida Police Department made a concerted effort to fix this system of criminalizing mental

---

[256] *Alternatives to Arrest* (Arnold Ventures). https://www.arnoldventures.org/work/alternatives-to-arrest.

[257] Reimagining America's Crisis Response Systems (Craft Media Bucket). https://craftmediabucket.s3.amazonaws.com/uploads/PDFs/A2A-RFP_FINAL5.pdf.

illness, substance abuse, and homelessness that had cost taxpayers over $13 million in just a few years. They decided to prioritize community services over incarceration. In just four years, the county had saved $12 million dollars and reduced the prison population from 7,000 to under 5,000 people.[258]

To start caring for and treating the mentally ill, substance abusers, and the homeless we must start reversing the persistent ignorance that exists about these populations. Police jurisdictions must work to identify the people who cycle through shelters, jails, and hospitals so that they can better understand the needs of the "frequent utilizer" population.[259] We must develop properly trained and equipped emergency response teams, post-crisis stabilization facilities, and treatment programs and services.[260] We must also act to legalize marijuana (which accounts from 40 percent of drug arrests alone) and decriminalize all drug addiction, mental illness, and homelessness nationwide.

BROAD SYSTEMIC REFORM

At the federal level, we must eliminate the clause in the Thirteenth Amendment that permits slavery as punishment for a crime. The prison labor system is effectively slavery, and it should not be tolerated in the 21st century. In every state, we must also act to reverse the harmful "tough-on-crime" laws that have ruined countless lives and torn families apart.

---

[258] Equitas. Miami-Dade County 11th Judicial Circuit Criminal Mental Health Project Criminal Justice/Mental Health Statistics and Project Outcomes. Equitas: 4. (2016). http://www.equitasusa.org/wp-content/uploads/2016/09/CMHP-Data-Criminal-Mental-Health-Project-06082016.pdf.

[259] *Modern Justice: Using Data to Reinvent America's Crisis Response Systems* (Craft Media Bucket). https://craftmediabucket.s3.amazonaws.com/uploads/PDFs/DDJ-MODERN-JUSTICE.pdf, 14.

[260] Reimagining America's Crisis Response Systems (Craft Media Bucket). https://craftmediabucket.s3.amazonaws.com/uploads/PDFs/A2A-RFP_FINAL5.pdf., 3-5.

Fortunately, criminal justice reform has become an issue worth discussing for Democrats in recent years, and many plans to reverse mass incarceration were created by 2020 presidential candidates. I believe the Douglass Plan, developed by former 2020 Democrat Party primary candidate Pete Buttigieg, is the most comprehensive and practical criminal justice reform plan laid out in full by a political candidate to date. The plan, which would reduce the prison population by 50 percent, calls for the reversal of mandatory minimums, the elimination of incarceration for drug possession, and the legalization of marijuana and the expunging of past convictions, among other measures.[261] I believe the Douglass Plan should be revived and enacted in its totality in order to set us on the right path towards a fairer and more equitable justice system.

THE END OF CASH BAIL

We must also act to reverse the injustice of cash bail and the broken pretrial justice system. When bail was established, it was intended to act as a monetary incentive to ensure people appeared for their scheduled day in court. It was not intended to jail people who couldn't afford to pay their bail. Today, unlike when bail was first established, there are already systems in place to effectively monitor people and ensure they appear for their scheduled day in court.

Under the current cash bail system, if two people commit the same crime and have their bail set for the same amount of money, the one who can afford to pay the bail would go home and wait for their trial date, under supervision. The person who could not afford to post bail would have to stay in jail until their case was heard. Today, 75 percent of people detained in local jails are there

---

[261] *THE DOUGLASS PLAN: A Comprehensive Investment in the Empowerment of Black America* (Courthouse News, 2019). https://www.courthousenews.com/wp-content/uploads/2019/07/douglass-plan.pdf.

because they cannot afford to pay bail. Staying in jail is not only traumatizing; it also increases the chance of conviction. In our example, the person who could not afford bail and who is forced to stay in jail before their trial is three times as likely to be convicted, and on average, their sentence is three times as long as those who could afford bail. Cash bail treads on the quintessential American value of "innocent until proven guilty".

Ending cash bail is not dangerous or unfair, it's the opposite. Those with the financial means already live in a country where cash bail is no obstacle to their freedom. Ending cash bail simply levels the playing field and ends one of the means by which poor Americans are oppressed. It should also be noted that ending cash bail would *not* lead to scores of dangerous criminals lurking the streets. An overwhelming majority of people who commit serious violent crimes are not even given the option of bail; extremely high-risk individuals will not be set free if we end cash bail.

It must be acknowledged that the bail industry hurts the average American too. The bail industry costs taxpayers $14 billion each year, and when accounting for damages done to families, communities and social services, the true economic cost of pretrial incarceration is $140 billion annually.[262] This is in addition to the previously mentioned $80 billion dollar burden that the prison system imposes on us. Many overlook the bail crisis in this country because they incorrectly believe there are bigger problems to solve within the criminal justice system. However, because 500,000 people are incarcerated before their trial due to unaffordable bail, and since *99 percent* of jail growth over the last 20 years has been the result of pre-incarceration,[263] it is clear that righting the injustice of bail policy is paramount to dismantling the system of mass incarceration.

---

[262] The Bail Project. *After Cash Bail: A Framework for Reimagining Pretrial Justice.*

[263] Steinberg, R. *What if We Ended the Injustice of Bail.* https://youtu.be/3B24RaqA33k?

So, what do we do? How do we end the injustice of bail? Fortunately, a solution has already been developed and is being successfully implemented on local levels: the Bail Project.[264] We must scale The Bail Project to a national level. *So how do we do that?* Lucky for us the organization has already outlined the framework for extending their program nationwide. The program calls for the end of cash bail, in the belief that eliminating this would in turn eliminate the system's exploitation of the poor.[265] It calls for people to be returned to their communities with support systems. This is to ensure they appear for court dates by solving common obstacles such as childcare or work schedules, to afford social services if they are struggling with drug addiction or mental illness, and to provide other supportive measures to ease the pretrial process.[266] The program calls for an end to risk evaluation algorithms that perpetuate racial bias and do not accurately predict risks.[267] It limits the use of pretrial detention to only extreme circumstances and calls for mandatory usage of noncustodial citations in place of arrests, noting the trauma associated with being handcuffed and the damages done to individuals, families and communities that results from pretrial detention.[268] Moving towards non-custodial citations means moving away from the violent encounters between police and citizens. Police would no longer ever have a reason to handcuff anyone pulled over for a traffic violation or a minor crime. They would simply write the offender a non-custodial citation for a court appearance.

Additionally, the program states that to ensure that "decarceration is lasting and continues to drive progress, we need to invest in

---

[264] The Bail Project. *After Cash Bail: A Framework for Reimagining Pretrial Justice.*

[265] Ibid.

[266] Ibid.

[267] Ibid.

[268] Ibid; Pretrial detention rips parents away from their children, forces them to miss work and many times lose their job, and damages mental health as it crushes an individual's spirit.

diverting resources away from policing and incarceration, increase transparency to monitor success, and—perhaps most importantly—enable communities to direct reform".[269] The Bail Project must be enacted as a step to end mass incarceration and help us become a more humane society.

REHABILITATION NOT PUNISHMENT

A further instance of widely held ignorance that must be reversed is the belief in deterrence theory. It has been statistically proven that the threat of incarceration does not reduce crime, yet we, as a country, choose to dismiss this evidence and ignorantly continue to support a criminal justice system based on deterrence and punishment. We continue to throw people in cages and treat people like animals. When they consistently emerge from prison not rehabilitated, we are disappointed. As Einstein said, "Doing the same thing over and over again and expecting a different result is insanity."

What we need is a system not based on punishment, but one grounded in restorative justice and rehabilitation. We must follow the lead of countries such as Norway, which has the lowest recidivism rate in the world at 20 percent. They employ a system of restorative justice instead of the system of retributive justice we have in the United States. Journalist Linn Chloe Hagstrøm elaborates:

> In Norway's restorative approach, removing someone's liberty is punishment enough, which is evident when looking at Norwegian sentencing. Over 89 percent of Norwegian jail sentences are shorter than a year. Comparatively, "in U.S. federal prisons, longer sentences are much more common, with fewer than 2 percent serving a year or less, according to the Federal Bureau of Prisons" (CNN). The maximum sentence a person can get in Norway is 21 years with the

---

[269] Ibid.

exception of genocide and war crimes, in which case one can be sentenced to a maximum of 30 years... However, if there is a clear risk for recurrence in a serious criminal case, an indefinite sentence of detention can be imposed every five years. Prison life in Norway may sound very pleasant and luxurious, yet this is not a product of naïveté. It is meant to prepare inmates for "difficult or painful internal reformation." Imprisonment is a way of treating people for the social or psychological issues that led them to commit crimes.[270]

Now I know you may be thinking, *"That all sounds great, but does it really work?"* Well, the honest answer is *yes*. Restorative justice, when implemented correctly, reduces crime, reduces recidivism rates, and saves our country boatloads of money by reducing the costs of imprisoning criminals.[271]

Of course, we cannot transform our justice system and turn it into Norway's overnight. We can, however, follow the lead of the organizations, such as Common Justice,[272] that are practicing restorative justice on local levels today. Common Justice is an organization that has formed and implemented successful strategies in the effort to disrupt cycles of violence. The organization practices restorative justice to ensure safety, healing, and justice for violence survivors and their communities. To reduce the recidivism rate, we must also support prisoner halfway houses, which help former prisoners transition back into society, as well as other rehabilitation programs and support groups for former prisoners.

---

[270] Hagstrøm, L. *What is Restorative Justice* (The Norwegian American, 2016). https://www.norwegianamerican.com/what-is-restorative-justice/.
[271] Fisher, M. *A Different Justice: Why Anders Breivik Only Got 21 Years for Killing 77 People* (The Atlantic, 2012).
[272] Common Justice is an organization that has formed and implemented successful strategies in the effort to disrupt cycles of violence. The organization practices restorative justice to ensure safety, healing, and justice for violence survivors and their communities. See Common Justice, Our Work.

Punishment does not work. Rehabilitation does. Understanding this is crucial in our mission to improve the criminal justice system and implementing restorative justice policies will aid in our mission of creating a culture that recognizes the dignity of the incarcerated.

LEVERAGING THE POWER OF COMMUNITY

We must also leverage the power of communities in our fight against mass incarceration. Many who are facing criminal charges are represented by an under-resourced, over-extended public defender. The accused face prosecutors who strive for high rates of convictions, are subject to mandatory minimum laws, and face racial bias in myriad ways throughout the legal process. Our goal to reform the criminal justice system must include increasing funding for public defense offices and increasing the salary of public defenders as to incentivize more lawyers to become public defenders. But this process will take time and it's important to provide adequate resources to those in immediate need as well.

Community organizer Raj Jayadev and the team at the Participatory Defense Network believe they have found a way for communities to play an active role in reforming the U.S. court system.[273] The Participatory Defense Network organizes weekly community meetings in which the participants are those with loved ones facing charges and community members who act as allies and advocates for the accused.

At these meetings, community members develop plans to help the public defender and the judge "get to know" those on trial. Through compiling photo albums that show their loved ones have a family who depends on them, finding faults in police investigations, or providing statements of support from community members

---

[273] The Participatory Defense Network. https://www.participatorydefense.org/about; Jayadev R. *Community Powered Criminal Justice Reform* (Ted Talk, 2019). https://www.ted.com/talks/raj_jayadev_community_powered_criminal_justice_reform?language=en.

who know them best, this community driven activism has been widely successful. The Participatory Defense Network has saved individuals from a cumulative total of 6,500 years of incarceration and is currently in communities across the country.[274] I believe that the Participatory Defense Network must be extended, especially to all communities with high incarceration rates. These community programs don't just save prisoners from serving time, they are also essential in building a culture that recognizes everyone's inherent dignity as humans. Community involvement must play an integral role if we are serious about the fight to end mass incarceration as quickly as possible.

DOING WHAT WORKS

Finally, we must better explore the social conditions that often lead to high rates of incarceration in certain neighborhoods. Rising socioeconomic inequity combined with ineffective crime prevention approaches have been directly linked to a rise in incarceration. Clearly, we must address and amend these two social problems and practices. Supporting more effective education geared toward achieving higher graduation rates and college attendance leads to a decrease in incarceration. A better, more equal education system, especially one that is conscious of ending the school to prison pipeline, must be a top priority for our country.[275] Furthermore, the opportunity for prisoners to enroll in higher education programs while they serve their sentence (such as the Bard College Initiative) has been proven to reduce the rate of recidivism, and therefore it is crucial that these programs become more accessible and widespread.

The plans I have proposed (and many more effective solutions that I have not mentioned) to end mass incarceration have already been developed. The reasons they have not been implemented on a

---

[274] Ibid.
[275] Kirkpatrick, 2016.

national scale can be traced back mainly to the existence of widely held ignorance created by those elites profiting and empowering themselves via the current system. As a mechanism of ignorance creation, the politicians who advocate for the preservation of our current criminal justice system intentionally dismiss the logic, reason, and evidence that proves how ineffective and expensive this broken system is. That is how we have found ourselves in the position we are in.

To get out of this unsustainable position and end mass incarceration, we must reverse public ignorance. Americans must be made aware of the failings of the criminal justice system, the racism baked into the system, and how these injustices negatively affect everyone. Americans must also become aware of the plans to end mass incarceration that I have laid out in this section, and they must understand how these solutions will help *everyone*.

For those who believe they are not affected by this issue, we must remind them that ending mass incarceration would lower their taxes, stimulate the economy, and reduce crime. Moreover, the money our government will save by reversing the harmful policies of the criminal justice system can and should be redirected to efforts to deter crime and improve education. We must pressure our state and federal politicians to implement these plans, which have been proven successful on local levels. We must hold our politicians accountable and vote them out of office when they dismiss logic, reason, facts, and evidence in support of ill-intentioned mass incarceration. Our police and criminal justice systems must operate driven by data and evidence, not by the greed and self-interest of the elites. Reversing ignorance is our greatest tool in creating a movement that prioritizes human dignity over the interests of the elite. By doing so, we can end mass incarceration.

5

The Risk Of Gun Violence

*Whoever lives for the sake of combatting an enemy has
an interest in the enemy's staying alive.*
– Friedrich Nietzsche

Americans have always owned guns. From the outset, farmers and frontiersmen possessed guns out of necessity. Although guns have always been around, the existence of a "gun culture" is relatively modern. Gun culture emerged in the mid-19th century when the primary purpose of gun ownership shifted from hunting for food to hunting and shooting as a form of serious recreation.[276] As hunting and shooting for sport grew in popularity, the National Rifle Association (NRA) was founded in 1871 and served as an organization that promoted good marksmanship and shooting for sport. Gun culture, however, like many other subcultures in our society, soon became driven and controlled by the elite who, as

---

[276] Yamane, D. *The sociology of U.S. gun culture* (Sociology Compass, 2017).

we know, create ignorance to create and amplify risks that enrich and empower them.

As the economy boomed in the post-WWII decades, gun culture began to evolve into what Wake Forest University sociologist David Yamane calls "Recreational Gun Culture" or "Gun Culture 1.0".[277] As wages and income increased among all demographics, and as consumer culture erupted and swept across the country, mass advertising of guns by corporate America prompted many Americans to buy guns—lots of guns. Owning a gun began to be seen as a symbol of masculinity, "A rite of passage that signified a transition from boyhood into manhood."[278] The pastime of collecting guns soon became widely popular.

While many people owned guns during the era of Gun Culture 1.0, there were relatively few mass shootings compared to today.[279] Ultimately, however, the responsible gun ownership fostered by Gun Culture 1.0 began to fade. Gun Culture 2.0—a culture driven by fear and the perceived need for self-protection—took hold in its place.

Economic trends in the late 20th century created an environment ripe for the public's adoption of Gun Culture 2.0. In the mid-1970s, the United States experienced "stagflation", a time in which the economic boom of post WWII America was grinding to a halt, the economy stopped growing, and inflation increased as wages and income remained the same. Practically, stagflation meant that a male breadwinner could no longer be the sole source of income for a middle-class family looking to make ends meet; the traditional family structure was no longer economically feasible. As women began to assert themselves both at home and in the workplace, and as the rise of feminism led to an age of women empowerment, many men began to feel

---

[277] Ibid.

[278] Ibid.

[279] Farrell, D. *A Solution to Gun Violence Found in American History* (TED, 2018).

"emasculated". In response, buying guns to protect oneself and one's family began to be viewed as a mechanism for men to reassert their masculinity.[280]

The development of a culture based on fear and punishment was also essential in establishing Gun Culture 2.0. As we have discussed in previous chapters, the election of Richard Nixon in 1972 marked the beginning of an era of "tough-on-crime" attitudes in households throughout this country. Simultaneously, over the last half century, the use of rhetorical fear mongering as a mechanism of ignorance creation has skyrocketed.

As ownership of media has consolidated into the hands of a few companies, the coverage of crime stories on the news increased dramatically. This was not only because sensationalizing the news made for good TV and drove up the bottom line for media conglomerates, but also because deliberate scare tactics and fear mongering used in the media were key to the establishment of Gun Culture 2.0. To be specific, from 1990 to 1996 the coverage of crime stories in the media tripled.[281] Additionally, the rhetoric of fear was used in newspaper headlines, in TV ads and commercials, and by influential organizations like the NRA to encourage people to purchase a gun for self-defense. This use of the "rhetoric of fear" created public ignorance that was necessary for Gun Culture 2.0.

These two macro-developments ushered in Gun Culture 2.0 as the era of "armed citizenship" took form. We have been living with it and solidifying this culture ever since. We have shifted from a country that owns guns for sport to a country that owns guns to kill; in 1999, 28 percent of gun owners cited the need for protection as their primary reason for owning a gun. In 2015, that number rose to 63 percent.[282]

---

[280] Yamane, 2017.

[281] Moyers, B. *Moyers on America* (The New Press, 2004). 92.

[282] Ibid.

The rise of fearmongering in political and media rhetoric didn't just lead to an increase in gun sales—it led to a rise in gun violence. Gun Safety Advocate, David Farrell, attributes this phenomenon directly to Gun Culture 2.0 and the purchase of guns for self-defense. He says, "When one buys a gun for self-defense purposes, two lines have been crossed: 1) you have decided that you are willing to take a human life, and 2) you are willingly to use a gun to do so."[283] Contrary to the age-old adage of previous generations that "violence is never the answer", the rhetoric of fear has created a culture in our country where violence sometimes *is* the answer.

To understand why the elites created the risk of gun violence, we must examine the monetary motivations at play.

THE BUSINESS OF GUNS AND GUN VIOLENCE

The creation and perpetuation of a gun culture in the U.S. has been extremely profitable for gun and ammunition manufacturers and retailers. Through the strategic promotion of anecdotal narratives and phrases—the idea that having a gun for self-defense is sensible and practical or the current motif of the NRA that *"the only thing that stops a bad guy with a gun is a good guy with a gun"*—the sale of guns has become a $28 billion industry.[284]

Thanks to researchers at the Harvard School of Public Health we know for certain that the opposite of those statements is the truth. These researchers found that very few "criminals" are shot by law-abiding citizens, guns are far more likely to be used as a form of intimidation than as self-defense, and self-defense gun use is extremely rare and actually not more effective at preventing

---

[283] Farrell, 2018.
[284] Macbride, E. *America's Gun Business Is $28B. The Gun Violence Business Is Bigger* (Forbes, 2018).

injuries of property loss than other protective measures.[285] The researchers also discovered that "most purported self-defense gun uses are gun uses in escalating arguments and are both socially undesirable and illegal".[286] Basically, the evidence suggests that the very notion that gun ownership is important, or even useful, for self-defense is misleading and inaccurate.

The NRA and gun corporations, of course, do not take these findings into consideration when they market guns as tools of self-defense. Instead, they create ignorance by flooding conservative media with misleading pro-gun talking points, then they capitalize on this public ignorance as scores of people deem it necessary to stockpile guns for self-protection. Their common refrains are intentionally misleading. They serve the purpose of creating the public ignorance that creates the risk of gun violence. And because the widespread acceptance of these misleading claims is fundamental to the $28 billion industry of gun sales, the industry is dependent on the propagation of the same public ignorance initially created by these refrains. Thus, they are continuously promoted. Consequently, this leads to the creation of further ignorance, and the dangerous risk of gun violence is amplified.

Alarmingly, the multi-billion-dollar business of the manufacturing and selling of guns is far from the whole story. As we discussed earlier, in the age of Gun Culture 2.0, pro-gun organizations have created a market for guns by establishing the widespread fear that one is not safe without a gun. Logically, to scare people into buying a gun for self-defense, there must be something tangible for people to fear. That "something" is violence, specifically gun violence. The money made from the business of manufacturing and selling guns pales in comparison to the profits of the business of gun violence.

---

[285] *Gun Threats and Self-Defense Gun Use* (Harvard T.H. Chan School of Public Health).
[286] Ibid.

The elites have effectively created ignorance by duping the public into accepting the idea that gun violence is here to stay. They have coaxed many into believing that no policy or gun control measures will be successful in addressing gun violence, so our only recourse is to protect ourselves from it.

Forbes writer Elizabeth MacBride asserts that this public ignorance has become essential to the survival of the many multi-billion-dollar industries that comprise the "gun violence industry". MacBride describes the gun violence industry as all the businesses whose business model is dependent on the existence of gun violence. One example is the $25 billion per year security alarm business. The author elaborates on just how deeply rooted gun violence has become in our economy, stating:

> You can argue that all the political firms and nonprofits in this space, from the NRA to gun control groups, are part of the gun violence "industry", with their vested interests growing the longer they are engaged in battle... You can even argue that the amount spent on health care (estimated at $2.8 billion a year for hospitals alone), though a cost to taxpayers, is also revenue to the health care companies and therefore part of the gun violence business.[287]

Gun violence has become so deeply entrenched in our society that many seemingly unrelated sectors of the business world have found ways to profit from it. This is what constitutes the industry of gun violence.

Meanwhile, as a relatively small number of corporations, powerful people, and organizations are making enormous profits from the existence of gun violence, every year 100,000 people are shot and injured,[288] 36,000 people die from gun violence (61 percent

---

[287] Macbride, 2018.
[288] *Gun Violence Statistics* (Giffords Law Center).

of which are suicides),[289] and there are destructive consequences for the economic health of our communities.[290] In total, gun violence costs our nation in excess of $229 billion annually (for perspective, this is more than double the size of New Mexico's economy).[291]

Essentially, the creation of public ignorance through the establishment of Gun Culture 2.0 created the risk of gun violence. Today, many powerful people, organizations, and corporations have an active monetary interest in preserving gun violence. Therefore, they have used their influence to do the following: 1) flood conservative media with talking points that promote gun ownership and preach the effectiveness of guns in stopping crime and in self-protection, 2) pass legislation (such as the stand-your-ground laws) to give gun owners more freedoms and create more instances of gun violence, 3) support pro-gun political candidates and tank anti-gun political candidates, and, perhaps most importantly, 4) continuously create ignorance about the issue of gun violence to distract citizens from the fact that they are being deceived into buying guns to appease the interests of billionaires and billion dollar corporations.

We are living in a society where the profits of a few have been given more importance than the lives of hundreds of thousands. Gun violence is a clear example of this. We must consider that the issue of gun violence does not exist in a vacuum. That is, we must ask ourselves, *whose lives are being disregarded in the name of profit? Whose lives don't matter as much as others'?* As has been alluded to in the previous two chapters, gun violence is intimately tied to race. Thomas Abt, criminologist and author of *Bleeding Out*, explains how racism has been an obstacle to reducing gun violence:

> It must be remembered that violence does not concentrate in poor communities of color by accident... Disparities

---

[289] Ibid.

[290] *Economic Impacts of Gun Violence* (Urban Institute).

[291] Heinrich, M. *America Can't Afford Gun Violence* (Joint Economic Committee Democrats, 2018).

in crime and violence that were created by white racism are now perpetuated by white indifference. Today, racial apathy, not racial hatred, is a major obstacle to progress. Hatred may be the greater sin, but it is less pervasive. White people's collective unconcern for their fellow black and brown citizens is more prevalent and more damaging.[292]

As Martin Luther King Jr. said in his *Letter from Birmingham Jail*, "The Negro's great stumbling block in the stride toward freedom is not the White Citizen's Council-er or the Ku Klux Klanner, but the White moderate who is more devoted to "order" than to justice; who prefers a negative peace which is the absence of tension to a positive peace which is the presence of justice."

For the elite, gun violence is not only a profitable business, but it is also a key factor in the creation and assertion of racist ideas and "tough-on-crime" attitudes that serve to oppress communities of color and preserve the rigged economic system and power structure currently in place. In other words, creating and amplifying the risk of gun violence also amplifies the risks of racism and mass incarceration. Our society has been deluded by the elite who have fed us lies and false information regarding gun violence. We have been kept ignorant of the solutions to reduce and eradicate gun violence because there are profits at stake. Let's now take a deeper look at the ignorance that has been created and just how detrimental this ignorance has been.

THE IGNORANCE OF GUN VIOLENCE

Gun violence has swept through countless communities across our nation, effectively transforming them into war zones and taking lives at an alarming rate. Although a world without gun violence

---

[292] Lopez, G. *How to dramatically reduce gun violence in American cities* (Vox, 2019).

seems far-fetched, the problem *is* solvable. Countless studies have confirmed the fact that if addressed properly, gun violence can be reduced dramatically.

The current gun violence "solutions" being implemented throughout the United States have not reduced gun violence because they are misguided—and not accidently misguided; they are deliberately designed to fail. Instead of treating gun violence like the policy issue it is and enacting evidence-based solutions, our lawmakers have attempted to address gun violence as a moral issue. This position that gun violence is an issue of good people versus bad people is a false narrative and is completely ineffective in terms of reducing gun violence. We cannot simply incarcerate our way out of gun violence by locking up the "bad people" until there are none left on the streets.

Yet, conservative politicians and media figures have pushed this narrative of the moral issue of gun violence to create a problem that cannot be solved. Creating ignorance ensures the existence gun violence. By designating this issue as one of morality, the public comes to falsely believe that all policy solutions are futile; if the issue is one of personal responsibility and morality, no amount of policy or money can stop people from killing each other with guns. As the saying goes, *"Guns don't kill people, people kill people."*

However, gun violence is an issue of public health, not morality. In fact, it spreads, "infects", and kills remarkably like viral epidemics. Recognizing that gun violence is, in essence, a contagious disease going untreated shifts the debate from determining punishments to deliberating on best treatments. Trusting the science and treating gun violence like the health crisis that it truly is constitutes the most effective way to decrease gun-related deaths and injuries.

Now, I know you might be thinking, *"Hold on, are you telling me that gun violence is a disease? How is that possible? How can an intentional act to injure or kill be similar to health epidemics such as COVID-19, AIDS, or Ebola?"* I know gun violence does not appear to be a public health crisis on the surface. Nonetheless, when we investigate deeper and listen, read, and analyze the research, this fact becomes abundantly clear.

Gun violence, like any public health crisis, is contagious and spreads through contact. Using the same research method used to measure contagions, researchers at Harvard and Yale, led by Dr. Andrew V. Papachristos, found that, "The frequency and duration of exposure to gun violence accounted for two-thirds of the 11,000 shooting episodes studied."[293] In other words, gun violence is passed from one person to another in the same manner any viral disease is. Those who are surrounded by gun violence often feel the need to protect themselves and turn to gun ownership as a solution. Unsurprisingly, these gun owners take matters into their own hands and use guns to kill. In this context, gun violence is a social contagion. The more a person is exposed to guns and gun violence, the more likely that person will become either a victim or a perpetrator of gun violence.

A public health crisis is one that affects people in certain geographic areas via the loss of life, a decline in community health, and negative effects on the economy.[294] In the United States, 310 people are shot every day and 100 of these victims suffer fatal wounds.[295] Homicide due to gun violence is killing young Americans at appalling rates, so much so that it is more likely for children under the age of four to die from gun violence than from cancer.[296] There are countless stories of families being torn apart by gun violence, mothers burying their teenage children, kids growing up without a father because he was fatally shot, little children being caught in the crossfire of a gunfight, and people of all ages using a gun to take their own life.

---

[293] Zhu, J. *We Need to Treat Gun Violence Like a Public Health Problem* (Huffington Post, 2017).

[294] *Health Crisis* (Wikipedia). https://en.wikipedia.org/wiki/Health_crisis.

[295] Dennis, B. *Why We Should Think of Gun Violence as a Disease, and Study It Accordingly* (The Washington Post, 2019).

[296] Humikowski, C. *Our Terrifying Children's Epidemic: Gun Violence* (Chicago Tribune, 2019).

Additionally, gun violence destroys community businesses and costs the U.S. hundreds of billions of dollars annually, placing a significant strain on the economy. Specifically, according to a report by U.S. Senator Martin Heinrich:

> The economic health of local communities is hampered by gun violence. Sharp increases in gun violence can reduce the growth rate of new businesses and slow home value appreciation. In Minneapolis, for example, each additional gun homicide in a given year was associated with 80 fewer jobs in the neighborhood the following year. Across six different American cities, from Baton Rouge to San Francisco, neighborhood surges in gun violence slowed home value appreciation by about 4 percent.[297]

Accordingly, it should be clear that, yes, gun violence most certainly meets the definition of a public health crisis.

If gun violence is clearly a public health crisis, why are we not treating it as such? Answer: the intentional creation and manipulation of public ignorance has prevented us from labeling, studying, and acting on gun violence as a public health crisis. If you recall from the introduction of this book, in 1996, the NRA and other pro-gun organizations successfully lobbied Congress to institute the Dickey Amendment. The American Psychological Association described the effect of this Amendment as follows:

> The Dickey Amendment... restricted funds for injury prevention and firearms control at the federal Centers for Disease Control and Prevention from being used to advocate or promote gun control. This move has had a chilling effect, halting vital prevention research at the CDC for more than 20 years...To make matters worse, the Bureau of Alcohol, Tobacco, Firearms and Explosives is prohibited from

---

[297] Heinrich, 2018.

releasing information about its firearms database to the CDC and the National Institutes of Health.[298]

Twenty-five years later, the epidemic of gun violence in this country remains undiagnosed, untreated, and uncured, and the public debate surrounding the topic is misguided.

While many researchers have determined that gun violence is a public health issue, the Dickey Amendment has left us with extremely insufficient data on gun violence. The data shortage has been particularly detrimental to society because it has significantly hampered researchers' ability to develop effective intervention methods. The amendment has created ignorance so effectively that even researchers are kept in the dark.

Moreover, the absence of data permits pro-gun activists to claim that there is no evidence that gun control or intervention methods are effective. In other words, pro-gun activists successfully prevented the collection of any data that would promote gun control reforms, and now they discredit all gun control proponents because they don't have enough proven data to support their reforms.

The lack of funding for public health-oriented research on gun violence is keeping people totally in the dark, including many of our legislators, governors, and mayors who are supposed to be focused on solving this problem. This ignorance is, to a great extent, responsible for the thousands upon thousands of lives lost from gun violence every year. Most devastatingly, the ignorance of the fact that the most effective way to reduce gun violence is through public health solutions and not through buying more guns for self-defense or solely through gun control methods has enabled corporations to continue to profit immensely from the business of gun violence.

Our ignorance about the nature of gun violence has also harmed us in areas other than loss of life. Since we don't view gun violence and other forms of violence as public health and policy issues, we

---

[298] Evans, A., Anthony, C. *Gun Violence: A Public Health Problem* (American Psychological Association, 2018).

have been manipulated into categorizing them as moral issues. We have determined that good people don't commit crimes, so those who do commit crimes must be bad people. This overly simplistic notion has had a profound impact on our culture. It has led to our acceptance of and indifference towards mass incarceration, our disdain for welfare programs designed to help the most vulnerable communities (which are often riddled with crime and violence), and our eagerness to label and dismiss people based on the worst things they've done. It has obscured our view of everyone's inherent human dignity.

Gun violence is having negative economic and social impacts on poor communities. The people growing up in these communities are being labeled as bad people not worthy of our assistance. And the political will to fix the problems in these communities has become virtually nonexistent. These factors converge to perpetuate the existence of gun violence, bolster the belief in racist and anti-government-assistance ideas, rationalize the existence of mass incarceration, and oppress poor communities. Meanwhile, as I've mentioned *ad nauseum*, corporations have been able to make enormous profits from the business of gun violence. Since they have been able to manipulate people into accepting, behaving, and voting according to racist and anti-government-assistance beliefs, they have been able to preserve the economic structures from which they profit greatly.

Ignorance of the risk of gun violence has been created because conservatives, pro-gun organizations and businesses, and corporate elites have an active interest in maintaining its existence. The elite purposely ensure that tens of thousands of people die from gun violence. They watch as the economic prospects of low-income communities are decimated, and they ignore the cries of those traumatized by gun violence. They do this because of their avarice. The creation of ignorance initially created the risk of gun violence. It has since prevented the needed government-led studies of gun violence as a public health issue, stifled the implementation of effective solutions, and led to Gun Culture 2.0

and the "tough-on-crime", anti-assistance, punitive culture that has corrupted the conscience of our society. Until we reverse the ignorance surrounding the very real issue of gun violence, we will never resolve this risk.

SOLUTIONS

When discussing how to reduce gun violence, it is extremely important to understand the factors that lead to crime. Poverty, unemployment, homelessness, untreated mental illness, inadequate education, an inability to appropriately handle emotions (usually due to a lack of social emotional education), and hopelessness are the main factors that lead to crime and violence in any society. Every solution that I will offer in this section will be aimed at reducing gun violence on its surface, rather than attempting to solve all the underlying factors that lead to gun violence.

But, make no mistake, these "crime-causing" social risks can all be dramatically reduced, and some of them can even be eradicated (we will discuss how to do that in the coming chapters). *If the above-mentioned social risks are the main factors that lead to crime, isn't every other solution pointless?* Absolutely not. When someone has lung cancer, doctors do not say, "Well, if you didn't smoke cigarettes, you wouldn't have cancer. Now there's nothing I can do to help you." Just because there are underlying causes to an illness does not mean we cannot treat it effectively.

The idea that "every problem on earth" must first be solved in order for there to be any progress is what Gary Slutkin, an epidemiologist, innovator in violence reduction, and the Founder and Executive Director of Cure Violence calls the "everything theory".[299] Many people, politicians, and activists call on society to fix the issues of poverty, poor schools, broken families, absent

---

[299] Slutkin, G. *Let's treat violence as a contagious disease.* (TED, 2013). www.youtube.com/watch?v=CZNrOzgNWf4.

fathers, drugs, and racism before we attempt to reduce gun violence by other means. While fixing every single root cause would certainly be ideal, Slutkin acknowledges that it isn't paramount to reducing gun violence. As an analogy, he points out that many epidemics, such as AIDS, were reversed in countries without fixing the problem of their failing economies.

The solution lies more in how we regard and understand the issue of gun violence than in fixing every problem that contributes to it. Looking at the epidemic of gun violence as one that requires only policing or gun control solutions leads to more complex solutions than are necessary. And because the issue is so polarizing in politics, no real effective solutions are ever implemented. Thus, reducing ignorance of this risk is our only hope.

REFORMING A PUNITIVE CULTURE

As you have read, and will continue to read throughout this book, the punitive culture we have created in our society is one of the most-threatening risks we are facing. We have chosen to ignore the reasons that lead one into a life of crime, instead judging everybody by the same "no excuses" moral code. While this culture stands in total opposition to the ideals of human dignity laid out by the Founding Fathers in the Declaration of Independence, we have chosen to become blind to our hypocrisy.

The concept of punishment has been a staple of our society's response to violent crime for centuries. Yet, as we read in Chapter 4, punishment is largely ineffective. Gary Slutkin has called punishment "highly overvalued."[300] In his Ted Talk, Slutkin points to multiple studies that illustrate the facts that punishment does not: 1) function as an effective deterrent of crime, 2) act as a main driver of behavior, or 3) result in behavioral changes. Instead, incarceration reinforces criminal norms and values and effectively eliminates any possibility

---

[300] Ibid.

of rehabilitation; essentially, offenders become "educated" and "trained" to behave as a criminal instead of being rehabilitated into positively functioning members of society. As you read last chapter, deterrence theory has been debunked, and overly harsh punishments and the legal discrimination that follows formerly incarcerated people frequently forces them back into a life of crime.

Slutkin goes on to address the false notion of the existence of bad and good people. He says that the idea that crime is committed by bad people and that to stop crime we must lock up these bad people, is very similar to the mishandled treatment of ancient epidemics. Plagues, leprosy, and other epidemics were blamed on "bad people" or "bad humors", and the deemed solution was to confine the sick in dungeons, persecute them, or isolate them. Obviously, this didn't help anything or anyone.[301] Today, incarceration is having little to no impact on curbing gun violence, and its continued existence is one of the main reasons we see no progress.

Abandoning our punitive culture is not only the right thing to do morally, but also the right thing to do if we want to reduce violence and save lives.

REVERSING IGNORANCE

The ignorance that preserves the risk of gun violence has in large part been created through the Dickey Amendment. Fortunately, amendments can be… amended. It is imperative that we reverse the Dickey Amendment if we are serious about reducing gun violence. By reversing the amendment, we will give researchers and experts the data they need to better understand gun violence and create effective solutions to reduce gun violence and the ongoing risk it poses.

We will also be able to enlighten the American people to show them that gun violence is an issue of public health. Ignorance

---

[301] Ibid.

is amplifying this risk ten-fold because very few people are pressuring their politicians to take the right path of action, there are no widespread social movements calling upon our leaders to treat gun violence as a public health crisis, and the "solutions" that are being proposed are largely misguided. By reversing the Dickey Amendment, we can change this. We can bring people out of the dark and create a movement to control the gun violence epidemic.

Reversing ignorance also requires that we invest heavily in education. Incorporating social emotional learning in schools to teach children how to resolve conflicts properly and productively and how to manage their emotions when they are angry or upset, among other things, will reap huge benefits for our children.

Additionally, we must reverse the ignorance of the effectiveness of gun control. Many people on the political right have been preaching the so-called ineffectiveness of gun control for years. They claim that gun control doesn't work, that "The only thing that stops a bad guy with a gun is a good guy with a gun", and that "guns don't kill people, people kill people." These common refrains are simply false. If the political right was correct by claiming that more guns equal more safety, we would be the safest country in the world. After all, we have more guns than people in the United States.[302] As sociologist and author DaShanne Stokes puts it:

> When a country with less than five percent of the world's population has nearly half of the world's privately owned guns and makes up nearly a third of the world's mass shootings, it's time to stop saying guns make us safer.[303]

We must educate Americans and expose these baseless, evidence-less claims coming from the pro-gun right.

---

[302] Ingraham, C. *There are more guns than people in the United States, according to a new study of global firearm ownership.* (Washington Post, 2018).

[303] Stokes, D. (Twitter, 2018). https://twitter.com/DaShanneStokes/status/1056273207081271299.

We should also look at the effective gun control measures implemented in other countries. In Australia in 1996, a lone gunman shot and killed 35 people and wounded 18 more when he opened fire with a semi-automatic weapon. The Australian Government quickly said, "enough is enough", and implemented sweeping gun control legislation. They banned the sale of assault weapons and created an assault weapon buyback program. Since then, the country had reported no mass shootings until 2002, when another gunman wielding six handguns went on to shoot and kill two people and injure five at Monash University in Melbourne. Australia again passed more gun control legislation, this time in the form of a National Handgun Agreement, a separate National Handgun Buyback Act in 2003, and a new and improved gun trafficking policy.

Since the passage of these policies, there have been no shooting sprees like the one in Melbourne. And, yet, even with all these new restrictions on gun ownership, the fears of gun control that are spewed by those on the political right did not become reality. As journalist Clinton Leaf explains:

> Australian independence didn't end. Tyranny didn't come. Australians still hunted and explored and big-wave surfed to their hearts' content. Their economy didn't crash; Invaders never arrived. Violence, in many forms, went down across the country, not up. Somehow, lawmakers on either side of the gun debate managed to get along and legislate.[304]

To offer some statistics, suicides have dropped by 80 percent, there have been no mass shootings or smaller shooting sprees, and the murder rate has dropped to just 1 killing per 100,000 people (and only 32 homicides have been committed with guns).[305]

Gun control works. Plain and simple. It's time for our country to reverse our ignorance and acknowledge this fact.

---

[304] Leaf, C. *How Australia All but Ended Gun Violence* (Fortune, 2018).
[305] Ibid.

The Risk Of Gun Violence

STICKY SOLUTIONS

Gun violence is "sticky". You may have just asked yourself, *"What does that mean?"* To offer some clarity, Thomas Abt elaborates on what exactly we mean when we talk about the sticky nature of gun violence:

> In the cities that struggle with high rates of violence, shootings are concentrated among a surprisingly small set of people and places. It doesn't concentrate in entire communities or neighborhoods. Even in the most allegedly dangerous places, the vast majority of people are not violent, and there are plenty of safe spaces... In fact, in most cities, about 4 percent of city blocks account for approximately 50 percent of crime. In Oakland, 60 percent of murders happen within a social network of approximately one to two thousand high-risk individuals—about 0.3 percent of the city's population.[306]

The stickiness of gun violence is why this risk is much easier to solve than most people believe. Building off the idea of concentrated violence, in his book, *Bleeding Out*, Thomas Abt offers evidence-based solutions that he claims would save 12,000 lives over the next eight years.

Abt's solution revolves around the idea of "focused deterrence". Focused deterrence is a method that combines the threat of law enforcement with community assistance. Basically, law enforcement officials and community leaders identify the most at risk of violence individuals and send a clear message that sounds something like this, "We know who you are. We want the best for you, but we can't and don't approve of what you're doing. We will crack down quickly and harshly if you continue down a path of violence. But if you agree

---

[306] Abt, T. *My eight-year plan to dramatically reduce urban gun violence* (The Guardian, 2019).

to stop, we'll give you an array of services—jobs, education, health care, and so on—to help you build a better, violence-free life."[307]

Abt's plan has three essential components: focus, balance, and fairness. It focuses on the highest risk individuals, seeks to balance the threat of law enforcement with community assistance, and it promotes fairness as it requires transparency from officials and an open line of communication and feedback from the community. The plan doesn't just sound good in theory; there are multiple studies and real-world implementations that have proven that focused deterrence works. For example, in Boston in the 1990s, focused deterrence reduced violent crime by 79 percent.[308] Abt's plan would reduce violence by 50 percent in the 40 most violent cities, save 12,000 lives, and only cost $100 million per year (and when you consider the $229 billion price tag of gun violence, it's clear that investing a mere $100 million is a huge cost-saver).

Another solution that focuses on the sticky nature of violence is Place-Based Investigations of Violent Offender Territories, also known by the acronym PIVOT. This plan was implemented in Cincinnati and has seen remarkable results. As described in an analysis by the National Civic League, the program "uses data to systematically dismantle criminal networks and eliminate safe havens for criminal activity. PIVOT empowers residents to reclaim their streets through confidential informants, visibility, and place-making".[309] The PIVOT method has reduced crime by 75 percent in the most violent neighborhoods in Cincinnati.[310]

We must implement the PIVOT program and Thomas Abt's solution throughout the entire country. These solutions are evidence-based, cost-effective, and will save tens of thousands of lives.

---

[307] Lopez, 2019.

[308] Ibid.

[309] *The Promising Practices Database: Time to PIVOT – Cincinnati, OH* (National Civic League). https://www.nationalcivicleague.org/promising-practices/time-to-pivot-cincinnati-oh/

[310] Ibid.

POLICE REFORM

As we discussed in Chapter 3 and 4, we need a whole lot of police reform in the United States. When discussing gun violence specifically, we must focus on solutions that increase community trust of the police. Police brutality, racial profiling, a concerted focus on low-level crimes, and low murder solve rates all contribute to low police trust. Journalist George Lopez explains the consequences of this distrust:

> The resulting distrust likely leads to more violence: When people don't trust the police or the criminal justice system, they're less likely to work with either. This not only makes it harder for detectives to catch people who may go on to commit more crimes or murders, but if someone gets into a dangerous or heated situation, his distrust in the police may lead him to take matters into his own hands—potentially resorting to violence—instead of calling 911.[311]

When you live in a neighborhood where the murder solve rate is extremely low and the police seem to be concerned with only low-level offenses, trust in police naturally declines, people instead take matters into their own hands, and a vicious cycle of violence is created.

Logically, it follows that to decrease crime we must increase police trust. Luckily, the Justice Collaboratory at Yale Law School has been working on just that. They have developed The National Initiative for Building Community Trust and Justice, which has "played an instrumental role in disseminating research, best practices and training on the use of procedural justice as a tool to improve police trust with the communities they serve".[312] The Justice

---

[311] Lopez, 2019.

[312] *The National Initiative for Building Community Trust and Justice* (Yale Law School). https://law.yale.edu/justice-collaboratory/our-work/projects/national-initiative-building-community-trust-and-justice.

Collaboratory has created comprehensive projects to increase police trust. We must start implementing these evidence-based projects in police precincts across the nation.

PUBLIC HEALTH SOLUTIONS

Gun violence can be treated in much the same way as other public health issues, such as tobacco, motor vehicle safety, and poison control. In the article, *Curbing Gun Violence: Lessons from Public Health Successes*, Dariush Mozaffarian, emphasizes the exigency of shifting our social norms as well as the way that we think and act on gun violence. While many people focus on passing gun control laws, the article challenges us to look at and treat gun violence by adopting a different perspective.

Similar to how we dramatically reduced the amount of tobacco smokers in the U.S. by raising taxes on tobacco products, we can tax the sale of guns and ammunition. Moreover, in the same manner that we launched anti-smoking campaigns, we can launch media and educational campaigns to reduce gun violence and suicide and teach people how to recognize at-risk individuals. We must call for a shift in social and cultural norms, specifically how we portray gun violence in the media, television, and movies.

We should also look at the progress we made in auto-vehicle safety and apply the lessons to gun safety. For example, we can require gun safety classes just as we require driver's education, we can enact safety standards to reduce clip sizes and firing speeds, require periodic safety inspections, and install automatic locks on guns. We can reduce gun violence if we simply look at the parallels between guns and other public health issues.[313]

Another public health solution to gun violence can be found in the method of "violence prevention". Gary Slutkin and his

---

[313] Mozaffarian, D. *Curbing Gun Violence: Lessons from Public Health Successes* (JAMA, American Medical Association, 2013).

organization, Cure Violence, found that "the greatest predictor of a case of violence is a preceding case of violence". This realization that gun violence is infectious and spreading like a disease has led to new ideas of how to curb violence. The Cure Violence organization decided to apply the same type of treatment to people who were likely to commit an act of violence that they applied to people in areas affected by epidemics, such as cholera or AIDS.

Slutkin's team knew that to reverse epidemics, they must interrupt transmissions and identify first causes, so they hired people whom they called "violence interrupters". Violence interrupters are people from the community (often former gang members or people with backgrounds in gun violence) who are credible, trusted, and specifically trained to find someone who is angry and likely to commit a violent crime (for instance, if someone owes them money or killed their friend) and talk them out of committing said crime.

A critical step to reversing epidemics is preventing further spread. Therefore, violence interrupters also find people who may not be likely to commit violence at that moment, but who are involved with a violent crowd or hanging out in a violent neighborhood and may be susceptible to committing a violent act in the future. These people are managed too. The organization then hires outreach workers who monitor and keep these people on therapy for 6–24 months. Lastly, the organization challenged and changed social norms through community activities, remodeling, and public education.

In its first trial, this method proved dramatically successful, witnessing a 67 percent decrease in homicides in the most violent police district in America at the time.[314] The method has sustained success in 20 other trials in the U.S, and the movement is starting to gain traction internationally as well.[315] Additionally, Thomas Abt has stated that the Cure Violence method would be an effective complement to his plan. We must employ violence interrupters in violence-ridden neighborhoods throughout the country.

---

[314] Slutkin, 2013.
[315] Ibid.

GUN CONTROL

Of course, one of the best ways to reduce gun violence is by getting guns off the street and out of the hands of potentially dangerous individuals. In other words, we need to enact stricter gun control laws. Gun control was a hot topic for Democrats in the primaries leading up to the 2020 presidential election, and many of the candidates drafted comprehensive gun control plans. I believe that the best plan was that proposed by Senator Elizabeth Warren. Most notably, Senator Warren's plan includes holding gun dealers and manufacturers accountable for the violence they contribute to, universal background checks, a federal assault weapon ban, and democratic reforms to release politicians from the stranglehold of pro-gun special interest groups.[316] All of Senator Warren's plans are evidence-based and would greatly contribute to reducing gun violence.

We should also create buyback programs like those seen in Australia, a policy not included in Senator Warren's plan.

One of the main obstacles to passing gun control legislation has been the extremely misleading fearmongering by conservative media and politicians who claim that the political left wants to repeal the Second Amendment and "take all your guns away". They spread fear of a tyrannical society without guns in which people cannot defend themselves. Given this extreme rhetoric, it is no surprise that there is always a surge in gun sales after a mass shooting when gun control legislation inevitably becomes a hot topic.[317]

However, as discussed earlier, when sweeping gun control measures were enacted in Australia, none of these fears of a tyrannical authoritarian state came true. Additionally, we should acknowledge the absurdity of the idea that any number of guns

---

[316] *Protecting Our Communities From Gun Violence* (Warren). https://elizabethwarren.com/plans/gun-violence.

[317] Liu, G., Wiebe, DJ. *A Time-Series Analysis of Firearm Purchasing After Mass Shooting Events in the United States (JAMA Network Open,* 2019).

in the hands of citizens would be able to protect Americans from the most powerful military in the history of the world during an authoritarian takeover.

Despite the ridiculousness of this baseless fear, we must work towards eliminating extreme fearmongering from media and political rhetoric. We must call the false claims that the left wants to repeal the Second Amendment and that gun control would lead to tyranny, what they are, *utter nonsense*. The best way forward is to reverse ignorance surrounding this topic so that the American people can see through the lies being spread by pro-gun corporations who are profiting from the gun sales and gun violence industries.

DEPARTMENT OF PEACE

Similar to how I suggested that we develop a cabinet office for racial justice, we must also establish the Department of Peace, an idea suggested by former presidential candidate, Marianne Williamson. This department is essential to making sure our values and goals of achieving peace domestically and abroad guide the implementation of all the above-mentioned policies. Williamson explains that the department will work to teach violence prevention in schools, decrease gang violence through treating gang psychology, and build peace-making efforts, both domestically and overseas, among other initiatives.[318] Elaborating on the goal of the Department, Williamson writes:

> As its mission, the U.S. Department of Peace will; hold peace as an organizing principle; promote justice and democratic principles to expand human rights; coordinate restorative justice programs; address white supremacy; strengthen nonmilitary means of peacemaking; work to prevent armed

---

[318] Plan for U.S. Department of Peace (Marianne 2020). https://marianne2020.com/issues/us-department-of-peace-plan.

conflict; address the epidemic of gun violence; develop new structures of nonviolent dispute resolution; and proactively and systematically promote national and international conflict prevention, mediation, and resolution. In short, we must wage peace. "Large groups of desperate people", said Williamson, "should be seen as a national security risk."[319]

The development and implementation of the Department of Peace is a crucial component of what it will take to truly increase safety and peace in the United States, and it will also push us in the right direction of abandoning our culture's punitive disposition.

NO NOTORIETY CAMPAIGN

Our final solution is known as the No Notoriety Campaign, which acknowledges that many mass shooters commit tragic acts of senseless violence that are in part motivated by the quest for notoriety and infamy. It calls on the media to be more responsible in their coverage of mass shootings by limiting the number of times the name of the shooter is mentioned, refusing to broadcast any manifesto written by the shooter, and not showing any photo of the shooter. Instead, the media should "elevate the names and likenesses of all victims killed and or injured to send the message their lives are more important than the killer's actions".[320] While it is uncomfortable to plan for mass shootings, it is irresponsible to dismiss an effective solution because of an uneasiness with what it aims to address.

---

[319] Ibid.
[320] No Notoriety. https://nonotoriety.com.

The Risk Of Gun Violence

IN SUM

Gun violence is treatable. It is not inevitable. Like countless other epidemics, the risk of future cases can be drastically diminished. If we shift the discourse surrounding the issue of gun violence from one of morality to one of public health, we will begin to understand how to solve this problem. We can enable the CDC to research gun violence as a public health crisis and gain a greater understanding of the epidemic. We can compare gun violence to similar public health crises to formulate public policy ideas that will reduce gun violence on a national scale. We can enact smart gun violence reducing solutions like PIVOT and focused deterrence, and we can pass sweeping gun control legislation.

Above all, we must reverse our ignorance about this risk. As with any other risk, widespread ignorance has spawned the risk of gun violence. Gun violence continues to plague our society because certain people, groups, and companies continue to make billions of dollars from the industry of gun violence and gun sales, and they are doing everything in their power to create the ignorance necessary to this industry's survival. We must make this common knowledge and we must start a movement to put an end to this injustice. Reducing gun violence will save lives, save taxpayers' money, and improve the quality of life for multitudes of Americans in violence-ridden neighborhoods.

Ignorance and the manipulation of that ignorance through fear mongering as well as the spreading of misleading and outright false common refrains have made this risk exponentially more dangerous and harder to solve. We can change that. We must change it. We have developed evidenced-based solutions. We know what to do. We must elect leaders at all levels who are committed to *solving* problems, instead of merely creating ways to live through them. Gun violence can be dramatically reduced; all we have to do is implement the correct policies, programs, and prevention methods.

6

The Risk Of Poor Health

The problem in America is not just that our current healthcare system fails to adequately treat sickness. The problem is also that our current economic system, based as it is on an inordinate focus on short-term profit, actually increases the probability of sickness.
– Marianne Williamson

It is no secret that many Americans are unhealthy. Poor diets, lack of exercise, and low health literacy have been so detrimental to the collective health of our nation that we are now simultaneously facing several life-threatening health challenges. These include high rates of obesity, cancer, diabetes, heart disease, stress, depression, and anxiety. Yet, we are not confronting these health crises with the appropriate sense of urgency and understanding. This is due to ignorance being created and preserved by the elites. This ignorance protects the corporations whose actions spawn these health problems. Our high-cost, inefficient healthcare system is designed to profit from illness not wellness. We also have a large misinformed group of anti-vaccine zealots whose negligent actions have contributed to the comeback of once eradicated diseases and have made it extremely challenging to end the COVID-19 pandemic.

This chapter seeks to address how ignorance has created and amplified these health crises. We will examine how public ignorance has developed, why ignorance has been maintained, and of course, we will discuss what our society can do to mitigate these health risks. The health risks facing our country are abundant. Accordingly, this chapter does not attempt to cover every single health issue in the United States. Instead, we will focus on the following topics: 1) health literacy, 2) the obesity and chronic illness epidemics, 3) the negative repercussions of our for-profit healthcare system, 4) the increasing rates of mental health difficulties, and 5) the anti-vaccine movement.

The biggest misconception regarding individual health is the idea that calling on people to take more personal responsibility in managing their health is effective. Our society tends to dismiss obesity as a "real" problem by claiming that losing weight is simply a matter of taking some personal responsibility to eat better, eat less, and exercise more. We do the same when we talk about mental health, telling someone with anxiety to "just calm down". Similarly, we blame anti-vaxxers for their own ignorance without even trying to understand how they have been misled into denying the necessity and immense benefits of vaccination.

To mitigate the dangers posed by the wide array of health risks facing our society, we must understand the systems, environments, policies, and monetary motivations underlying the risks. We must reverse ignorance to improve the health of our nation. This goal is very attainable, and it should be a priority for our society.

We have the power to create a healthier society, with longer life expectancies for all Americans, less chronic disease, better mental health, and higher standards of living. It's time we abandon the notion that calling for more rugged individualism and personal responsibility is an appropriate responses to our myriad health problems. We cannot solve these problems by telling people they simply must make better choices. Instead, we must make systemic changes such as: improving health literacy and education, restructuring our food and physical environments, placing a greater emphasis on improving mental health, and radically altering the profit-oriented business models of the healthcare and pharmaceutical industries.

So, let's get started by examining why and how ignorance has developed for each of these issues.

WHY AND HOW HAS IGNORANCE DEVELOPED

Just like other risks we have discussed, the pursuit of profit underlies the ignorance of health risks in our society. To fully grasp how money drives these risks, we first must understand a basic tenet of capitalism. As a blunt oversimplification, capitalism thrives when people spend money. And to be clear, it doesn't matter how people are spending their money. *All that matters is that they are spending money.* Spending grows the GDP. Historian and author Rutger Bregman elaborates on this attribute of capitalism in his book *Utopia for Realists*:

> The GDP benefits from all manner of human suffering… If you were the GDP, your ideal citizen would be a compulsive gambler with cancer who's going through a drawn-out divorce that he copes with by popping fistfuls of Prozac and going berserk on Black Friday…Mental illness, obesity, pollution, crime—in terms of the GDP, the more the better. That's also why the country with the highest GDP, the United States, also leads in social problems.[321]

---

[321] Bregman, R. *Utopia for Realists* (Bay Back Books, 2018). 105-106.

That's exactly what we've been discussing so far. Inherent in our definition of a risk is the potential for the elites to profit. Where there are risks, there is money to be made by entrepreneurs and corporations… and when there is money to be made, ignorance is created and preserved to ensure the survival of the risk.

But how has ignorance developed in the health sector? How have we become so ignorant about food, diets, mental health, and general health? As we will see, most of the ignorance regarding health issues has been maintained through intentional efforts. I am not proposing that "evil" people have intentionally hid health information from the public, but rather that the public has gradually grown ignorant of a health industry constantly growing in complexity. Wealthy people and corporations within the healthcare industrial complex have benefited from this ignorance. Therefore, they have had an active interest in maintaining it.

HEALTH LITERACY

Low health literacy is one of the core varieties of ignorance causing the health risks facing our nation. According to the Center for Health Care Strategies, approximately 90 million Americans are said to have low health literacy. Low health literacy, as the organization defines it, is "The degree to which individuals have the capacity to obtain, process, and understand basic health information and services needed to make appropriate health decisions."[322] I imagine it won't surprise you to learn that those 90 million Americans are mostly comprised of the following demographics: the elderly, those in lower socioeconomic classes, those with lower levels of education, those who speak English as a second language, and those who receive public assistance in any

---

[322] *What is Health Literacy* (Center for Health Care Strategies). https://www.chcs.org/media/What_is_Health_Literacy.pdf.

form.[323] It is the marginalized groups in our society who suffer the most from the creation and preservation of ignorance and the consequent amplification of risks.

90 million Americans have low health literacy largely because it has become much harder to be health literate. Due to advances in science and medicine, the healthcare industry has grown increasingly perplexing to the common person over the last 70 years. Now more than ever, navigating this system requires the skills of health and science literacy.

The attainment of these skills increases when one has advanced education levels, high individual incomes, and greater professional success.[324] Conversely, health literacy skills become harder to acquire when a person has little (or low quality) education, a learning disability or cognitive disability, and when their cognitive ability declines (usually in old age).[325]

We have reached this point because we have not made a concerted effort as a nation to help people keep up with the growing complexities of the health and medicine industry, nor have we made a serious effort to improve health literacy across all demographics. We have instead opted to create a system in which only those among higher socioeconomic classes receive the education necessary to become health literate, whereas the poor, elderly, and immigrant populations have been left in the dust.

There is an active interest among the elite to maintain such a high level of low health literacy because low health literacy enriches and empowers them. Compared to those who are health literate, people with low health literacy generate bigger profits for hospitals, Big Pharmaceutical companies, and health insurance companies. The Partnership for Clear Health Communication at the National

---

[323] Ibid.

[324] *How Poor Health Literacy Impacts Vulnerable Populations* (Rider University). https://online.rider.edu/blog/how-poor-health-literacy-impacts-vulnerable-populations/.

[325] Ibid.

Patient Safety Foundation reports that, "Compared to those with proficient health literacy, adults with low health literacy experience: 4 times higher health care costs, 6 percent more hospital visits, and 2 day-longer hospital stay."[326] Meanwhile, as low health literacy is generating greater profits for the health industry, it is estimated to cost the U.S. economy approximately $236 billion annually.[327]

Poor health literacy poses a great risk because it permeates many aspects of one's life from income level and occupation to housing, education, and of course, good medical care.[328] Meanwhile, as marginalized communities suffer, the elite are enriched and empowered. The negative consequences that stem from low health literacy serve to oppress vulnerable communities while simultaneously reasserting racist and classist stereotypes that are weaponized to rationalize the existence of the challenges that afflict them. Pivotally, the affirmation of these stereotypes leads voters to dismiss low health literacy as a societal problem, instead deeming it to be a problem of personal responsibility. This lack of political will gives politicians no electoral incentive to focus on the problem. And when you couple this lack of political will with the lobbying and campaign financing efforts of large corporations and powerful players in the health industry, the incentive for politicians to act to solve public health issues vanishes. These factors contribute to the maintenance of widespread low health literacy among vulnerable communities and the ignorance that justifies it in the minds of many.

These marginalized groups, who already face significant obstacles to upward socioeconomic mobility, suffer negative health and financial consequences because of their low health literacy, and as a direct consequence, their opportunities to move up the socioeconomic ladder decrease even more drastically.

This factor means that subgroup of elites who profit from the health industry are not the only ones with a vested interest in

---

[326] Ibid.
[327] Ibid.
[328] Ibid.

maintaining widespread low health literacy. In fact, every member of the elite class who wants to preserve the current socioeconomic stratification has this perverted incentive to maintain this form of ignorance. Since the elite exert tremendous influence over the political sphere, they can ensure that their own interests are met. Ignorance in the form of low health literacy has been cultivated in American society because the elite class has an interest in benefitting from the risks it creates.

DIET

In addition to low health literacy, the ignorance of what constitutes a healthy diet and how to maintain a healthy weight is dangerously widespread. Poor diets have caused too many health problems to count. Today, two-thirds of adults in the United States are either overweight or obese; one out of every four deaths are from cancer; the CDC predicts that in the next 25 years, one out of every three Americans will have diabetes; and approximately 70 percent of deaths are largely lifestyle related and preventable.[329]

Processed and sugary foods dominate our diets. As a result, we are now experiencing disastrous health effects. Research has suggested that every 10 percent increase in one's consumption of ultra-processed foods increases one's risk of cancer by 12 percent.[330] Similarly, eating high amounts of sugar significantly increases a person's risk of obesity, heart disease, diabetes, and other chronic health issues that can also increase the risk of cancer.[331] I can go on and on, and you would probably get sicker and sicker just reading about it.

---

[329] *FACTS* (What the Health Film). https://www.whatthehealthfilm.com/facts.
[330] Reinberg, S. *Highly Processed Foods Tied to Higher Cancer Risk* (WebMD, 2018).
[331] Ndumele, C. *Obesity, Sugar and Heart Health*. (Johns Hopkins Medicine). https://www.hopkinsmedicine.org/health/wellness-and-prevention/obesity-sugar-and-heart-health; *Does Sugar Cause Diabetes? Fact vs Fiction* (Healthline). https://www.healthline.com/nutrition/does-sugar-cause-diabetes.

If Only We Knew

These negative health trends are a result of public ignorance regarding what it means to eat healthy and how to maintain a healthy weight. The rise of ignorance concerning how to reduce the rates of obesity and chronic illnesses has come about in a very similar manner as that of low health literacy. As time has marched on, the world, specifically our food landscape, has changed. Market forces have led to the production of foods that are more processed and higher in sugar content. Additionally, since the mid-20th century, we have developed lifestyles and eating habits that have made us more prone to obesity, diabetes, and cancer.

However, as Jonathan Engel explains in his book, *Fat Nation*, it isn't obvious to recognize these changes to our world as "obesity-inducing" changes. Consequently, the public has developed false ideas of what causes obesity instead of recognizing the true causes. In a study conducted by University of Chicago researcher Jennifer Benz, it was found that as much as 75 percent of Americans believe the main cause of obesity is a lack of willpower.[332] This belief is simply not true. As Engel puts it:

> If being less heavy were simply a matter of eating less and moving more, we might have made progress against obesity. But the more we study fat the more complicated it seems to be. There is more to fat than meets the eye.[333]

Contrary to the popular, ignorant belief in the efficacy of taking personal responsibility, the rise in obesity has largely been caused by changes to our environment and lifestyles. I'm talking about changes such as the increase of sugary foods being sold, the expansion of the suburbs that drastically decreased "walkability", the move to more sedentary work environments where we sit in front

---

[332] Kolata, G. *Americans Blame Obesity on Willpower, Despite Evidence It's Genetic* (New York Times, 2016).

[333] Engel, J. *Fat Nation: A History of Obesity in America* (Rowman & Littlefield Publishing Group, Inc., 2018). 14.

of a desk all day, and the rise of an indifference towards obesity in our social lives.[334] These changes in our physical, social, and food environments have largely gone unnoticed. As a result, the public has become ignorant of the true causes of obesity.

While these changes in our environment took shape free from perverse intentions to negatively affect our health, many sectors of the health industry have had monetary incentives to ensure the survival of the negative consequences that followed those environmental transformations. Let's look at some examples.

As obesity rates increased throughout the nation, the diet and weight-loss industry became engorged as well. Yet, despite the extremely broad selection of diets and weight-loss programs currently on the market, virtually none of them provide lasting results. We ignorantly preach to obese people telling them to eat less and eat "better", but we completely ignore the fact that 97 percent of people who go on a diet regain the weight they lost (and often add more weight) within three years.[335]

Despite the shocking lack of evidence to suggest diets are an effective way to lose weight, 45 million Americans "go on a diet" every year. Our ignorance about how to effectively lose weight pushes us to dieting. When this doesn't work and people remain obese or regain the weight they lost, "Plan B" is to try another diet. This leads to enormous profits for the diet industry. To offer some perspective, the diet and weight-loss industry is worth $66 billion dollars.[336]

The potential to reign in enormous profits incentivizes those in the diet industry to perpetuate the ignorant claims that losing weight only requires willpower. Since the major players in the diet and weight-loss industry have a business model that is dependent on the existence of obese people, their business thrives when ignorance

---

[334] Engel, 2018.

[335] Brown, H. *The Weight of the Evidence: It's time to stop telling fat people to become thin* (Slate, 2015).

[336] Engel, 2018.

drives people to diets that intentionally fail and result in more and more people becoming or remaining obese. The existence of public ignorance creates a seemingly never-ending cycle of dieting.

The diet industry, however, is just one part of a bigger conglomerate of industries that profit from the ignorance of what constitutes a good diet and how to maintain a healthy weight. Ignorance has been perpetuated because of the profits produced from the selling of addictive processed and sugary foods, along with the treatment and care that is needed when millions of people become obese (a $190 billion industry) or are diagnosed with a chronic disease.[337] We are witnessing food companies choosing profit over social responsibility, and our society is paying the costs, both financially and in poor health.

Make no mistake about it, corporations in the food industry and the health care industry are well aware of the negative health consequences that come with a poor diet. Journalist and author Michael Moss has gone as far as to say there is "a conscious effort—taking place in labs and marketing meetings and grocery-store aisles—to get people hooked on foods that are convenient and inexpensive."[338] His claim is substantiated by statistics.

Our consumption of sugar has skyrocketed since 1950. In terms of sugar sweetened beverages alone, our annual consumption of these drinks rose 38.5 gallons per person between 1950 and 2000.[339] And this rise in sugar intake is not slowing down. The sugar industry made $10.4 billion in revenue in 2018.

These corporations in the sugar industry have chosen to directly feed into narratives that create and preserve ignorance about the dangers of sugar. One clear example of food companies creating ignorance can be seen in the actions of Coca-Cola. In an attempt

---

[337] Ibid.

[338] Godelnik, R. *Salt, Sugar, Fat & CSR: When Food Companies Choose Profit Over Responsibility* (Triple Pundit, 2013).

[339] Bray, G., Popkin, B. *Dietary sugar and body weight: Have we reached a crisis in the epidemic of obesity and diabetes?: Health be damned! Pour on the sugar* (Diabetes Care, 2014).

to create ignorance and shift the blame of the obesity epidemic away from bad diets and high consumption of sugar, the Coca-Cola corporation funds "researchers" to conduct "research" that disputes the evidence that high sugar foods lead to obesity; they claim that consuming too many calories or foods high in fat content is the issue instead.

When opponents of Coca-Cola object to the corporation's claims that the consumption of sugar doesn't play a role in obesity, Coca-Cola can accuse them of denying scientific evidence. But they don't even have to go that far. Because if there is not a clear consensus in the scientific research that the consumption of sugar is directly linked to obesity and chronic metabolic diseases, the sugar industry can continue to function without strong opposition.[340]

Coca-Cola is just one example of a large corporation in the sugar industry choosing to value profit instead of taking responsibility and attempting to mitigate the negative health consequences they are causing. Hospitals and large pharmaceutical companies have made enormous profits from necessary treatment that results from low health literacy and poor diets as well. However, these profits do not even come close to those currently being raked in by the health insurance industry. Let's look.

THE HEALTHCARE INDUSTRY

In 1974, researchers Thomas Bodenheimer, Steven Cummings, and Elizabeth Harding published an article they entitled, "Capitalizing on Illness: The Health Insurance Industry". The article went as far as to say, "Unless insurance companies are barred from the health care field and a public financing mechanism based on progressive

---

[340] *That Sugar Film.* (2015). https://www.youtube.com/watch?v=SNr7loGoZC8&has_verified=1; O'Connor, A. *Coca-Cola Funds Scientists Who Shift Blame for Obesity Away from Bad Diets.* (New York Times, 2015).

taxation is introduced, health care will never be an equal right for everyone in the United States."[341] The authors lambasted the insurance industry for reigning in annual profits of approximately $312 billion (adjusted for inflation) from the illness of Americans. Today, just seven companies in the health insurance industry rake in almost triple that number, combining to profit $913 billion annually to be exact.[342]

Considering the enormous profits being made by health insurance companies, it is no surprise that all proposals to restructure our healthcare system have been met with vehement opposition by the lobbyists employed by health insurance corporations. Representative Brian Higgins, a Democrat from New York, explains this opposition to attempts at healthcare reform:

> Insurance companies are fighting it because they are afraid of the prospect of a potent new competitor that will cut into their profits…Medicare has lower administrative costs and lower executive salaries and could use its bargaining power to get better deals from hospitals and other health care providers.[343]

Private health insurance companies' opposition to healthcare reform does more than just block legislation to reform healthcare, however. It also creates ignorance among the public. The relentless opposition to healthcare reform that comes from insurance companies and many conservatives creates the narrative that any attempt at healthcare reform is a transition to socialized medicine, which according to conservatives will disrupt the fabric of society—that's barely even an exaggeration.

---

[341] Bodenheimer, T., et al. *Capitalizing on Illness: The Health Insurance Industry* (International Journal of Health Ser-vices, 1974).

[342] Payne, E. *Top health insurers' revenues soared to almost $1 trillion in 2019* (BenefitsPro, 2020).

[343] Pear, R. *Health Care and Insurance Industries Mobilize to Kill 'Medicare for All'* (NPR, 2019).

Representative Higgins, the chief sponsor behind a moderate Medicare buy-in program drafted in the House of Representatives, laments this misleading rhetoric espoused by conservatives saying, "The critics lump our bill with the bigger Medicare-for-all proposal. That's strategic, and I think it's deliberate." This strategy has created ignorance about what even modest healthcare reform would mean for everyday Americans. It has instilled real fear in many Americans, making a large swath of the population resistant to any change.

This rhetoric also neglects the facts that we already have socialized medicine in the United States. It's called Medicare and Medicaid, and it's more efficient and cost-effective than private insurance. However, by creating ignorance, the elites can instill in the wider public this completely illogical fear of socialized medicine.

This ignorant fear should not be overlooked when discussing healthcare reform. William Hsiao, a retired health care economist from Harvard University and designer of Taiwan's national healthcare system, believes that the biggest obstacle to healthcare reform is the public ignorance being created and manipulated by healthcare companies. In a conversation with *Politico*'s Maura Reynolds, Hsiao stated that most people who study the economics of healthcare agree that a single payer insurance system is the most efficient system economically, that it would lead to greater healthcare quality, and that it would actually cut costs for up to 90 percent of Americans.[344] Hsiao, however, thinks that a single payer system is far from becoming reality in the United States because of the manipulation of public ignorance. He elaborates, saying:

> The common, average American is not educated yet and there is a lot of misinformation being directed at them. And you haven't even seen the insurance industry and

---

[344] Reynolds, M. *There's a Fear Factor, a Fear of Change. William Hsiao knows more about single payer systems than pretty much any other American. What does he think about 'Medicare for All'?* (Politico, 2019).

pharmaceutical industry come out yet with really well-organized campaigns against it. The private insurance industry's annual revenue is $1.3 trillion. The pharmaceutical industry's annual income is $400 billion. They only have to use one-thousandth of 1 percent of their revenue to fight [this]. They can elect the key decision-makers in Congress, the Senate and the House of Representatives, because they can mobilize literally a billion dollars. And those powerful, wealthy, well-organized, vested interest groups have not come out openly yet. That's the reality of American money, politics.[345]

The healthcare industry makes enormous profits from an inefficient healthcare system that exploits the consumer. Healthcare corporations then create ignorance among the public to convince them that the healthcare system cannot, and must not, be reformed. Finally, they manipulate the ignorant public into voting to maintain this corrupt system from which they profit. And because the business model of health insurance companies is to profit from the illness of Americans, it is no surprise they support the corporations and industries, such as the sugar and processed food industries, that also perpetuate a state of ignorance to make people unhealthy. Of course, these companies have had an active interest in maintaining widespread ignorance about what constitutes a healthy diet and how to stay a healthy weight; their business depends on unhealthy Americans.

MENTAL HEALTH

While this may not come as a surprise, our society is woefully ignorant about mental health. The risk of mental health is rooted in power and profit motivations. By proliferating ignorance of mental illnesses, those who are not diagnosed with an illness become privileged.

---

[345] Ibid.

Ignorance about mental health contributes to what we call the "stigma". The stigma around mental health is the negative connotations that come with being deemed mentally unhealthy. This stigma leads to a fear of being exposed as mentally ill, as well as the discomfort of talking about one's mental health. The stigma survives because of widespread misinformation and false beliefs about mental health.

Compared to 1950, twice as many people today believe that the mentally ill are more violent than the average person. However, the opposite is true. The mentally ill are no more likely to be violent than the average population, but they are 2.5 times as likely to be the victim of violence compared to the general population.[346] The ignorant beliefs about mental health are more than just unfortunate misunderstandings; they come at a real cost to society. As stigma researcher Bernice Pescosolido explains it:

> An estimated one in four adults has a diagnosable mental illness, according to the National Institute of Mental Health. That's about 76 million Americans who live with the fear that others may find out about their disorder and think less of them or even keep them from getting jobs or promotions.[347]

Additionally, Pescosolido notes that the stigma extends into the home and workplace. According to the researcher, 68 percent of people don't want someone with mental illness to be married into their family, and 58 percent of people don't want to work with someone who has a mental illness.[348] The stigma also negatively affects the physical health of mentally unhealthy people, how they perform on tests, and it can act as a deterrent to taking medication for many patients.[349]

---

[346] Dingfelder, S. *Stigma: Alive and well (American Psychological Association, 2009); Mental Health Myths and Facts.* (Mentalhealth.gov) https://www.mentalhealth.gov/basics/mental-health-myths-facts.

[347] Ibid.

[348] Ibid.

[349] Ibid.

At this point you may be thinking to yourself, *"Ok, I understand how damaging the stigma is, but I always see ads and information posts on social media about ending the stigma, how can it possibly be getting worse?"* Unfortunately, many of those "anti-stigma" campaigns haven't been all that beneficial. Many focus on the prevalence of mental illness by emphasizing that any one of us can suffer from mental illness. While this, of course, is an attempt to reverse the ostracization that those with mental illnesses continue to experience, these campaigns have been shown to reinforce the already existing fear of mental illness in our society. If people already fear others with mental illness, telling them that there may be more mentally ill people than it appears only increases the number of people to fear.[350]

Anti-stigma campaigns have, for the most part, yielded unintended negative consequences because the way they present mental illness does not reverse ignorance, but rather, it reinforces it. To begin to reduce the stigma, we must start by reversing the public's ignorance of mental illness. This is done not by saying that everyone might be afflicted by mental illness. Rather, it is done by presenting the true facts of mental illness to dispel irrational fears and by telling positive stories that show people with mental illness are functioning members of society too, not the prone-to-violence outcasts we imagine they are.

In addition to the power motivations that inspired the demonization of the mentally ill, the ignorance of mental illness is driven by corporations seeking to maximize the productivity of their employees. Mental illness and disorders are on the rise among American teens.[351] There is reason to speculate that increasing levels of competition in school (a result of a culture that obsesses over financial success) have driven the stigma of mental health and have contributed to worsening mental health throughout the nation.

---

[350] Ibid.

[351] McCarthy, C. *Anxiety in Teens is Rising: What's Going On?* (HealthyChildren. org, 2019).

Competition and the desire to maximize productivity have similarly affected mental health in the workforce. Despite declining mental health among students and workers, we have chosen not to address these trends through policy.

One policy we have chosen not to enact is requiring all workers to take vacation days. The United States is the only developed country in the world where paid vacation days are not mandatory.[352] This is largely because ignorance has developed among employers who fear that they cannot afford to give vacation days. Not only is that idea grounded in ignorance, but it is having a profoundly negative impact on mental health. Journalist Samantha Stevens reported that, "83 percent of workers in the U.S. suffer from work-life induced stress… Approximately 1 in 5 U.S. adults (that comprises of 18.3 percent or 44.7 million people) are affected by mental illness due to imbalanced work life…[and] 71 percent of adults show symptoms of stress like headaches and intense anxiety."[353]

Ignorance regarding mental health has always existed and created a stigma. During biblical times, mental illness was often blamed on demon possession. As recently as 1955, the year deinstitutionalization began, we were still locking the mentally ill in asylums where they were severely mistreated. Today, we know better. Research on mental health, from the perspectives of many different disciplines, is abundant, and the solutions to create a mentally healthier society are out there waiting to be implemented. However, public ignorance of what these solutions are and how to best implement these solutions is holding us back and amplifying this risk.

---

[352] Stevens, S. *Vacation Days and Productivity in the U.S. vs. Other Countries Paid Vacation Days in the United States.* (Global Call Forwarding, 2018)
[353] Ibid.

If Only We Knew

THE ANTI-VACCINE MOVEMENT

The last health risk facing our society that we will discuss is the anti-vaccine movement. While anti-vaccines sentiments have for the most part always been around, the recent anti-vaccine movement in the United States really started to take off when celebrity Jenny McCarthy came out publicly as an "anti-vaxxer" in 2007. The people who are part of the movement are skeptical of vaccines and large pharmaceutical corporations, a.k.a. "Big Pharma", and have thus decided to opt for "natural remedies" as a replacement for vaccines.

Most of us can see how dangerous and ill-advised this movement is. These dangers have become even clearer as anti-vaccine sentiment has spread doubt about the effectiveness and safety of the COVID-19 vaccine. In the summer of 2021, we saw in real-time how dangerous this rhetoric can be. The COVID-19 Delta Variant swept through the country, ravaging areas with low vaccination rates, yet despite constant vaccine information campaigns backed by the latest research in behavior science, and the widespread availability of vaccines, encouraging people to get the vaccine proved extremely difficult.

However, the misleading information fueling the anti-vaccine movement is just that, misleading. Vaccines have been enormously important and effective at controlling and eliminating devastating diseases throughout history—and the COVID-19 vaccine was no exception.

There is no doubt that the anti-vax movement has done great damage to the strides we have made in our fight against harmful, contagious diseases. Before the recent surge of the anti-vax movement, vaccines were producing great results. In 2000, vaccines effectively eliminated measles from the United States. Since the recent anti-vax movement, however, measles has re-emerged; there were three large breakouts among unvaccinated children from 2013-2015.

So, how have we gotten to this point? Why do so many people not trust vaccines? Why are they so afraid? The anti-vax movement has two main roots: 1) mistrust in Big Pharma, and 2) ignorant beliefs about the safety of vaccines fueled by misleading rhetoric in the media and politics. Let's examine the mistrust in Big Pharma first.

As with other sectors of the health industry, Big Pharma is motivated by profit. As mentioned earlier in the section regarding healthcare, the pharmaceutical industry generates $400 billion annually. The for-profit nature of the industry has resulted in many cases of price gouging and other untrustworthy behaviors. While we won't go too deep into these dubious behaviors in this chapter, if you read anything about Purdue's role in the opioid epidemic or Mylan's role in the price gouging of EpiPens, you will see what I'm talking about. The point I'm trying to make is that these exploitative and unethical practices of Big Pharma have in large part led to the development of mistrust of Big Pharma by the public. This mistrust is one of the driving forces behind the anti-vaccine movement.

While this mistrust of Big Pharma is not unwarranted, mistrust in vaccines is dangerously misguided. At its core, the anti-vax movement is a dangerous and unfortunate dismissal of scientific research and beneficial medical intervention. Data and empirical evidence have proven that vaccines are safe. However, mistrust in the pharmaceutical industry has led many to distrust vaccines, solely because they are products of Big Pharma. The anti-vax movement is therefore a representation of misplaced mistrust.

Ironically, this misplaced mistrust in vaccines has spurred a wide-spread investment in a completely unregulated, untested, unproven market of "natural" remedies, such as herbal supplements, essential oils, etc. During the COVID-19 pandemic, we even saw many resorting to treating themselves with horse and cow dewormer instead of taking the vaccine. As a result, some states, like Texas, saw over a 500 percent increase in calls to the poison control center regarding ingestion of horse and cow dewormers.[354]

---

[354] Joy, W. *Texas sees 550% spike in poison calls for horse and cow dewormer, despite FDA warning* (ABC, 2021).

Anti-vaxxers oppose vaccines because they claim they aren't safe, yet their alternative is to turn to remedies and supplements that are less regulated, not approved by doctors, and less safe than vaccines. People are placing trust in products that are much less trustworthy than mainstream drugs and medical practices. Instead of investing in reforming the perverse incentives of a for-profit health industry, anti-vaxxers are bypassing the regulated industry of vaccines completely.

The so-called evidence on which most anti-vaxxers base their mistrust of vaccines is a since debunked research paper by British Doctor Andrew Wakefield in 1998, which tried to link the Measles, Mumps, and Rubella (MMR) vaccine to autism in children.[355] This paper was officially debunked in 2011, and since then there has been widespread consensus among the medical and science community that the claims made in the paper are wholly inaccurate—there is no causal relationship between vaccines and autism. There is no wiggle room in this statement, as there is no evidence to substantiate a claim that a vaccine has ever caused, nor will cause, autism.

Since the debunking of his paper, Wakefield was stripped of his medical license, and there was even an investigation conducted by the *British Medical Journal* that found evidence of outright fraud in Wakefield's paper.[356] But the damage had already been done. Wakefield's report had given the public the "evidence" they needed to create an anti-vaccine movement. Ignorance has been created. For anti-vaxxers, the debunking of the paper and the stripping of Wakefield's credentials simply points to the bigger conspiracy of Big Pharma trying to silence people who oppose them.

The rise in autism spectrum disorders (ASDs) has not been definitively linked to any specific cause, however, researchers today have found strong links between the rise in autism and the increased prevalence of exposure to pesticides contaminating our

---

[355] The anti-vaccination movement (Measles & Rubella Initiative). https://measlesrubellainitiative.org/anti-vaccination-movement/.
[356] Ibid.

food supply and environment.[357] The fear of vaccines is an outgrowth of ignorance. The media and our politicians have chosen not to discuss or act on the dangers of pesticides because they are linked to the industries that profit from the spraying of chemicals in our environment. Thus, they have created ignorance by irresponsibly promoting anti-vaccine sentiment instead.

As I mentioned earlier, the recent anti-vax movement started to gain serious momentum when celebrity Jenny McCarthy came out publicly in support for the movement. You may have also been aware that former President Donald Trump has a long history of support for the movement, claiming on multiple occasions that vaccines cause autism. In Chapter 1, we discussed the fact that the rhetoric of powerful people has a greater influence than the words of an everyday person. When anti-vax claims are made by celebrities and politicians, they carry more weight and have more devastating effects.

During the measles outbreaks of 2013, 2014, and 2015, many conservative politicians blamed the outbreak on illegal immigration from Latin American countries. They claimed that illegal aliens were not subject to the same healthcare screening process as lawful immigrants and thus they were bringing measles into the United States and infecting our children. This claim was false.

It neglected the facts that almost all of the cases of measles reported in the U.S. were reported in unvaccinated individuals and that an extremely small number (only 3 out of 288, .01 percent) of measles cases originated from someone from Latin America.[358] Conservatives back up their assertion that illegal immigration has caused the measles outbreak by claiming that the Latin American countries from which illegal immigrants come from don't have the same vaccination standards that we have in the United States. This is also false. Elaborating on this point, author Dave Levitan writes:

---

[357] Shelton, J., et. al. *Tipping the Balance of Autism Risk: Potential Mechanisms Linking Pesticides and Autism* (Environmental Health Perspectives, 2012).

[358] Centers for Disease Control and Prevention. https://www.cdc.gov/measles/cases-outbreaks.html.

According to the World Health Organization, the United States in 2013 had a measles vaccination rate for 1-year-olds of 91 percent. Though Mexico's rate dropped to 89 percent in 2013, it had been at 95 percent or higher for every other year since 2000. Guatemala's 2013 rate was 85 percent, down from 93 percent the previous year. Honduras also had a coverage rate of 89 percent, down from above 90 percent in previous years. El Salvador's rate was 94 percent in 2013.[359]

Yet even though the anti-immigrant explanations for measles outbreaks are false, they have proven to be very convincing. Conservative politicians employed this same tactic when there was a rise in COVID-19 cases in the summer of 2021. When the Delta Variant was ravaging "red" states, governors blamed immigrants to distract the public from the true causes behind the spread: banning mask mandates, low vaccination rates, and poor or non-existent mitigation strategies.

The reaction of conservative politicians to the anti-vaccine movement provides us with yet another example of the intentional creation and preservation of ignorance. This preservation of ignorance creates and amplifies the risk of the anti-vax movement. Instead of urging anti-vaxxers to abandon their ignorant position, many conservative politicians have used the harmful consequences of the anti-vax movement for their own political gain. They have taken this "opportunity" to spread anti-immigrant sentiment that amplifies the risk of racism. They have once again neglected to act in the interests of the health of the American people, instead opting to serve their own political interests.

Similarly, conservative media companies spread anti-vax rhetoric because it generates ratings. We can see this clearly in *Fox News*'s coverage of the COVID-19 vaccine, which was filled with debunked myths about the safety of the vaccine and wild conspiracies about

---

[359] Levitan, D. False Narrative on Measles Outbreak. (Factcheck.org, 2015). https://www.factcheck.org/2015/02/false-narrative-on-measles-outbreak/.

the government's intentions behind pushing the vaccine. While this is, of course, not journalism, it was aired because *Fox News* viewers were eating it up. They loved it and they made sure to tune in to *Fox News* to listen to the latest development in the vaccine conspiracy.

The anti-vax movement is a clear example of public ignorance creating and amplifying a risk that should never have been a risk in the first place.

Ignorance amplifies every risk in the health industry. However, as is almost always the case, many solutions to mitigate these risks have been developed and are just waiting to be discovered by the mass population before being scaled to a national level.

SOLUTIONS

The poor health of our nation is one of the most serious risks we face. Our poor health choices in terms of diet, lack of exercise, and a lack of attention and care for mental health is unnecessarily killing hundreds of thousands of Americans each year while degrading the quality of life for millions of other Americans. Ignorance leads people to make bad decisions for their own health while also preventing us from enacting the solutions and policies that would make us healthier as a country. As a result, we have been becoming less and less healthy, so much so that the average lifespan in the United States has decreased in recent years.[360] All the while, powerful people and corporations are benefitting from the business of making Americans unhealthy. However, there is hope because many solutions and policy proposals to alleviate these risks have been developed.

As seen in previous chapters, the most effective way to reduce risks is to reverse our ignorance of the issue and follow the evidence

---

[360] Saiidi, U. US life expectancy has been declining. *Here's why* (CNBC, 2019) https://www.cnbc.com/2019/07/09/us-life-expectancy-has-been-declining-heres-why.html.

to implement solutions that will effectively mitigate the risks. Often, following the evidence means confronting and changing our position on ideas or solutions that we believe will work. When we think about ignorance, we often believe increasing education on the issue at hand is always an effective solution, but this is not always the case. For example, many of us believe that one of the ways to curb the obesity epidemic is to educate the public on what and how much to eat. However, as we will discuss in more detail later in this section, according to Jonathan Engel, nutrition education has very little impact on obesity rates.[361] In order to truly start reducing the health risks in this country, we need to abandon our prior convictions and follow the evidence to enact comprehensive health policies.

THE WHOLE HEALTH PLAN

During the 2020 Democrat Party Primaries, former candidate Marianne Williamson hit the nail on the head when addressing our health crisis. While her campaign never gained any serious momentum, Williamson proposed several solutions regarding improving the health of Americans under a plan she called "The Whole Health Plan". The plan differs from that of almost all other candidates in recent memory because it focuses on treating the causes of our illnesses, not just treating the symptoms. In her plan, Williamson proposed enacting policies and launching initiatives to improve food quality, tackle the issue of unclean water and air, and keep pesticides, herbicides, and other toxins out of our food and environment.[362]

In the spirit of reversing ignorance, Williamson called on the need for greater investments in research of these issues so that we

---

[361] Engel, 2018.
[362] Williamson, M. *The Whole Health Plan* https://marianne2020.com/issues/the-whole-health-plan.

can develop more evidenced-based solutions to make us healthier as a nation. Although we have made great strides in researching how to become healthier as a society, there is always more work to be done. Investing in ongoing evidence-based research is essential to reversing ignorance among the public about health issues.

The Whole Health Plan provides us with a framework to start preventing illnesses and holding corporate interests accountable for their actions that have exacerbated health risks in our nation. For this reason, the Whole Health Plan must be implemented.

FOOD SOLUTIONS

With the same approach as her Whole Health Plan, Marianne Williamson also developed a "Food" plan that aimed to accomplish five main goals: 1) putting an end to the corruption occurring between the Big Agriculture corporations and government, 2) restore the strength and authority of the FDA, 3) rid our food and water of the toxins, pesticides/herbicides/fertilizers, and other harmful chemicals that are making us sick, 4) protecting and aiding small farmers, and 5) revamping outdated nutrition guidelines and implementing policies and initiatives to protect the health and improve the nutrition of our children.[363] Through a slew of plans, Williamson's food platform can accomplish these goals.

Earlier, we discussed the fact that our food supply is causing an increase in chronic illnesses. Instead of solely investing in drugs and medicine to symptomatically treat these diseases, it would prove much more beneficial if we demanded a decontamination of our toxic food supply. We must pass legislation to do this. We cannot continue down the path of eating contaminated food just so Big Agriculture corporations can widen their profit margin while health insurance companies and for-profit hospitals can bankrupt us with the seemingly never-ending expenses that are associated with

---

[363] Williamson, M. *Food.* https://marianne2020.com/issues/food.

chronic illness. We must enact a plan like Marianne Williamson's Food plan to start reducing the risk of chronic illnesses, diabetes, and obesity caused by poor diets and food contamination.

OBESITY SOLUTIONS

One of the greatest risks within the "health risk umbrella" is the risk of obesity. Obesity kills. Plain and simple. However, the fact that obesity has emerged to be such a pervasive risk only in the last 70 years shows us that obesity is not inevitable. As mentioned earlier, the obesity epidemic has emerged because of changes to our lifestyles, physical environment, and food environment. To start to reduce national obesity rates, we must give up the ignorant notion that the answer to the obesity epidemic lies in personal responsibility and willpower. We must acknowledge that we have much less control than we think over what we eat, how active we are, and how able (or unable) we are to resist the temptation of sugar and junk food.[364] The way to reduce the obesity epidemic is to change our physical and food environments.

Changing our environments is, of course, no easy task. Luckily for us, in the last chapter of his book, *Fat Nation*, Jonathan Engel offers us what he believes we must do to make the necessary changes to our environments. To change our food environment, Engel claims the first step is to increase the regulations on unhealthy foods, especially sugar. As Engel explains, and as many studies have found, sugar is essentially a legalized drug. Engel elaborates:

> People have been eating sugar for millennia, and in doses that are appropriate (and bound to fiber), it does us no harm. However, cheap ubiquitous sugar is playing havoc with our biology, our brain chemistry, our moods, and our

---

[364] Engel, 2018. 150-152.

weight-regulation systems. The answer must not be to outlaw the stuff but regulate it reasonably.[365]

Engel believes the regulation of sugar could come in the form of regulating where it can be sold, the quantities it can be sold in, imposing high taxes on high-sugar content items to discourage price sensitive consumers like children from buying it, and even banning food from certain public locations such as subways, buses, and trains. No matter what regulations we decide to impose, Engel stresses that implementing regulations is an essential component of the mission to reduce obesity.

In addition to regulating unhealthy foods, Engel also believes we must encourage healthier eating habits. These habits include eating at designated times and places and eating with other people. The recent trend of eating on the run, eating out more, and eating alone has greatly contributed to the rise in obesity. To encourage better habits, Engel suggests teaching cooking classes for all school children again, as well as banning school activities during dinner time, extending lunch time, and as mentioned above, banning eating from public places to discourage eating on the run.[366]

We must do more than change our food environment, we also must change our physical environment. The rise of suburbia has led to a significant decline in walking, the easiest and most effective form of daily physical exercise. To reverse this decline, we must increase the walkability of suburbs through what is known as "new urbanism", a way of redesigning suburbs to make them more pedestrian friendly. Another way to encourage people to walk more, according to Engel, is to disincentivize driving. Through more expensive gas, parking taxes, and other anti-driving policies, people will theoretically respond rationally and start to more frequently opt for walking, carpooling, and public transportation.[367] Moreover,

---

[365] Ibid. 153.
[366] Ibid. 154.
[367] Ibid. 155.

incentivizing walking will also lead to lower exhaust and carbon emissions, which will help the environment, and if new urbanism is conducted correctly, walking can even help improve race relations by integrating largely segregated neighborhoods.

These obesity reducing solutions are not just abstract ideas that we think will work, they have been put into practice in real life. In 2012, the mayor of Oklahoma City, Mike Cornett, called on the residents of his city, which was ranked as one of the most obese in the nation, to go on a diet. He set a goal for the city to lose 1 million pounds, and they actually did it. Cornett created a website that allowed people to track how much weight they had lost and how much weight the city had lost. He called it *This City Is Going on A Diet*. The website enabled people to be part of something bigger than themselves. This sense of belonging played an extremely vital role in inspiring people to accomplish the goal their mayor had set for them.

Through motivating residents, launching massive public awareness campaigns to encourage healthier eating choices, and engaging with local employers and businesses to commence weight-loss competitions among them, 47,000 OKC residents were able to shed a collective total of 1 million pounds.[368] But the progress did not stop there. Since launching this weight loss campaign, OKC has invested in making their city healthier by building parks, increasing the city's walkability, building gyms in every grade school, and building senior wellness centers.[369] These changes to the city's physical environment have also helped the city grow economically; the new pedestrian friendly, pro-healthy living city is slowly becoming an attractive destination for highly educated millennials.[370]

---

[368] Leber, J. *This City Lost 1 Million Pounds–Now It's Redesigning Itself to Keep Them Off* (Fast Company, 2014). https://www.fastcompany.com/3035899/this-city-lost-1-million-pounds-now-its-redesigning-itself-to-keep-them-off.
[369] Ibid.
[370] Ibid.

The Risk Of Poor Health

The lesson we must learn from the success of Oklahoma City is that the design of a city has an enormous impact on the health of its residents. We also must recognize the power of good leadership and collective goal setting. Mayor Cornett was able to galvanize an obese city to lose weight. This was a pretty unpopular idea, but he was able to do so by being honest with his constituents and setting a collective goal for the city. This honesty and passionate appeal to residents made redesigning the city much less controversial.

As Cornett put it, "The success of the awareness campaign led me to believe that the message had penetrated enough that we could get voter's approval to start redesigning the city around people, not cars."[371] Cornett was right. He has been able to redesign OKC, and as a result the city is now ranked as one of the nation's most fit.

Finally, we should consider the policy recommendations by experts in the public health field who study obesity. In an academic article entitled *Role of Government Policy in Nutrition—Barriers to and Opportunities for Healthier Eating*, public health expert Dariush Mozaffarian and his colleagues proposed a multitude of policies that would improve nutrition and reduce obesity.[372] Among these policies are point of labelling purchasing, fiscal disincentives via taxes on unhealthy foods, and worksite wellness programs. All the policies proposed in the article should be seriously considered as effective means to reducing the risk of obesity.

While the proposed solutions I have mentioned in this section may seem radical, Jonathan Engel urges us to consider the fact that we have been here before. The last time was with tobacco. The sugar and junk food industry have attempted to avoid these major reforms by making their unhealthy food products "safer" through low-fat or reduced sugar options. The tobacco industry used very similar tactics when it was under fire. After tobacco was declared unhealthy, the industry attempted to circumvent the proposed bans

---

[371] Ibid.

[372] Mozzaffarian, D., et al. *Role of government policy in nutrition—barriers to and opportunities for healthier eating* (BMJ, 2018).

of cigarettes from public places by pushing for filters in cigarettes as well as "low-tar" and "low-nicotine" options. The similarities between the responses of the two industries are extensive and shocking.

Today, even though anti-tobacco measures once seemed radical and impractical, it is hard for many of us, especially millennials and Gen-Z, to imagine smoking being as prevalent as it once was. We must enact policies to reduce the risk of obesogenic physical and food environments because eventually the radical changes we make now will be accepted and celebrated. Our children and grandchildren will be in shock about how we lived prior to these changes.

DOING WHAT WORKS

One of the most important lessons we must learn from our study of obesity is that the solutions aren't always obvious. We often believe that the answers are common sense, when in reality, they aren't so simple. As a result, our ignorance blinds us from following the evidence of what works. If we want to reduce obesity rates and chronic illnesses, we need policies that will change our physical and food environments. There are many ideas about how to reduce obesity (including the ideas of personal responsibility and willpower) that simply are not supported by evidence. Our ignorant belief that these ideas are effective is amplifying the risk by distracting us from the policies that we know work.

For example, many people have claimed that a primary cause of obesity in poor communities is the existence of food deserts. This is the idea that since poor communities don't have access to supermarkets and fresh produce, they have limited opportunities to buy healthy foods and thus they become obese at higher rates. While there is no disputing that food deserts exist and that poorer people would be healthier if they ate more fruits and vegetables, there is absolutely no evidence that it would reduce obesity. As Engel explains:

Obesity is more an artifact of what we *do* eat than what we *don't*. It is more important to eat fewer candy bars and refined starchy foods and to drink less fruit juice than it is to eat more fruits and vegetables... If vegetables displace starches and sugars then they are a welcome addition to the diet; but if vegetables are simply added to a starch-laden diet, they will do little beyond possibly controlling spiking insulin levels. Americans, with their consumerist culture, seem obsessed with the idea of finding the right food to buy and consume, but the better response is simply to consume less.[373]

Another misconception is that nutrition education and anti-junk food advertising are extremely important. They're not. Eating is mostly a product of our subconscious reaction to our physical and food environments, so these programs have very little effect on our dietary habits.

It is extremely important to follow the evidence-based solutions for reducing every risk, but it is especially important that we maintain this attitude when the evidence points us in a different direction than we thought we would be going. When it comes to reducing obesity, we know what works. It is vitally important that we don't let our preconceived notions get in the way of following the evidence that will save and improve countless lives.

MENTAL HEALTH SOLUTIONS

To improve mental health in our nation, we must focus on five main goals: 1) ending the stigma of mental illness, 2) fostering a stronger sense of belonging in our communities, 3) increasing access to mental health services for people of all ages, especially young people, 4) improving work-life balance, and 5) understanding how to be happy and enacting policies that can increase happiness.

---

[373] Engel, 2018. 157-158.

ENDING THE STIGMA

Ending the stigma towards mental illness has proved a very difficult task. As we discussed earlier, many attempts have backfired drastically. It is of utmost importance that we learn from these failures and follow the evidence to effectively make progress on this mission to end the stigma. The evidence shows us that: 1) there most certainly is a stigma around mental illness, 2) trying to end the stigma by saying more people are mentally ill than the average person may think only reinforces, and worsens, the stigma of mental illness, and 3) there are a few anti-stigma efforts that have shown promise but have not been sufficiently tested to be determined as effective.

Ignorance about how to end the stigma has made it much worse. Our ignorance has led us to develop detrimental anti-stigma campaigns, and our lack of funding to research how to reduce the stigma has stifled our ability to devise potentially effective solutions. We must devote more time and resources into studying and solving the issue of the stigma surrounding mental health. We also must do a better job of teaching children how to manage their emotions through incorporating social-emotional learning into education and by teaching children and young adults how to talk about mental illness.

RESTORING BELONGING AND TRUST

One of the most serious problems in our society is the crisis of belonging. In the 2020 Democrat Party primaries, Pete Buttigieg ran on restoring this sense of belonging as his key issue. He believes that the consequences of automation and globalization in the workplace that have displaced millions of workers along with the abundance of divisive rhetoric in media and politics has damaged our ability as a nation to see the commonalities we all share. We have chosen to instead focus on our differences. In short, these changes have led many to lose their sense of identity and belonging in this country.

Buttigieg believes that restoring solidarity and building diverse coalitions is essential to restoring this lost sense of belonging. A sense of belonging to something greater than oneself is at the core of our evolutionary psychology. Without this sense of belonging, many fall into depression, become extremely anxious, or succumb to drug and alcohol addiction. It is for this reason that it is essential to enact a plan modeled after Buttigieg's National Service Plan, which aimed to restore a sense of belonging in people. It is also extremely important to elect and appoint leaders who seek to sow unity instead of division.

Similarly, Buttigieg believes we must act to restore greater levels of trust in each other, our elected leaders, and our institutions. In fact, he wrote a whole book about it (it's called *Trust: America's Best Chance*). In recent decades, trust has been declining steadily and rapidly in our country. Restoring trust is essential to reducing political polarization and increasing mental wellness. Additionally, trust in one's neighbors, politicians, and institutions has been found to be directly correlated to a country's overall happiness.[374]

We must not dismiss Buttigieg's calls for an increase in belonging and trust as abstract ideals. Instead, we must focus on enacting policies that make these ideals realities. On a deeper level, we must build a culture in which all people feel welcomed and can trust their neighbor (we will discuss this further in Chapter 8).

EXPANDING ACCESS TO MENTAL HEALTH CARE

We must increase access to mental health by integrating more mental health services to schools, pediatric offices, and other areas of public health. Research shows that catching and addressing mental health struggles early is extremely beneficial for young adults and

---

[374] Miething, A., et. al. *Trust, happiness and mortality: Findings from a prospective US population-based survey.* (Social Science and Medicine, 2020).

children. Becoming more demographically strategic by expanding mental health services in places such as schools, will greatly improve our ability to mitigate this risk of deteriorating mental health.

VACATION DAYS

We must also improve the focus on work-life balance. As stated earlier, the United States is the only nation in the developed world that does not require employers to provide paid vacation days.[375] For comparison, other developed countries, like Germany and Portugal, have 34 and 35 required paid vacation days respectively.[376] The absence of vacation days in the United States is wreaking havoc on our mental health, as well as counterintuitively harming our productivity. As journalist Samantha Stevens explains:

> In a study by the Society for Human Resource Management (SHRM) for Project: Time Off, HR managers believe that taking vacation time leads to greatly improved performance (75 percent) and better job satisfaction (78 percent). In other words, vacation gives a person the chance to "recharge their batteries" and mentally rest from their job. When they finally return to their desk, morale (and overall productivity) is improved.[377]

If we continue to work without employers mandating vacation days simply because we ignorantly believe it results in increased productivity, we will continue to see a rise in anxiety and a decrease in overall job satisfaction. Even if it were true that fewer vacation days and working extra hours led to greater productivity, what is the point if this increased productivity is not making us any happier?

---

[375] Stevens, 2018.
[376] Ibid.
[377] Ibid.

HOW TO BE HAPPIER

To increase happiness in our society, we need to understand our evolution as humans. Being happy was an important trait for the earliest humans, because it made humans more fit for their environments.[378] Happy individuals were energetic, social, and aware of their surroundings, which aided them in survival. The feeling of happiness is driven by the body's release of large amounts of dopamine, a process that occurs when humans receive an unexpected reward.

Early humans learned that reward seeking behavior leads to happiness, and they acted accordingly. This pursuit of happiness led to fundamental evolutionary changes. As contributing writer for Quartz Oliver Staley explains, "Dopamine heightened our ancestors' awareness and focused their attention on what they wanted; they craved the feelings it produced and it guided them toward comfort and love, conditions that help make us human."[379] Over time, natural selection proved to favor happy people.

Yet even though our evolution leans towards happiness, it has been determined that we are not substantially happier today than our hunter-gatherer ancestors. Currently, the average happiness level around the world can be empirically measured as a 5.5 out of 10.[380] The question then becomes, *"If we have not become any happier over time, is greater happiness even possible, and if so, how can we achieve it?"*

An evolutionary perspective tells us that a primary way to achieve greater happiness is to improve the living conditions in our society at the macro-level, to improve the ability for workers to be happy at the organizational level, and to improve the ability for people to be happy at the individual level. At the macro-level

---

[378] Staley, O. *What Is the Evolutionary Purpose of Happiness?* (Quartz, 2017).
[379] Ibid.
[380] Veenhoven, R. *Can We Get Happier Than We Are?* (The Human Pursuit of Well-Being, 2011).

increasing happiness is directly linked to a country's ability to stimulate the potentials of the workforce. Ruut Veenhoven, a Dutch sociologist and founder of the World Happiness Database, explains why this is evolutionarily necessary:

> Like most animals, we have an innate need to use our potentials. The biological function of this need is to keep us sharp, in the human case, in particular, to keep the brain in shape. The human species evolved under the conditions of a hunter-gatherer existence that involved a lot of challenge. In today's conditions, as an industrial society, we still need some challenges and most of us find them mainly in our work life.[381]

It is important for society to provide all its citizens with an opportunity to utilize their talents for happiness to be achieved on a national scale.

At the organizational level, encouraging people to find work they enjoy is a key to increasing happiness. Additionally, work-life balance initiatives must be taken to improve happiness of employees. Unfortunately, there is not sufficient research on quality of life within institutions, so the first step must be to fund and conduct research on this matter.[382]

Finally, and perhaps most importantly, we must teach individuals how to be happier by educating them on how to enjoy and take pleasure in the simple things in life, how to foster lifelong personal development by participating in challenging physical and mental activities, and how to find meaning in all facets of our lives.[383] Most significantly, we must reverse ignorance and provide everyone with more information so that they can make better choices that lead to happiness. As Veenhoven explains:

---

[381] Ibid.
[382] Ibid.
[383] Ibid.

Another way of improving happiness at the individual level is to inform people about the consequences of major choices in life. We have to realize that we live in a "multiple-choice society", in which about 40 percent of the differences in happiness seems to be due to "intentional activity". Better informed choices will give rise to greater happiness.[384]

All these abilities must be taught to students as they progress through their K-12 education.

Furthermore, there should be an expansion of the field of life-counselors who specialize in providing guidance to lead a happier life within our educations systems and workplaces.[385] If we take an evolutionary perspective and address the faults on the macro, organizational, and micro-levels of society, we can achieve greater happiness.

HEALTHCARE

Healthcare is one of the most complex issues in politics. Although almost all experts in the healthcare economics and delivery systems field agree that a single-payer system would be the most efficient system for better health and a better economy, the path to get to this system is complex to say the least. An immediate (or rapid) and complete government takeover of the health industry would put dozens of multi-billion-dollar insurance companies out of business and displace tens of thousands of workers in that industry. On the other hand, maintaining our current system leaves millions uninsured or underinsured and continues to amplify the health risks we discussed above. What we must do, as Andrew Yang said in his 2020 presidential campaign, is, "Be laser focused on how to bring the costs of coverage down by solving the root problems plaguing

---

[384] Ibid.
[385] Ibid.

the American healthcare system."[386] We must focus on the problems that need to be solved and we must focus on creating a smooth and quick glidepath to a single payer system.

DISPELLING ANTI-VAX ANXIETY

Revamping our healthcare system to prioritize people over profits should have a significant effect on mitigating the risk of the anti-vax movement. Remember, the root cause of the movement is a misplacement of warranted mistrust in Big Pharma and the healthcare industry. Increasing accountability and regulation in these industries should act to restore trust and turn people away from the ill-advised anti-vax movement.

We must also start calling out politicians and media figures who skew vaccine statistics to further their anti-immigrant agendas, and, as we do this, we must highlight the statistics that show the remarkable effectiveness of vaccines. Electing leaders who we can trust to tell us the truth is a vital component of reducing this risk.

The solutions we discussed in Chapter 1 are vital to stopping the spread of ignorance that leads to anti-vax sentiments. Those solutions are thus the most important solutions for addressing the anti-vax risk.

A HEALTHIER SOCIETY

The goal to create a healthier society is not some far-fetched idea. This movement to become healthier will not be easy. However, we can achieve this goal. We do this by reversing ignorance about the profit motive that exists in the health industry, the truth about how to reduce the rates of obesity and chronic illness, the true effective ways to start improving mental health, and the falsehoods

---

[386] Yang, A. *Medicare for All – Yang* (2020).

the anti-vax movement is built upon. Ignorance has transformed our health problems into risks that are constantly worsening, but the evidence shows us that we can reverse this trend. Creating a healthier society is vitally important to improving the happiness and satisfaction for all people, and that should be our top priority.

7

The Risk Of Poverty And Privilege

> *It is not great wealth in a few individuals that proves a country is prosperous, but great general wealth evenly distributed among the people . . . It is the struggling masses who are the foundation [of this country]; and if the foundation be rotten or insecure, the rest of the structure must eventually crumble.*
> – Victoria Woodhull, first woman to run for President of the United States in 1872

Since Captain John Smith declared, "If you don't work, you don't eat", at the Jamestown colonial settlement in 1607, the American ideal of rugged individualism has been preached from the mountain on high. America is the land of opportunity, we are told. The United States is the country of the "American Dream". The idea that no matter where you come from, what you look like, or how much money you start with, you can "make it" if you work hard enough. You can be successful and "get rich".

If Only We Knew

In his famous collection of poems, *Song of Myself*, American poet and historical icon Walt Whitman proudly wrote, "I celebrate myself, and sing myself, and what I assume you shall assume, for every atom belonging to me as good belongs to you."[387] In just a few lines, Whitman emphasizes the ideals of individuality and personal responsibility. He calls for everyone to recognize that we all start on an "equal playing field". We have all heard the common refrain that one should "pull themselves up by their bootstraps". We have been told that the key to success is personal responsibility. Social inequities can't be fixed by policy alone, it is said. Rather, inequities will resolve themselves when everyone takes personal responsibility to secure a well-paying job, attain a good education, and take care of their health. These ideas, however, are not grounded in truth, nor are they expressed in good faith by those in the media and political spheres; they are instruments of ignorance creation.

These misleading statements and adages serve to distract the public from the reality that this nation is, and always has been, designed by and for the wealthy and powerful. In fact, one of the Founding Fathers James Madison explicitly stated that the nation should be designed to protect the wealthy. Michelle Alexander elaborates on the original intent behind the constitution in her book, *The New Jim Crow*:

> Northern white elites were sympathetic to the demand for their "property rights" to be respected, as they, too, wanted the Constitution to protect their property interests. As James Madison put it, the nation ought to be constituted "to protect the minority of the opulent against the majority". Consequently, the Constitution was designed so the federal government would be weak, not only in its relationship to private property, but also in relationship to the rights of states to conduct their own affairs.[388]

---

[387] Whitman, W. *Song of Myself*, 1855.
[388] Alexander, 2012. 25.

But this is not what we learn in high school history class, *is it?* Instead, we learn that the United States of America was founded on the ideal of equal opportunity for all.

Both explicitly and implicitly, we are taught that the poor deserve to be poor because they don't "work hard enough". We are told that the wealthy deserve to be wealthy because they earned their money and worked hard to be successful. And this must be true, because in the United States, *anyone can make it*. Look at Bezos, they say, look at Obama, Lebron, and Bill Gates. If they can make it, you can make it. Everyone can.

These sentiments are crucial to the preservation of a system designed to serve the interests of elite people. Generally, if people believe the socioeconomic system gives everyone a fair shot, no serious threats of upheaval to the social, political, or economic status quo will materialize.

Economic opportunity and social mobility are much less dependent on taking personal responsibility and working hard than the elites would have you believe. In recent decades, the United States has functioned increasingly as a "meritocracy". That is, a society in which those who are the "most deserving" reach the top of the socioeconomic ladder, whereas those who are the "least deserving" with the least amount of "merit" fall to or remain at the bottom. The idea of a meritocracy sounds like a great thing, *doesn't it? Why shouldn't the best and the brightest be the ones who make it to the top of society?*

While a meritocracy may sound like the most fair and equitable system, and while it must be acknowledged that, in some regards, it has contributed to reducing racial and gender inequalities, this existing system is also causing great damage to our nation, particularly because it reinforces the view that rugged individualism and personal responsibility are the primary (and some suggest sole) drivers of one's personal outcome.

The meritocracy has led to historic increases in income inequality. When the wealthy are indoctrinated to believe they deserve all the money they make because they earned it through their own merit, they feel little responsibility to share their wealth and income with those less fortunate.[389] Hence, they oppose estate taxes, higher income taxes, and government programs to aid the poor. Worse yet, the elite feel justified in their creation of ignorance to maximize their own interests. After all, they (or their ancestors) worked hard to be in the position they are in; it's every man for themselves why shouldn't they prioritize their interests above the public's?

All those who don't reach the top quintile of the socioeconomic ladder (i.e., the bottom 80 percent) are told they have no one to blame for their plight but themselves, and this leads to a significant increase in despair and disengagement among this demographic.[390]

The privileged are endowed with opportunities to accumulate more and more merit, then they hoard those opportunities, naturally locking out the bottom 80 percent from a fair chance at upward mobility. The subsequent increase in economic inequality fortifies the unfair structure that exists by increasing the opportunities afforded to the wealthy and decreasing those available for the masses. Unsurprisingly, as we move up the income ladder, we see that the top 20 percent has less opportunities than the top 10 percent, and the top 10 percent has less opportunities than the top 1 percent. This opportunity hoarding by the upper-middle class, the wealthy, and most significantly the elite, serves as a mechanism for the powerful to stay in power for generations.

It is true that there are exceptions to this system. There are always outliers. Sometimes, people who grow up in abject poverty rise to the top against all odds and become wealthy. However, it must be acknowledged that a system in which there is absolutely no social mobility or social change would *weaken* the elite's ability to stay in power. While a meritocracy allows for a few "outsiders" to gain power and wealth, it also allows the elite to reproduce their

---

[389] Reeves, R. *What Is Meritocracy?* (The Institute of Art and Ideas, 2019). https://www.youtube.com/watch?v=SBYcN4ypm0U.
[390] Ibid.

socioeconomic status while maintaining public ignorance about the fairness of the system.

This is a point social theorist Immanuel Wallerstein made in his *World Systems Analysis*. Wallerstein states that the elites have always known that by permitting slow, incremental progress, "The 'dangerous classes' would become less dangerous and those with 'merit' would play the key roles in political, economic, and social institutions."[391] In other words, allowing for some slow change allows powerful groups to adjust strategies to maintain power and social control.

The creation of ignorance leads people to accept the notion that the system is fair. This ignorance serves to maintain this "rigged" social stratification.

In this chapter, we will explore the mechanisms of ignorance creation and opportunity hoarding more deeply, and ultimately, discuss why social mobility is critical to the well-being of the nation and how we can create a more equitable society.

THE CREATION OF IGNORANCE

At the end of Chapter 3, I argued that, in a society where the public subscribes to racist ideas, it is understandable that an economically conservative President and Congress are elected at a time when 78 percent of Americans are living paycheck to paycheck. However, this position must be taken one step further. The acceptance and neglect of such appalling economic inequality is also fueled by the ignorant belief that everyone's chances to be economically successful are fair and equal. Essentially, while people may not necessarily be happy with high levels of economic inequality, they do not view this inequality as indicative of a broken system. Instead, they fall back to the common explanations that

---

[391] Wallerstein, I. *World-systems Analysis: An Introduction* (Duke University Press, 2004). 52.

inequality exists due to individual failures, and people simply need to work harder if they want to succeed. We may say, "It's not about race, it's about work ethic." To paint a clearer picture of this phenomenon, let's look at the numbers.

According to a 2018 Gallup poll, 63 percent of Americans are "satisfied with a person's opportunity to get ahead".[392] Among conservatives, 86 percent are satisfied with one's chances for upward economic mobility. These numbers are truly staggering considering that, in reality, upward mobility in the United States is extremely limited.

Consider the following: in a perfectly socially mobile society, each quintile (that is each block of 20 percent of the income distribution) would have an equal chance to move up in society. Someone in the bottom 20 percent would have an equal chance as someone in the top 20 percent of reaching the top quintile of income distribution (or any quintile for that matter); everyone would have a 20 percent chance of landing in each quintile. Based on the results of the Gallup poll, it appears that most people, particularly conservatives, feel that one's chances to move up economically are roughly equal to this 20 percent chance. However, this is not the case. The following excerpt from a report from the Hamilton Project, entitled *Thirteen Economic Facts about Social Mobility and the Role of Education*, explains the reality of social mobility in the United States:

> Children of well-off families are disproportionately likely to stay well off and children of poor families are very likely to remain poor. For example, a child born to parents with income in the lowest quintile is more than ten times more likely to end up in the lowest quintile than the highest as an adult (43 percent versus 4 percent). And, a child born to parents in the highest quintile is five times more likely to

---

[392] Newport, F. *Majority in U.S. Satisfied with Opportunity to Get Ahead* (Gallup, 2018).

end up in the highest quintile than the lowest (40 percent versus 8 percent). These results run counter to the historic vision of the United States as a land of equal opportunity.[393]

However, these numbers, which clearly fall short of those that would be expected in a society that is socially mobile, are easily justified by the idea that people from wealthy families simply work harder than people from low-income families. Many believe that children from low-income families simply don't work hard enough, but if they did, they would undoubtedly move up the socioeconomic ladder. In fact, researchers from Northwestern University have found that when respondents are told that certain children from low-income families are from "very hard-working" families, they give much higher estimates for those children's chances of future success.[394]

Polls have consistently shown that conservative Americans believe if one works hard, they can be economically successful. They believe that the system *is* fair. What would not be fair, according to these people, are income and wealth redistribution policies or policies that strengthen the social safety net.

Conservative voters do not support wealth redistribution policies because they feel the problem of inequality is a problem of personal responsibility, it is not a problem the government has the capacity to solve.[395] In fact, many conservatives believe the opposite; not only should the government refrain from enacting redistribution policies, but it should also cut government welfare programs and focus on "freeing the economy" to decrease inequality.[396] For they believe it is unfair to "punish" hard-working, economically successful

---

[393] Greenstone, M., et. al. *Thirteen Economic Facts about Social Mobility and the Role of Education* (The Hamilton Project, 2013).

[394] Alesnia, A., et. al. *How Closely Do Our Beliefs About Social Mobility Match Reality?* (Kellogg Insight, 2018).

[395] Ibid.

[396] Ibid.

individuals by forcing them to pay taxes to fund assistance programs for "lazy", low-income individuals.

Candidly explaining this belief among conservatives, historian Steve Hochstadt commented on a study by the Pew Research Center, writing, "Most Republicans believe that hard work alone is the guarantee of success; those who are poor need to work harder. Poverty is their own fault."[397]

This notion that government programs or redistribution efforts are part of the problem, not the solution, when it comes to inequality is completely contradictory to what statistics and evidence reveal about economic inequality. In the most equitable countries, most notably the Nordic countries such as Denmark and Finland, the social safety net is the strongest and redistribution policies are the most prevalent. However, in the United States a large swath of the population rejects the notion that these facts are causally related. *Why?* Quite simply, because ignorance is created and spread by conservative politicians and conservative news and media outlets.

As discussed in previous chapters, conservative politicians have lambasted the poor—most notably poor people of color—who rely on government assistance for decades. Conservative politicians directly and indirectly further the false narratives that welfare is actually bad for low-income people and that people are poor because they are lazy and trying to cheat the government for "handouts". Ronald Reagan, who spoke fervently about ever-present "welfare queens" and other free riders, perfectly exemplified this model of an ignorance creating politician.

Moreover, politicians, as well as influential think tanks, heap praise on and award conservative media figures who expound on these false ideas about the poor and their chances for upward mobility. President Reagan commemorated Rush Limbaugh (perhaps the most notorious and influential individual ignorance creator of the last 50 years) as "the number one voice for conservatism in

---

[397] Hochstadt, S. *Do Poor People Deserve Help?* (LA Progressive, 2014).

our country".[398] In February of 2020, President Trump awarded Limbaugh the Medal of Freedom. This praise for ignorance creating conservative media figures by "well-respected", established people and organizations only enhances the apparent credibility of the false ideas that media figures preach to their audience.

I now implore you to remember our discussion of the ignorance creating mechanisms of *Fox News* in Chapter 1. Ignorance is created directly by hosts on this most watched "news" channel in the United States. Prior to the sexual harassment scandals that led to his demise and firing, Bill O'Reilly, who for years had the most watched prime time news show in the nation, repeatedly preached to his audience about the importance of hard work. In a *New York Times* opinion article, journalist Charles Blow sums up O'Reilly's ignorance creating on this issue:

> In 2004, Bill O'Reilly, arguably the face of *Fox News*, said: "You gotta look people in the eye and tell 'em they're irresponsible and lazy. And who's gonna wanna do that? Because that's what poverty is, ladies and gentlemen. In this country, you can succeed if you get educated and work hard. Period. Period." In 2012, O'Reilly listed what he called the "true causes of poverty" including "poor education, addiction, irresponsible behavior and laziness."[399]

The work of demeaning the laziness of the poor and upholding personal responsibility as the sole requirement for upward mobility has been continued by today's notable *Fox News* hosts, such as Tucker Carlson and Laura Ingraham. Never does their rhetoric consider the prejudicial and oppressive treatment the poor and people of color have experienced for generation upon generation. *How could hundreds of years of oppression and non-access to opportunity be irrelevant?* It isn't—refer to Chapter 3.

---

[398] Ibid.

[399] Blow, C. *The President, Fox News and the Poor* (New York Times, 2015).

The creation of ignorance regarding this risk can also be attributed to the preservation of unintentionally developed ignorance. Much of today's ignorance about social mobility comes from our older generations' collective experiences of social mobility. In his book, *Capital*, economist Thomas Piketty explains that the mid-20th century was unique (especially in the United States) in its low levels of wealth and income inequality. This occurred due to the multiple shocks to the value of capital (e.g., the value of real estate and stocks) in the period of 1914–1945 (a period that included two World Wars and the Great Depression) as well as economic policies such as the GI Bill and extremely high tax rates for the very wealthy, both of which led to a more equal distribution of wealth.

The decrease in the value of capital coupled with more egalitarian wealth distribution policies led to the greatest wealth building period in American history (almost exclusively for White families). In the three decades following WWII, it had appeared that "old" society, in which the heirs of wealthy families inherited extreme wealth and dominated society, had ended. It appeared that a new era where anyone could rise to the top had come to be the "new normal".

What defined this era was the idea that education can take you to the top.

This was in contrast to the past where it was widely accepted (even among the wealthy) that the wealthy were wealthy not because of merit but because of birthright. However, in the mid-20th century the economy was booming, and mid and high skilled jobs were in high demand. As a result, an individual's level of education played a more prominent role in where one would be placed in the labor market. And because the cost of obtaining a college education was affordable, many took advantage of the opportunity to get educated and gain marketable skills. Thus, during this period many were able to move up from their childhood class status.

Piketty describes the collective attitude of the working masses during this period, writing, "There was a fundamental unity to this society, in which everyone participated in the communion of labor and honored the meritocratic ideal. People believed that the arbitrary inequalities of inherited wealth were a thing of the past."[400] This period of wealth-building for the middle class and high taxation on the extremely wealthy, however, did not last. Soon, the value of capital began to recover from the shocks of the first half of the 20th century and conservative economic policies of deregulation, reducing the power of unions, lowering the real value of the minimum wage, tax cuts for the wealthy, and a creation of "loopholes" and other benefits for the wealthy in the tax code re-established a society dominated by inherited wealth and extreme inequality.

Nevertheless, older generations who experienced living in this era of remarkable opportunity refuse to accept any notion that, today, personal responsibility and hard work are not at the crux of what is necessary for success. The reality is that while education has become extremely important in our society, there is no evidence that our society is now (or ever was) a land of equal opportunity. Piketty spells out this fact clearly writing:

> It is obvious that education plays a more important role today than in the eighteenth century. However, it does not follow that society has become more meritocratic. In particular, it does not follow that the share of national income going to labor has actually increased, and it certainly does not follow that everyone has equal access to the same opportunities to acquire skills of every variety. Indeed, inequalities of training have to a large extent simply been translated upward, and there is no evidence that education has really increased intergenerational mobility.[401]

Ironically, education has served the opposite purpose in our meritocracy. Education has been one of the most important factors

---

[400] Piketty, T. *Capital in the Twenty-First Century* (The Belknap Press of the Harvard University Press, 2017). 516.
[401] Ibid. 532.

in creating inequalities in our society and reasserting the ignorant notions that the poor deserve to be poor, while the wealthy deserve to be wealthy.[402]

Nevertheless, it should not be difficult to understand how the generations who came of age in a more egalitarian society would be easily convinced by the notions that success is the product of hard work and not influenced by the income level of one's family. Given these older voters from generations past comprise the largest voting bloc, it is also not surprising that their attitudes have been reflected in the implementation of conservative policies that have led to increased inequality and declining social mobility.

The last form of ignorance that we will discuss in this section is the ignorance created among the upper-middle class (i.e., the top 20 percent of the income distribution). In the next section, we will closely examine how the top 20 percent "hoard opportunities", in turn creating a wealth trap for their children and creating a ceiling for the bottom 80 percent trying to move up the socioeconomic ladder. What is important to discuss at this point is how ignorance has been created among this demographic to justify this opportunity hoarding.

Most of this ignorance developed unintentionally, but it's important to connect its preserved existence to the elite's vested interests that it serves. There are two factors contributing to the existing ignorance among the top 20 percent of income earners in the United States: 1) the top 20 percent can see others who are wealthier than them and use this as justification that they are not in fact privileged, and 2) social movements and angry rhetoric aimed against the top 1 percent create the notion that the bottom 99 percent are all suffering equally.

According to Gallup (who has been surveying this statistic since 1939), up to 90 percent of Americans consider themselves middle class while only 1–2 percent of people consider themselves

---

[402] Delbanco, A. *College: What It Was, Is, and Should Be* (Princeton University Press, 2012). 135.

upper class.[403] The top 20 percent of income earners do not consider themselves wealthy or as part of the elite, and they use this to justify actions to give their children a competitive advantage. After all, the only "bad guys" are those in the top 1 percent of the income distribution; they are not among them. The top 20 percent's misconception of their own class position leads them to vote, support, and advocate (with no remorse, might I add) for policies and practices that give them and their children an unfair competitive advantage over the bottom 80 percent. I'm talking about exclusionary zoning practices, college admissions policies that favor the upper-middle class (such as standardized testing, legacy seats, and the ability to visit campuses), and securing internships and employment opportunities for their children.

Let us also think back to a point made earlier in this chapter about the public's attitudes towards the fairness of the system. Convincing the public that the system is fair is a vital mechanism for ensuring the unpopularity of wealth redistribution policies. The ignorance that is preserved among the top 20 percent, that is, the ignorant beliefs that they are not privileged and everything they do to give their children an advantage is fair and justifiable, is very much connected to the elites' interest in preventing the implementation of wealth redistribution policies.

The white collar, college-educated voters who comprise the top 20 percent of the income distribution are by all accounts the most important voting bloc. This large group has money available to donate to political campaigns and they have extremely high percentages of voter turnout. Unsurprisingly, securing the support of this voting bloc is of particular interest to the elites.

The ignorance created among the masses (in general) and the top 20 percent (in particular) insulates the public from the fact that the existing social stratification and economic inequality is the result of a strategically rigged system. It prevents voters from collectively

---

[403] Covert, B. *We Are the 99 Percent—Except for the Top 20 Percent of Us* (The Nation, 2017).

acting to restructure our economy to create a fair system where social mobility is widely attainable.

Further, and perhaps more devastatingly, the false belief that the system is fair, that the wealthy deserve to be wealthy, and the poor deserve to be poor, leads to apathy for improving the social safety net and economic reality of the bottom 80 percent. *After all, if the system is fair, why should the wealthy give away their hard-earned money to the lazy, irresponsible poor?*

Ignorance is created to assert the notion that poverty is the fault of the poor, and that privilege is irrelevant in the age of meritocracy. This creates the risk of poverty and privilege; the risk that allows the wealthy to maintain their power and preserve the economic system from which they benefit tremendously while the public sees their wages decline, their chances for upward mobility diminish, and their social assistance programs evaporate into thin air. This ignorance then amplifies the economic risks facing our society as the public grows apathetic towards the growth in inequality and the decrease in one's chances for upward economic mobility.

THE TRUE CAUSES OF INEQUALITY

Since the 1980s, economic inequality has skyrocketed; there are now more millionaires and billionaires than ever and the incomes and wealth of those in the top 20, 10, 1, and .01 percentiles represent more of the national income and wealth than ever. Meanwhile the average American's chances for upward socioeconomic mobility have plummeted. These trends are the result of policies designed to enrich and empower the elite at the expense of the public. The creation of ignorance regarding socioeconomic mobility has been vital in justifying these trends and quelling any possibility of social, political, or economic revolt.

Unfortunately, there is no reason to believe the current trend toward extreme levels of inequality will simply solve itself. If ignorance concerning this risk persists, the risk of inequality will continue to be amplified. Thomas Piketty explains this relationship between inequality and ignorance as follows:

> Indeed, whether such extreme inequality is or is not sustainable depends not only on the effectiveness of the repressive apparatus but also, and perhaps primarily, on the effectiveness of the apparatus of justification. If inequalities are seen as justified, say because they seem to be a consequence of the choice by the rich to work harder or more efficiently than the poor, or because preventing the rich from earning more would inevitably harm the worst-off members of society, then it is perfectly possible for the concentration of income to set new historical records.[404]

An important point to recognize here is that our labor market does reward merit. We live in a meritocracy, that is for certain. However, the opportunities to accumulate merit are much more accessible to those at the top end of the income ladder than to those at the bottom. This inequality of merit accumulating opportunities is exacerbated by the growing economic inequality that has resulted from conservative economic policies, such as the push for deregulation of corporate industries, enormous tax cuts for wealthy individuals and corporations, and a failure to enact effective policies to offset the negative effects of globalization and the rapid growth of technology.

The problem with our meritocracy is not that the majority of those who are reaching the top are "rich kids" who are not qualified to rise to the top. The problem is that most of those rich kids *are* qualified to reach the top. Overwhelmingly, the evidence shows us that kids from the top 20 percent of the income distribution perform better on their SATs, attend college (especially more selective colleges) at higher rates, finish college at higher rates, and eventually land jobs that place them in the top 20 percent of

---

[404] Piketty, 2017. 330.

the income distribution at higher rates.[405] This is not because those children work harder or are naturally smarter than the rest of the population. Rather, it can be attributed to their opportunities to accumulate merit, which are not available to most of the population.

When a child grows up in an upper-middle class family, they are afforded continuous opportunities to accumulate merit that others who come from lower-income families do not have. While the created ignorance tells us that in the United States there is an equal playing field, this "equal playing field" metaphor is completely misleading. Richard Reeves, author of *Dream Hoarders*, describes the shortcomings of this metaphor when contrasting it with reality, writing:

> But in real life there is no clear starting whistle for a single contest. Rather, there is a series of continuous competitions, with victory in one often leading to the opportunity to prepare more thoroughly for the next. As the philosopher Clare Chambers puts it, "each outcome is another opportunity". This is most obvious when we are still making our way through childhood and early adulthood, with one educational outcome tending to take the form of another opportunity. Getting into a good high school increases your odds of entering a selective college, which will be a better preparation for the world of work.[406]

Studies of the cognitive ability of children at the earliest ages show us that there is not a statistically significant difference between the abilities and intelligence of children born in families of different income levels.[407] In other words, children *do* start on

---

[405] Reber, S., Sinclair, C. *Opportunity Engines: Middle-Class Mobility in Higher Education* (Brookings Institute, 2020).

[406] Reeves, R. *Dream Hoarders: How the American Upper Middle Class Is Leaving Everyone Else in the Dust, Why That Is a Problem, and What to Do About It Book* (Brookings Institution Press, 2018). 82.

[407] Greenstone, 2013.

an equal playing field in terms of intelligence. What is significantly different, however, are the opportunities presented to these children.

By the time children reach the age of three, children whose parents are on welfare have heard 30 million less words than children whose parents are professionals.[408] Additionally, three-year-old children of professional parents have vocabularies that are 50 percent larger than children of working families and 100 percent larger than children of parents receiving welfare. By age four, children from families in the top 20 percent of the income distribution are scoring in the 69th percentile for language and math tests whereas the children from the lowest quintile are scoring in the low 30s.[409] These statistics are especially relevant considering a child's brain grows to 80 percent of its adult size by age three and 90 percent by age five.[410]

As children age, these gaps continue to grow, and this growth has mirrored our nation's growing economic inequality since the 1970s. Since 1970, the achievement gap between high- and low-income middle school students has grown by over 40 percent; this is a result of the wealthy performing at higher levels while the poor's performance has stagnated.[411] Similarly, since 1980 college graduation rates for children from the top 20 percent have risen by 18 percent whereas children from the lowest quintile have seen their graduation rates rise by a mere 4 percent.[412] When we examine higher education more closely, we see that 70 percent of the children attending the most competitive schools are from the top 20 percent of the income distribution; students at these selective universities are fourteen times more likely to be from a family in the top 25 percent than the bottom 25 percent.[413]

---

[408] Ibid.

[409] Ibid.

[410] *Brain Development* (First Things First). https://www.firstthingsfirst.org/early-childhood-matters/brain-development/.

[411] Ibid.

[412] Ibid.

[413] Ibid.

The achievement gaps that result from the ability to accumulate market merit are also a product of the practice of what Richard Reeves calls "opportunity hoarding" by the upper-middle class. As Reeves defines it, "Opportunity hoarding takes place when valuable, scarce opportunities are allocated in an anti-competitive manner: that is, influenced by factors unrelated to an individual's performance."[414]

Upper-middle class parents, like all parents, simply want the best for their children. Usually, this desire translates economically into an aspiration for their children to be better off or at least as comfortable financially as they are. Unsurprisingly, this desire of upper-middle class parents has been intensified by the explosion of income inequality. Today, the fall from the top 20 percent to the middle 50 percent, for example, is much greater than it once was (relatively speaking). Naturally, these parents are motivated by these anxieties, and they engage in efforts to give their child the best chance at success.

However, this seemingly innocuous desire to improve your child's chances for success has negative consequences for children whose parents cannot afford to give them the opportunities available to the upper-middle class. Reeves explains the unfairness of opportunity hoarding as follows:

> While parents have every right to act in ways that will help their children's lives go well, they do not have the right to confer on them a competitive advantage, in other words, to ensure not just that they do well, but that they do better than others. This is because, in a society with finite rewards, improving the situation of one child necessarily worsens that of another, at least in relative terms.[415]

---

[414] Reeves, 2018. 102-103.
[415] Ibid. 101.

So, how does the upper-middle class hoard opportunities? Reeves identifies three foremost modes of opportunity hoarding: exclusionary zoning practices, unfair mechanisms for gaining admission to college, and informality in securing internships.[416]

EXCLUSIONARY ZONING PRACTICES

Exclusionary zoning practices include the limiting rules of land ordinances enacted in neighborhoods, such as limits on population density, preventing the development of affordable housing, and tax codes that benefit the wealthy at the expense of lower-income people. Zoning ordinances were first designed as racist mechanisms of segregation, but they have evolved to become classist mechanisms of segregation by income (which, of course, still has racist implications).

Homes in upper-middle class neighborhoods are scarce, valuable, and extremely sought after for several reasons. Key factors are that these neighborhoods are located next to the best schools, they benefit from favorable tax codes that allow families to convert their income into wealth, and they surround you with people in the same upper-middle class status and therefore foster networking connections for your children.[417] All these factors are extremely important in ensuring your child accumulates market merit and that you stay financially comfortable. Naturally, the upper-middle class population votes overwhelmingly to ensure the preservation of these exclusionary laws.

Reforming these zoning regulations to increase inclusivity would yield significant benefits regarding social mobility; reforms would shrink the housing cost gap and by extension narrow existing educational inequalities.[418] However, wealthy families place their financial desires and their desires for their children to be successful

---

[416] Ibid.
[417] Ibid. 104
[418] Ibid. 106.

over their desire to narrow these inequalities. If you are saying right now, *"What's wrong with that?"* and *"Why are these actions hurtful to others?"* then I encourage you to read on until the end of this chapter.

We have created a culture that conditions people to place their own interests above the interests of others (a topic we will dive into in the next chapter), so it is understandable that anyone would have those same questions. If you think everyone has a fair shot to be successful (or to be in a position in which they can live in a neighborhood with exclusionary zoning practices), then you see no problem with voting for your financial self-interests over those of others who clearly did not work hard enough to enjoy the benefits you are enjoying.

State and federal governments act and legislate in agreement with this sentiment. Federal tax policy favors high-income individuals and families who seek to buy homes in these neighborhoods by placing them in a higher tax bracket and granting them benefits such as larger mortgage deductions.[419] These benefits translate into proportionally lower real costs of living for high-income families than lower-income families. Additionally, these tax codes aid in the conversion of high incomes into wealth, an opportunity not available for lower-income families.[420] This wealth is extremely important because it acts as a safety net if one falls on hard times and allows them to make large investments in property, education, and stocks, which can provide additional sources of income.[421]

The class segregation that leads to the formation of these neighborhoods also creates a "bubble" of upper-middle class people. Residents in these neighborhoods interact only with people in their social and economic class and this social sorting creates a deeper ignorance among them. This bubble allows residents to network with

---

[419] Ibid. 106

[420] Ibid.

[421] Keeley, B. *"What are income and wealth?", in Income Inequality: The Gap between Rich and Poor*, (OECD Publishing, 2015).

each other, improving their professional careers as well as creating employment opportunities for their children. Often, however, they lose perspective of the plight of those in lower socioeconomic classes and hence develop less empathy for them.[422]

Consequently, the ignorant beliefs that the system is fair, that the poor don't deserve assistance, and that the wealthy deserve their wealth become more deeply ingrained in their psyches. *Of course they do!* If you grow up never seeing, meeting, or spending time with someone of a lower economic class (or of color), you will never develop proper perspective of the true suffering that results from the rigged economic system that favors your own opportunity hoarding. You become extremely vulnerable to accepting the sacred myths of hard work and personal responsibility as truth.

Like all risks, exclusionary zoning is not just beneficial for the elite and top 20 percent, it is detrimental to the nation as well; it is damaging to economic growth. According to researchers Enrico Moretti and Chang-Tai Hsieh, exclusionary zoning practice have "lowered aggregate U.S. growth by 36 percent from 1964–2009". They elaborate on this point writing:

> Although labor productivity and labor demand grew most rapidly in New York, San Francisco, and San Jose, thanks to the concentration of human capital-intensive industries like high tech and finance, growth in these three cities had limited benefits for the United States as a whole. In the presence of strong labor demand, tight housing supply constraints effectively limited employment growth in these cities. We estimate that holding constant land availability, lowering regulatory constraints in New York, San Francisco, and San Jose cities to the level of the median city would increase aggregate output and welfare growth.[423]

---

[422] Reeves, 2018. 108.

[423] Hsieh, C., Moretti, E. *Housing Constraints and Spatial Misallocation* (American Economic Journal: Macroeconomics, 2019).

Local exclusionary zoning practices have damaging national consequences.

UNFAIR COLLEGE ADMISSIONS AND INTERNSHIPS

The children of upper-middle class families also benefit greatly from unfair college admissions practices, the most notable of which is the practice of awarding legacy seats.[424] At many colleges and universities in the U.S., if your parents, grandparents, or siblings attended a specific university, you are considered a legacy student and your chances of being accepted to that school increase. Compared to other colleges and universities globally, those institutions in the United States are alone in their maintenance of the practice of awarding legacy seats; no other country has colleges or universities that have admissions policies that reward legacy status. This practice, along with "Z-list admissions",[425] allow for underqualified students to gain admission to the nation's most elite schools simply because they are well connected.

However, even without legacy seats, the college admission process in general is skewed in favor of those with greater financial resources. The heavily weighted SAT and ACTs reward those who can afford expensive prep classes, private tutoring, and multiple attempts at taking the test. Those with more disposable money on hand, can provide these resources for their children while those with less money cannot. Unsurprisingly, children from wealthier families perform better and are accepted into more selective schools. Yet, because their achievements are measured via test scores, these

---

[424] Legacy admission is the practice of admitting a student because one or both of their parents are alumni of the college or university.

[425] Z-list admissions is a common practice at elite universities in which prospective students are offered admissions but are asked to wait a year before enrolling. Two-thirds of these students were legacies and 9/10 of these students were not eligible for financial aid.

students come to believe they fairly earned their acceptance. After all, they scored higher, so they must be smarter.

Well-connected upper-middle class children can obtain more impressive reference letters, personally visit schools to show "strong interest", and they can apply to schools via the binding Early Decision option, enabling the for-profit university to accept them and provide little to no financial aid. These unfair, anticompetitive practices give upper-middle class students significant advantages in obtaining acceptance to the most selective colleges where they once again accumulate more market merit than their peers.[426]

As mentioned above, exclusionary zoning practices and unfair college admissions place upper-middle class people in a demographic bubble. This increases their networking opportunities and their ability to secure internships. Widespread nepotism present in securing internships is a key mechanism of opportunity hoarding. Internships are extremely important in one's journey to becoming a high income earning professional. In fact, many employers view internship experience as the most important factor in the hiring process.[427]

Internships often translate directly to full-time employment, and even when they don't, they greatly improve a resume. Yet, these internships are not available to everyone. For example, many internships are unpaid (or the compensation does not cover the costs of transportation, dress code, and meals away from home) and thus are unavailable or impractical for low-income students who cannot afford to spend a summer or semester without working a paid job close to home. Such internships are almost exclusively available to upper-middle-class and wealthy students attending selective colleges. Lower-income students and students from less selective institutions are customarily excluded from the opportunity to secure impressive internships.

---

[426] Reeves, 2018. 109-113.
[427] Ibid. 118.

THE FORTIFICATION OF IGNORANCE

The practices of opportunity hoarding by the upper-middle class reinforce the ignorant notion that the wealthy earned their position in society all on their own. The wealthy come to believe that their hard work alone is behind their success. In reality, inherited privilege and hoarded opportunities have been the driving forces. Meanwhile, as upper-middle class children benefit, their opportunity hoarding practices act as a seemingly impenetrable ceiling for most of the population (those in the lower 80 percent).

The gaps between high and low-income children and families are also intimately connected to race. As a society, we have preached the doctrines of meritocracy and colorblindness simultaneously. This has created the ignorant idea, accepted by both parents and children, that neither your race nor class play a factor in your chances of success. The problem with this worldview is that it is grounded entirely in fiction. Racial obstacles still exist for students of color, and this can clearly be seen in their lower standardized test scores and their lack of access to resources. Initiatives to close the racial achievement gap have been abandoned and replaced by the insistence of colorblindness, "race-neutral" policies, and meritocracy.[428] These so-called post-racial strategies unfortunately ignore the reality that racial inequities in schooling still exist.

These racial disparities are glaringly reflected in statistics concerning economic mobility. Evidence shows us that White Americans have greater rates of upward mobility and lower rates of downward mobility compared to Black Americans. This is due to generations of systemic racism, implicit bias, and the other challenges facing the black community that we discussed in greater detail in Chapters 3 and 4. The common racist objections that blame the shortcomings of Black Americans on Black Americans themselves (i.e., the claim that parental marital status is to blame

---

[428] Lewis-McCoy, R. *Inequality in the Promised Land: Race, Resources, and Suburban Schooling.* (Stanford University Press, 2014).

or that Black children simply aren't as smart or talented as White children) have been found to be wholly inadequate in explaining the racial income gap.[429]

Further, we see that the income level of one's parents does not make up for the challenges faced by Black Americans. Raj Chetty and other researchers for *Opportunity Insights* explain this fact, writing, "Controlling for parental income, black boys have lower incomes in adulthood than white boys in 99 percent of Census tracts. Both black and white boys have better outcomes in low-poverty areas, but black-white gaps are larger on average for boys who grow up in such neighborhoods."[430]

As we can see, the inequality and lack of social mobility that exists in the United States cannot simply be attributed to the bottom 80 percent's lack of hard work and personal responsibility. There are multiple factors, including but not limited to, conservative economic policies of tax cuts and deregulation, the born privileges of the top 20 percent, the practices of opportunity hoarding, lower quality education, and systemic racism. Restructuring our society and investing in people to create a more fair and equal society instead of the rigged, racist, and classist system in place would improve the economic prospects of the entire country. To create such transformational change, we must reverse ignorance.

THE IMPORTANCE OF SOCIAL MOBILITY

Throughout this chapter you may have found yourself asking things like, *"Is opportunity hoarding really that bad? Are legacy seats really that big of a deal? And is restrictive zoning really that determinantal to society?"* After all, *what is so wrong with trying to give your kids an advantage in a competitive labor market or*

---

[429] Chetty, R. *Race and Economic Opportunity in the United States: An Intergenerational Perspective* (Quarterly Journal of Economics, 2018).
[430] Ibid.

trying to maintain the high value of your suburban home? The practices and trends that have led to a decline in social mobility and a dramatic increase in economic inequality *really are that serious,* and their consequences extend further than simply preventing people with lower incomes from moving up economically.

We must open our eyes to the fact that improving social mobility is beneficial for everyone in society. Reuters explains this relationship between mobility and standard of living:

> If you have lots of social mobility, then the general standard of living is going to go up: you'll have lots of poor people becoming richer, and you'll also have the rich protecting their downside, in the likely event that they become poorer, by doing their best to improve the lot of the poor.[431]

Increasing social mobility will create a favorable political environment for stronger social safety net policies, which are necessary to improving quality of life in this country. So, before we dive into specific solutions, let's quickly look at the reasons why inequality and low levels of mobility are detrimental, and how improving mobility and decreasing inequality will be beneficial.

As we touched on earlier, ending practices of opportunity hoarding will grow the economy significantly. Logically, when more people can earn a decent living, we will witness economic growth as a result. And if we ensure that the fruits of this growth are distributed fairly, everyone will benefit and end up better off financially. Ending these uncompetitive practices of opportunity hoarding will also help to close racial and gender gaps in sectors such as education and wealth.

Moreover, a recent cause for concern among voters across the country (especially after insurrectionists stormed the Capitol building on January 6th, 2021) are rising levels of political polarization. Political polarization leads to gridlock in government

---

[431] *Why is Social Mobility Important* (Reuters, 2012).

that prevents the passing of legislation, it creates more social tension between people, and it pushes political parties to endorse fringe policy ideas. This polarization does not emerge in a vacuum. It is directly linked to income inequality.[432] When inequality increases, people become more inclined to abandon logic and reason; they become more vulnerable to internalizing radical ideas. Take, for example, the extreme inequality that preceded the rise of fascism in Europe (most notably Hitler's Germany). The solutions I am about to lay out, which are aimed at reducing inequality, will also have the consequence of decreasing such polarization.

Finally, income inequality decreases happiness in society. Writers at the *Harvard Business Review* examined Gallup polls to provide the following analysis on the relationship between inequality and happiness:

> The more income is concentrated in the hands of a few, the more likely individuals are to report lower levels of life satisfaction and more negative daily emotional experiences. That is, the higher the share of national income that is held by the top 1 percent, the lower the overall well-being of the general population.[433]

Inequality leaves the public unhappy. It lowers their productivity and leads them to take more and longer sick days, among other negative consequences for the labor market.[434] Not to mention the more important consideration that we should never accept social phenomena that make people unhappy without valid justification. Moreover, recent studies have found that greater inequality makes wealthy people unhappy as well; they become more prone to social and mental health difficulties such as anxiety, depression, and

---

[432] Makridis, C. *Are soaring levels of income inequality making us a more polarized nation?* (The Conversation, 2016).

[433] De Neve, J., Powdthavee, N. *Income Inequality Makes Whole Countries Less Happy* (Harvard Business Review, 2016).

[434] Ibid.

suspicion.[435] While this may be attributed to several factors, the fact that inequality contributes to unhappiness is certain.

SOLUTIONS

In this solutions section, I will outline how we can make our society more socially mobile and less economically unequal. Creating a more equitable, highly socially mobile society will not only mitigate the risk of poverty and privilege, but it will also aid in the mitigation of all the other risks we have discussed thus far. More importantly, the creation of this equitable society will further our mission to create a culture for others, the topic of the next chapter. This section offers a guideline for creating a future about which we can be excited, not afraid.

OUTLAWING FORMS OF OPPORTUNITY HOARDING

Ending opportunity hoarding practices is essential to creating a fairer, more competitive society. This means we must significantly loosen restrictive zoning ordinances, which will grow our economy significantly and open education opportunities in the short run. We also must make unpaid internships universally illegal as they give affluent young adults a significant advantage over their lower-income peers. Finally, we must mandate that college admissions are to be based on fair practices and prohibit the currently abundant unfair practices. This includes increasing transparency in these processes, adopting affirmative action policies for class as well as race, and simplifying the college application process.[436]

---

[435] Bregman, R. *Utopia for Realists: How We Can Build the Ideal World* (Back Bay Books, 2016). 67.
[436] Reeves, 2018. 90.

Let me also note that when I mention the necessity to end the practice of exclusionary zoning, I am not suggesting that to solve social mobility we should simply make it easier for poor people move to wealthier neighborhoods. Solely focusing on zoning laws neglects the fact that for everyone who gets the opportunity to move to a more affluent neighborhood, there are many others who do not have the opportunity to leave their disadvantaged, under resourced communities. It is essential that we focus on uplifting disadvantaged neighborhoods by providing them with equal resources. We must be committed to comprehensively and strategically investing more in these communities to lift them out of poverty, provide them with equal quality education, and create opportunities for residents to build wealth in these neighborhoods without having to move to different areas.

However, the existence of exclusionary zoning inevitably results in a stratification where those privileged to live in wealthy neighborhoods are afforded better resources and therefore experience better outcomes. Thus, it is essential to end the practice of exclusionary zoning while simultaneously investing in the uplifting of disadvantaged, under resourced communities.

While ending opportunity hoarding will yield some perceived "negative" consequences for the upper-middle class, it is an essential step to creating a society of which we can all be proud. We should not hesitate to implement these reforms that will aid our less fortunate neighbors and improve our entire society economically and socially. Richard Reeves elaborates on this point, writing:

> By definition, reducing opportunity hoarding will mean some losses for the upper–middle class. But they will be small. Our neighborhoods will be a little less upmarket— but also less boring. Our kids will rub shoulders with some poorer kids in the school corridor. They might not squeak into an Ivy League college, and they may have to be content going to an excellent public university. But if

we aren't willing to entertain even these sacrifices, there is little hope.[437]

Societies should be measured by how well they uplift the least among us not by how well they protect and enrich those with the most. Ending opportunity hoarding is a step in this right direction.

UNIVERSAL BASIC INCOME

Adopting Universal Basic Income (UBI) in the form of the Freedom Dividend, as Andrew Yang laid out in his presidential campaign in 2020, is a vital component of our mission to create a fairer society. This policy will eliminate poverty immediately and stimulate the economy indefinitely.

Adopting the Freedom Dividend is a good decision because, quite frankly, this policy has been proven to work much more efficiently and effectively than all other welfare policies. Studies on cash handout programs have shown that when people are given "free money", they put the money to good use (they pay bills, buy food, and other essentials). Despite common objections claiming poor people are lazy and make bad decisions due to their immorality, studies have shown us that when people are given cash handouts the vast majority do not stop working or spend the money on drugs or alcohol. The reality is the opposite: when given cash handouts, people work harder, spend less money on drugs and alcohol, and experience long term health benefits all while society sees an increase in tax revenue and a rise in incomes. UBI also allows individuals to save their money or secure a new high paying job without losing their UBI benefits. The cherry on top is that UBI would cost less than current alternatives.[438]

---

[437] Ibid. 124.
[438] Bregman, 2016.

Later in this section, we will discuss increased investments and reform in education, policies that many point to as the "be-all-end-all" of social mobility. However, education alone is not enough to ensure mobility. Often, poor children barely benefit from investments in education in large part due to the stresses of being poor.[439] Adopting UBI will help solve this problem and enable all children to benefit from investments in education.

In terms of benefits for the economy, Yang estimates that his proposed Freedom Dividend would grow the economy by about 13 percent (or $2.5 trillion) in just five years and it would add just under five million workers to the labor force.

PROVIDING SHELTER

In addition to offering everyone a basic income, we also must solve the disgrace of homelessness by providing every person experiencing homelessness with safe shelter and a "life coach". This is a policy that was enacted in Utah in the early 2000s and it has seen remarkable success. Utah is now on track to be the first state to end homelessness and it has saved vast amounts of money by enacting this policy. Whereas each homeless person previously cost the state about $16,000 per year in social services and criminal justice costs, the new policy only costs the state $11,000 to provide each homeless person with an apartment and life coach.[440]

More recent studies on similar policies have found that providing housing to the homeless reduces crime, increases employment, improves health, and empowers people to be less reliant on social services, rather than increasing their reliance. Further these studies found that 80 percent of the costs of such policies are covered by

---

[439] Ibid. 61.
[440] Ibid. 70.

the benefits that result from the policy in just 18 months.[441] This policy would end the injustice of homelessness and improve our economy all the while saving us money... *that's a homerun.* We should implement this plan immediately nationwide.

HUMAN-FIRST POLICIES

In the same spirit of creating a culture that puts others first, we must also create an economy that prioritizes people over the market. This is a concept that was at the center of Andrew Yang's presidential campaign, and the policies he proposed to create this economy should be implemented. Throughout history, many on the right side of the political aisle have upheld the value of protecting "free markets". However, the market doesn't always produce the best outcome for all people (as evidenced clearly by the abundance of social problems facing our nation). *What's the point of designing an economy that doesn't work for all the people?* We must design an economy that serves the interest of people not the interests of corporations.

Among the solutions Yang proposes, one of the most significant is improving the American Scorecard. This means abandoning old measurements like Gross Domestic Product (GDP), which inaccurately measure quality of life, and instead adopting measurements of happiness, childhood success rates, and inequality, among various others. This will help us orient our culture and economy towards the implementation of human-first policies.

---

[441] Cohen, E. *Housing the Homeless: The Effect of Housing Assistance on Recidivism to Homelessness, Economic, and Social Outcomes* (UCLA, 2020).

The Risk Of Poverty And Privilege

REFORMING EDUCATION AND PRIORITIZING OUR CHILDREN

In her 2020 presidential campaign, Marianne Williamson proposed four plans to reform education and prioritize children: 1) a plan for child advocacy, 2) the "Whole Student" plan K-12, 3) an education plan, and 4) a plan for U.S. Department of Children and Youth. These plans contain policies and procedures that are essential for creating a fairer more equal playing field for children. Moreover, we can expect to see a tremendous return on investment from these policies since well-educated children almost always grow into highly productive adult citizens. Williamson's plans include incorporating mindfulness and social emotional learning into school curriculums, ending high stakes state testing so teachers can teach more effectively, and creating a department that ensures the needs of children are being met in all other departments that directly or indirectly concern children.

In addition to Williamson's plans, we should also add the following five subjects recommended by best-selling author Mark Manson to our curriculum: personal finance, relationships, logic and reasoning, self-awareness, and skepticism.[442] Adapting our curriculum to meet the needs of the 21st century is important to ensuring that children become productive citizens and, more importantly, happy people.

In the same vein, we must also support bold reforms of our education system (particularly higher education) to become more personalized instead of standardized. The goal of education should be to inspire students to become intellectually curious individuals, to teach students how to interact and communicate with others who hold different perspectives, to equip students with the adequate skills for the labor market, and to assist students in finding meaning

---

[442] For more detail on these proposed educational subjects see: Manson, M. *5 Things That Should Be Taught in Every School* (markmanson.net). https://markmanson.net/taught-in-school.

and purpose in their careers and personal lives. We can create an education system that accomplishes these goals, but it will take significant reform both in curriculum and general structure. We must conjure up the courage to take the necessary steps to launch this education revolution. We know it's the right thing to do, now is not the time to be afraid.

Reforming our education system is important not only for social mobility, but also for increasing subjective well-being and happiness. That is why I believe in addition to all the reforms offered by Williamson and Manson we must also teach children how to find true happiness, or better, tranquility and inner peace. If the purpose of life (or at least one of the main goals of life) is to be happy (in the sense that we are wholly satisfied and content with our lives), we should be teaching ourselves and our children how to be happy! There are thousands of self-help books, philosophy courses, and spiritual teachings that guide us towards happiness, yet we are never taught how to achieve happiness in a formal setting—it is left to us to find happiness for ourselves. I believe we should create curriculums that introduce children at all levels of education to the concepts of how to achieve happiness.

TAX CODE REFORM AND REGULATING EXTREME WEALTH

In recent years, it has become very clear that the regulation of wealth is and will continue to be one of the most pressing issues of our young century. Thomas Piketty demonstrated this point with persistent logic and data in his book, *Capital*. In response to this crisis of rapid wealth concentration among those at the top of the wealth and income distribution, the author proposed what some consider to be radical solutions.

Piketty suggested a high progressive global tax on capital along with enforced transparency for all bank transactions, among a few other ideas. The daunting fact regarding Piketty's assessment of the reality of wealth and his proposed solutions is that all historical and contemporary data indicates that he is spot on. However, as Piketty himself acknowledged, his proposed solutions are "utopian ideas" that would require unprecedented international cooperation and cooperation of the world's "greedy" billionaires. One of our goals must be to make these ideas not seem so "utopian". To make Piketty's solutions a reality, we must effect a dramatic shift in our culture, which we will discuss in the next chapter.

Luckily, there are other reforms to our national tax code that we can enact to create a fairer society and fund social initiatives in the meantime. These reforms will ensure that the extremely wealthy are paying their fair share in taxes.

Currently the top marginal tax rate is 37 percent, however, those in this income bracket effectively end up paying the least amount of taxes due to mechanisms of legal and illegal tax avoidance. Many often point to the post-WWII period where inequality was the lowest and our top marginal income tax rate reached 91 percent, claiming we need to return to such a high level. However, while the rate during this period was indeed 91 percent, most elites only paid about 40 percent of their income in taxes because they were able to successfully utilize mechanisms of tax avoidance and loopholes (just like the wealthy of today).[443] What we must do now is close the loopholes that enable billionaires to pay only 13 percent in taxes and ensure they contribute their fair share of 37 percent.

One of the ways we do this is by fully funding the Internal Revenue Service (IRS) to ensure elites are paying what they are legally required to. President Biden has indicated that he plans to close some of these loopholes by implementing tax reforms such as eliminating the tax break for capital gains and raising the top marginal tax rate substantially. Additionally, we must adopt a Value Added Tax (VAT) of at least 10 percent so that we can pay for Universal Basic Income and enable everyday Americans to share

---

[443] Greenberg, S. *Taxes on the Rich Were Not That Much Higher in the 1950s* (The Tax Foundation, 2017).

in the success of multibillion-dollar corporations like Amazon. It is also important to remember that all the solutions I have proposed in this book will significantly reduce social problems that currently cost us hundreds of billions, if not trillions, of dollars. These savings can be reallocated to fund more social investments that will save us more money, and so on. We can re-allocate our budget to invest in areas like infrastructure and education with some of the money we are using for redundant military purposes. We have more than enough money to fund all the solutions offered in this book as well as many others we have not discussed.

SOCIAL MOBILITY SOLUTIONS

To increase social mobility, we must recreate the Office of Economic Opportunity that President Reagan cut in 1981. In an article for Brookings, Richard Reeves explains what the role of this office would be today, writing:

> The 2021 rebooted Office of Economic Opportunity should be explicitly tasked with improving rates of upward economic mobility, by setting high-profile goals for success; measuring progress with regular public reports, drawing especially on linked administrative data; coordinating efforts across the federal government; and rigorously evaluating pilot programs intended to improve opportunity outcomes.[444]

We must enact policies that target barriers to social mobility. Researchers at the Organization for Economic Co-operation and Development have found that increasing social mobility requires initiatives in five main sectors: 1) investments in early childhood education as well as in policies to prevent high school dropouts,

---

[444] Reeves, R. *Biden Should Restore the Office of Economic Opportunity Abolished by Reagan* (Brookings, 2020).

2) public investment in health and healthcare, 3) family policies that promote work and family balance and provide child care services, 4) policies that affect wealth accumulation and savings behavior (an important tool for social and economic mobility) as well as progressive taxes on wealth and income, and limiting tax avoidance, and 5) designing inclusionary zoning policies as opposed to exclusionary zoning policies.[445]

We also must close the racial and gender pay gaps through policies like the Equal Rights Amendment and others that increase transparency and ensure fairness in wages. We must also raise the federal minimum wage to $15 an hour to drive up wages for all workers.

Additionally, ending the digital divide in rural communities is vital to increasing social mobility. Lack of access to improved technology and internet in households in rural communities limits these populations' ability to benefit from the advances in technology.

We must invest in family planning initiatives across the country, and especially in rural communities, where unplanned pregnancies are most prevalent and detrimental to social mobility. These family planning initiatives include improving access to contraceptives and requiring relevant, comprehensive sexual education in all schools.

Finally, we must change our culture and abandon our glorification of individualism and the "American Dream" as we shift towards a culture that puts the needs of other first. This topic is the focus of our final chapter, so I will be brief in this section. Simply put, changing our culture is essential to increasing social mobility. Putting the interests of others, and society in general, above our own self-interest will create the political atmosphere necessary to enact the policies that will improve social mobility and economic fairness.

It is important to recognize the interconnectedness of social mobility and all the other risks we have covered in this book. The

---

[445] *A Broken Social Elevator? How to Promote Social Mobility* (OECD, 2019).

policy ideas I have suggested call for greater investments and reform in education, improvement in our health and healthcare sectors, and the implementation of economic policies to lift people out of poverty and regulate the enormous wealth of the elites. Implementing these solutions would greatly aid in the mission to mitigate the risks of racism, mass incarceration, gun violence, and health. Conversely, because social mobility is a multifaceted process, all the solutions I have proposed in this book will also directly or indirectly break down barriers to mobility.

REVERSING THE IGNORANCE OF POVERTY AND PRIVILEGE

Throughout our nation's history, we have been fed the simplified narrative that hard work can put anyone on the path to wealth and success regardless of class and race. Ignorance of the many other factors that determine one's wealth and success has been created and maintained to create the risk of an economic system that favors the wealthy at the expense of the poor and middle class. To see true success in the mitigation of this risk, we must reverse this ignorance. We must demonstrate that the "American Dream" is merely a dream, not a reality, in America. But we must open the public's eyes to the fact that *we can* make this dream a reality. Ignorance has amplified the risk of declining social mobility and increasing economic inequality, but as always, since ignorance created this risk, the reversal of this ignorance is our most powerful weapon in mitigating the risk. We can create a fairer, more equal society if we reverse our ignorance and follow the evidence that points us in the direction of implementing effective solutions.

8

Building A Culture For Others

The reason Heaven and Earth can last forever, is that they do not exist for themselves.
– Lao Tzu

Throughout this book, I have addressed what I consider to be the most threatening, pressing risks facing our society today. I have argued that the selfish pursuit of profit and power by the elite class in our society is the chief generator and preserver of public ignorance and that this public ignorance creates and amplifies risks. I explained that monetary motivations drive this creation of ignorance. Since the elite class gains wealth and power from the existence of large-scale material risks, they create ignorance among the public to ensure the risks' survival and amplification.

If enacted, the solutions I have proposed in this book will mitigate the risks we face. Given the chance, these solutions will produce transformational change and will improve the lives of countless individuals. However, if we do not reform the flaws in our culture, dangerous risks will continue to emerge, and they will never cease emerging. No amount of policy can prevent this reality.

Historically, irrespective of which economic system is in place—feudalism, capitalism, socialism, or communism—and regardless of the political system—democracy, monarchy, oligarchy, or authoritarianism—we have always witnessed greed pervert the intentions of the elite class and lead them to prioritize profits over people. We have consistently seen systemic hate and exploitation arise and dominate society because of this greed. Eliminating the inclination fostered by our culture to put one's own interests above or at the expense of others' is our greatest mission and the topic of this final chapter.

Currently, our culture nurtures and promotes the following values: 1) punitive attitudes, 2) finite thinking, and 3) a "dog-eat-dog", "only the strongest survive" mentality regarding personal success. These cultural values are flawed, and they are a product of ignorance. An ignorant view of how the world works and how to succeed in such a world led to the creation of this culture that encourages selfish, punitive, and greedy behavior. These values underlie the emergence of large-scale risks. The elites operate in accordance with these values and thus feel justified in their creation and amplification of risks. After all, it's every man for themselves in this world, isn't it?

If we want to build a better future, we do not have to create a perfect society in which we account for and solve every problem known to man, but we do have to stop the forces that encourage the powerful to promote and amplify risks at the expense of others.

Many claim that it is human nature to be selfish. Some even say that this selfishness is a good thing. In the 1987 film, *Wall Street*, the protagonist, Gordon Gekko, sums up this attitude in his now rather iconic speech, saying, "The point is, ladies and gentlemen, that greed, for lack of a better word, is good. Greed is right. Greed works. Greed clarifies, cuts through, and captures the essence of the evolutionary spirit." Evolutionary science, however, tells us the opposite.

At our core, we humans are not selfish or egotistic or inherently violent. Scientific studies have shown that as humans we are more altruistic than we are selfish. Altruism is actually a key component of our survival instinct. This is a fact made clear through dozens of studies of human behavior during natural disasters, which discovered a strong pattern of altruistic behavior among victims—victims actively look to lend a helping hand to their neighbors and to cooperate and work with each other.[446]

Furthermore, studies have revealed that selfish tendencies are correlated with unhappiness, and altruistic tendencies are correlated with happiness. Altruism is also strongly linked to success. We know, for example, that the most successful business models are ones that aim to contribute to something greater than profits. We also know that individuals who act as "givers" in their professional lives are more successful and more satisfied.

As we embark on the journey to mitigate risks by reversing public ignorance, we must examine our country's moral compass. We must take a long, hard look at the "soul of our nation" and ask ourselves if we are willing to continue to live in a society where it's every-man-for-himself. If this is the status quo (and I believe that it is), then we must no longer accept it. We must be active in learning why rugged individualism and punitive attitudes are not the best way forward for any of us, especially considering the evidence that shows us that living for others reaps greater rewards for everyone. We must build a community designed for others.

ABANDONING OUR OBSESSION WITH PUNISHMENT

In Chapters 4 and 5, we discussed how our punitive culture has contributed to the rise of both mass incarceration and apathy towards gun violence. I presented evidence that revealed how harsh punishments are an ineffective (and harmful) strategy for reducing crime and I exposed the illogical nature of condemning the morality of people

---

[446] Cutler, H., The 14th Dalai Lama. *The Art of Happiness* (Easton Press, 1998). 58-59.

who commit crimes. However, this obsession with punishing people, "giving them what they deserve", so to speak, is so deeply ingrained in our psyches that it is hard for us to imagine anything different.

For as long as we can remember, we have been taught that the world is divided between "good people" and "bad people"; "good guys" pitted against "bad guys". In the absence of logic and reason, the infamous lesson of Hammurabi's code—"an eye for an eye, a tooth for a tooth"—still beats strongly in the heart of our nation.

In the abstract, this moral divide is clear and simple. The murderer is a "bad guy". The heroic police officer who arrests the murderer is a "good guy". But none of this is completely accurate. There are no "good people" or "bad people"; there are only people. It is imperative that we move past the notion that "good people" and "bad people" exist. There are "bad" actions and "good" actions; the former we should condemn and the latter we should praise. However, we should never condemn the person. As a society, we must seek to understand the reasons (not to be confused with excuses) why people act the way they do. If a person commits a "bad" action, such as murder, we must not label them as an irredeemably "bad person". Instead, we must attempt to understand why they committed that action. We must engage in restorative justice, not punishment.

Humans are not perfect. Father Greg Boyle, Catholic priest and author of *Tattoos on the Heart*, maintains the belief that there exists a range of healthy, whole people, and sick, broken people. We must see past the flaws in our neighbors and locate the goodness that exists in them. Boyle preaches that the first step to healing wounds is acknowledging their presence in ourselves as well as in others. If we don't acknowledge our own wounds, we may come to despise the wounded around us. This leads to the very destructive notion that some lives are worth less than others. And we have seen this notion materialize to form cultural indifference towards large-scale risks such as racism, mass incarceration, gun violence, and the plight of the poor in general.

We must re-evaluate how we are treating and viewing the disadvantaged, marginalized, and impoverished in our society.

We must reflect and analyze the damage caused by generations of oppression and suppression imposed on marginalized peoples in our nation. We should stand in awe of the burdens of the marginalized, seeking to give them the tools to relieve their troubles. We must no longer stand in judgement of them. In 2021, it must no longer be acceptable to treat prisoners like animals, or to view the poor, marginalized, and imprisoned as disposable, second-class citizens.

As a nation, we must come to value love. We can look to the 14th Dalai Lama's definition of love, "an utter, absolute, and unqualified wish for the happiness of another individual",[447] or we can look to a Western definition of love, perhaps one offered by the great Catholic theologian and philosopher Thomas Aquinas: "willing the good of another". Regardless of which definition we connect with most, we must build a culture centered on love. That is, we must design new systems and lead our individual lives in a way that maximizes the ability for others to achieve true happiness.[448] In a conversation with Bill Moyers, Michele Alexander illustrated the importance of caring for everyone, saying:

> If I care about a young man serving 25 years to life for a minor drug crime. If I care about him and care about his humanity, ought I not also care equally about a young woman who's facing deportation back to a country she hardly knows and had lived in only as a child and can barely speak the language? And ought I not be as equally concerned about her fate as well?
>
> Ought I not be equally concerned about a family whose loved ones were just killed by drones in Afghanistan? Ought I not care equally for all?

---

[447] Cutler, 1998. 286.

[448] By happiness, I am alluding to Aristotle's concept of eudaimonia, rather than a utilitarian happiness based solely on the presence of more pleasure than pain. For more detail on eudaimonia, see Moore, C. *What is Eudaimonia? Aristotle and Eudaimonic Well-Being.* (Positive Psychology, 2021). https://positivepsychology.com/eudaimonia/.

So, I think we ought to commit ourselves to building a human rights movement in this country, a human rights movement for education, not incarceration, for jobs, not jails. A movement that will end all these forms of legal discrimination against people released from prison, discrimination that denies them basic human rights to work, to shelter, to education, to food.[449]

Expanding on Alexander's sentiment, I want to offer you another example. If we care about respecting the humanity of someone who committed a murder in a gang fight, we must also care about the police officer who murdered an unarmed Black man. That is not to say we should justify the officer's action or not hold him accountable for his wrongdoing, but it is to say that we should not renege on our principles and call for the death penalty or a life sentence for this officer.

It is imperative that we are committed to our moral principles, no matter how tempting it may be to abandon them. Everyone is outraged when someone they love is murdered. Calling for life sentences or the death penalty does not solve anything. This attitude is what led to the development of the risk of mass incarceration in the first place. We cannot logically fight for the end of mass incarceration and harsh prison sentences while simultaneously calling for life sentences for police officers (or anyone for that matter) who commit racially charged murders.

We must condemn the horrific act of hate crimes while also upholding the dignity of each and every person. All the while we must seek to understand what drove the offender to the point of committing a criminal offense, and we must seek to rehabilitate the offender and strive to create social conditions that are not criminogenic.

While the idea of abandoning punishment in favor of restorative justice and rehabilitation may seem naive (and to some, unfair), it

---

[449] *Michelle Alexander—Locked Out of America* (Billmoyers.com, 2013). https://billmoyers.com/segment/michelle-alexander-locked-out-of-the-american-dream/.

is necessary, and it is moral. When we begin to build systems that acknowledge the hopelessness and brokenness that drive someone to crime—systems intended to heal broken people, not punish them—we will witness society grow happier, more peaceful, and less violent. It is imperative that we create a compassionate culture to replace our punitive one.

OPERATING WITH AN INFINITE MINDSET

In his book, *The Infinite Game*, best-selling author and famous Ted Talk speaker Simon Sinek diagnosed what he believes is a fatal disease for businesses, as well as for the professional and personal fulfillment of individuals. The disease... a "finite mindset". Sinek explains that life, including the corporate world, is an "infinite game". That is, in life, as well as in business, there are no definitive rules, there are no time restrictions (the game never ends), and perhaps most importantly, there are no winners and losers. However, within the infinite game of life and business, far too many people operate with a finite mindset. People and businesses are trying to "win" or "be the best". But there are no winners, and there is no best in the infinite game. Playing an infinite game with a finite mindset is a flawed strategy.

Our culture primes individuals to adopt a finite mindset. We promote the glorification of profits and fantasizing and obsessing over wealth. A finite mindset is one in which one's life or one's business is operated with short-term goals at the forefront. Businesses with a finite mindset prioritize profits and sales growth instead of prioritizing their long term "just cause".[450] Yet, as Sinek points out, living with a finite mindset never brings fulfillment or sustainable business success.

Operating with an infinite mindset, conversely, requires a commitment to a just cause. This just cause is your *why*. It is one's

---

[450] Traynor, M. *The advantage of infinite thinking* (BenefitsPro, 2020).

"driving purpose", the reason why you live or the reason why your business does business. It is an infinite goal to contribute to something bigger than yourself. Sinek describes it as, "A specific vision of a future state that does not exist; a future state so appealing that people are willing to make sacrifices in order to help advance towards that vision."[451] The point of an infinite mindset is not that you accomplish goals, but rather that you never accomplish your goals. Under an infinite mindset you strive every day to make progress, to inch closer and closer to a goal you know you will never reach. Operating with an infinite mindset in pursuit of a just cause allows us to make real, rewarding change. Change that improves lives and increases happiness. Just imagine a world in which every business or corporation prioritized *improving lives* instead of maximizing their own profits. That is the world we can and must create.

Adopting an infinite mindset, however, is much more than a feel-good strategy. It does not mean turning every business into a charity that makes zero profits. In fact, it's the opposite. Sinek explains that the most profitable companies, the ones who achieve long-lasting success, are those that think infinitely. To build a world in which, "The vast majority of us wake up every single morning inspired, feel safe at work and return home fulfilled at the end of the day", as Sinek is striving for, we must build a culture that promotes the value of infinite thinking in individuals, businesses, and government. Building this aspect of our culture will give us the energy we need to implement the solutions I have laid out in this book. It will inspire each of us to make lasting positive change in the world. It will give us the courage to challenge the status quo to build systems that work for people, systems that give people meaning and make people happy.

---

[451] *Book Summary of - The Infinite Game: How Great Businesses Achieve Long-Lasting Success* (The Hopeful Institute, 2020).

BECOMING GIVERS

Like thinking infinitely, becoming a "giver" in our professional lives leads to greater success and improves our ability to find meaning and purpose in our work. Adam Grant, best-selling author of *Give and Take*, explains that, in business, there are three types of people: givers, matchers, and takers. Givers are people who give more to others than they get back in return—this giving can come in the form of doing favors, making time to meet new people in networking, etc. Matchers believe in giving only when they get something back in return. Takers take more than they give; they take for themselves first because they see the world as dog-eat-dog, take or be taken advantage of.

Our culture currently inclines us to be matchers and takers. As we've discussed in previous chapters, for instance, many Americans believe racial justice is a zero-sum game, and this leads them to become takers in the "game" of civil rights. The belief in zero-sum game theory also exists in professional life for many people. Many believe that if they don't hoard opportunities for themselves or if they "waste time" networking instead of working, they will fall behind. Doing someone a favor is only worth it if someone does you a favor. Once again, studies show us that this is not true.

Living as a matcher or taker is not productive, rewarding, or sustainable. The most successful people are givers who give without expecting anything in return. These people put others first. They genuinely want to see others succeed and are more than happy to assist others to achieve this end. What researchers have found is that givers are not just the most fulfilled people, but also the most successful.[452]

Currently, we have a culture in which nearly everyone subscribes to the notion that humans are inherently bad, strangers are not to be trusted, and when given the opportunity, everyone will act selfishly. As I have noted, this is far from the truth. Yet, the belief in this view of humanity, even though it is untrue, has real consequences. In his book, *Humankind*, historian Rutger Bregman elaborates:

---

[452] Grant, A. *Give and Take* (Penguin Books, 2013).

If you believe something enough it can become real… ideas are never *merely* ideas. We are what we believe. We find what we go looking for. And what we predict comes to pass… If we *believe* most people can't be trusted, that's how we'll treat each other, to everyone's detriment. Few ideas have as much power to shape the world as our view of other people… If we want to tackle the greatest challenges of our time… the place we need to start is our view of human nature.[453]

We must create a culture that encourages more people to be givers. However, people must become givers not because they are looking to be successful. Instead, they must be givers for the sake of being givers. Creating a society in which people give for the sake of giving, not for perceived personal gain, will increase social trust, personal success, and national success.

In a culture where the vast majority of people are givers, we can trust that our neighbors will always have our best interests in mind. If our politicians and leaders are givers, we can trust that they have our best interests in mind too. Being a giver leads to more success for both the giver and receiver. To build a society that prioritizes others is to build a society that prioritizes yourself. Creating a culture that produces "giving" individuals is crucial to creating a society that maximizes meaningful fulfillment and happiness for all people. Being givers is inherent in our nature. We must realize this and embrace it.

EDUCATING FOR AN EFFECTIVE DEMOCRACY

Effective democracy is dependent on an informed citizenry. As I hope it is clear to you now, the citizenry in the United States

---

[453] Bregman, R. *Humankind: A Hopeful History* (Hachette Book Group, 2020). 9.

is anything but well informed. Widespread ignorance is created in media and political spheres, and our educational system is woefully inadequate at producing citizens who can make knowledgeable decisions when participating in civic life. As we have discussed, public ignorance has created and then amplified risks exponentially. We must prioritize higher quality, more appropriate education and we must place higher value on honesty in media and politics.

In the above sections, I have argued that our culture must encourage people to be more understanding and forgiving instead of punitive. I wrote that we must think and live infinitely, leading our lives in ways in which we contribute to something greater than ourselves. And I suggested that we must all become givers who genuinely wish to see our neighbors succeed. In other words, we need to build systems of *love* (as defined by the 14th Dalai Lama and Thomas Aquinas). We must construct a society that lives up to the revolutionary American idea upon which our nation was founded, that all people are created equal with certain inalienable rights: life, liberty, and the pursuit of happiness. To construct such a society, we must utilize our most powerful tool: the reversal of ignorance.

As a society we must all collectively commit to continuously acknowledging and seeking to reverse our ignorance. Throughout this book, I have offered some solutions to set us on this path. I discussed restoring honesty in media as well as reforming education. However, creating a culture that truly values exposing ignorance requires more than policy reforms. It requires that we elect *moral, philosophical* leaders who lead by example. Leaders who admit their own ignorance, who aren't afraid to change their position in light of new evidence, and who implore us citizens to acknowledge and reverse our ignorance as well. Those are the leaders we can trust. The leaders who bring out the best in us, not the worst.

Franklin Delano Roosevelt captured this necessity for moral leadership when he said, "The Presidency is not merely an administrative office. That's the least of it.... It is pre-eminently a place of moral leadership." We must honor this sentiment and expect all political offices to be held by moral leaders. Of course, setting policy is important, but building community and calling people to their highest values, inspiring people to care for one another, think infinitely, and be givers, is, and must always be, the true task of our leaders.

The task of moral leadership must also be assigned to the faith leaders in our country. We must not shy away from the fact that the United States is overwhelmingly filled with people living faith-based lives. We must call on churches and faith leaders to preach a message of social salvation; one that inspires congregants to actively seek to improve society and care for their neighbors. Some of the most important social movements in our nation's history, from the abolition of slavery to the Civil Rights movement, were fueled by churches and faith leaders. We must harness the power of every church and inspire people to act in accordance with their highest morals.

When our society begins to value the pursuit of reversing ignorance, an education revolution will inevitably follow suit. We will design educational systems that are personalized instead of standardized. We will educate people not to teach them answers, but to guide them to ask the right questions. The goal of education will be to inspire students to seek out and reverse their own ignorance by asking questions and following their own personal educational path that guides them towards a meaningful, happy life. This new form of education will produce infinite thinkers and lifelong students. It will produce selfless givers who are eager to contribute to a just cause greater than themselves. It will produce citizens who demand that government honestly attempt to improve lives, and who are informed enough to hold the government accountable when it falls short of these duties.

Only by creating a culture that leads us to elect moral leaders and reform our education can we hope to truly produce an informed citizenry. With an informed citizenry that is committed to improving lives, democracy will function effectively, and we will be sufficiently able to mitigate emerging risks as they arise in the future.

Perhaps most significantly, creating this culture for others will change the values and mindset of the elite. The elite will come to accept the values of compassion, selflessness, and infinite thinking and they will no longer be interested in creating and amplifying risks for their personal gain. They will realize that they too will be happier when they prioritize the interests of others and use their talents and resources to improve conditions for all people.

THIS IS POSSIBLE

As you read this book, you may have dismissed some of my ideas as "utopian". You may scoff at the idea that people will ever care about anything other than money, or maybe, for example, you believe that it's impossible to eradicate systemic racism given the history of this country. I understand your cynicism. Human civilization has been in existence for thousands of years, and it appears that the world is approaching "Doomsday" at faster rates than ever. Today, it seems, we are challenged by more risks than ever before (and the future doesn't look so hot either). However, while reading about history can produce feelings of despair and hopelessness, it also shows us our potential to change.

For hundreds of years, slavery was the law of the land in the United States. Most people accepted that was just the way things are and that there was nothing we could do about it. But eventually radical ideas and revolutionary people challenged the status quo and ended the era of chattel slavery. For thousands of years, feudalism relegated 99 percent of the population to abject poverty. As recently as the 18th century, the average life expectancy in England was just 35 years. But things changed. In comparison to life just a few hundred years ago, many more of us are now living in the land of the plenty. Nothing, whether bad or good, lasts forever. Change is the only constant.

We must always strive to create a better world, and the commitment to seek out and reverse public ignorance is essential to this mission. We must not be held back by cynics who say things will never change, that our ideas will never be more than ideas. History shows us that we can change the world, but only if we think big.

In sports, the notion of striving for greatness is applauded. We celebrate the athletes who claim they want to be *the best*. These athletes ignore all the critics who tell them they are crazy, that their dreams are impossible. Some truly do achieve greatness. This commitment to continuously improving, always striving to be better than you were yesterday, has resulted in the most competitive, highest level of sports ever witnessed. We need to adopt this attitude in our view of improving the world. *Why not strive for utopia? Why listen to the critics who say it's impossible to improve society?* We can achieve the impossible if we create a culture and society that inspires its citizens to get up every day committed to improving the world for others.

I will leave you with a quote from Oscar Wilde:

> A map of the world that does not include Utopia is not worth even glancing at, for it leaves out the one country at which Humanity is always landing. And when Humanity lands there, it looks out, and, seeing a better country, sets sail. Progress is the realization of Utopias.[454]

At this moment, let us commit to chasing utopia. We must build a community for others by rooting out the evils of greed, hate, and apathy towards ignorance replacing them with the virtues of love and curiosity of the unknown. All this is possible, but it will require a collective commitment to reversing ignorance. Brick by brick, we can build a culture and society that works for us all.

---

[454] Wilde, O. *The Soul of a Man Under Socialism.* http://www.wilde-online.info/the-soul-of-man-under-socialism-page11.html.

About the Author

Peter S. Baron wrote *If Only We Knew* as an upper-class Dean's List student in the Honors Program at Fairfield University. Peter decided to personalize his education by designing his own major through the Individually Designed Major program offered by Fairfield. This interdisciplinary major is titled "Socioeconomic Inequities: Inevitable or Avoidable?". It is centered on a guiding question: *are socioeconomic inequities an inevitable product of human evolution or an avoidable product of the development of human culture and civilization, and is it possible, and in society's best interests, to seek to eliminate inequities?* Through his studies, Baron aimed to examine the causal relationship between a culture that fosters greed and the existence of socioeconomic inequities.

In the summer of 2021, Baron started his blog, *Pondering with Pete*, where he discusses the benefits of applying philosophy to our daily lives.

Outside of his academic and professional pursuits, Peter loves the beach, spending time with family, friends, and his dog, Julien.

Acknowledgments

First and foremost, I want to thank the entire team at Ultimate World Publishing. Thank you for giving me the opportunity to realize my dream.

Thank you, reader, for taking a chance on me and my message. I hope you enjoyed and learned something of value from this book.

Thank you to all the people who have believed in and challenged me over the years. Since eighth grade, I knew I wanted to write a book. I didn't know what I would write about, but I knew being a published author was something I wanted to accomplish. My eighth-grade English teacher never laughed at me or dismissed me when I told him this. He told me that he would be at my book signing. Mr. Molloy, wherever you are, thank you. You've inspired me more than you know.

I want to thank my professors at Fairfield University for encouraging and challenging me, but most of all, for being there for me. Dr. Lacy, thank you for your unwavering belief in me and your wisdom. In our first meeting, you saw my vision and potential, and you never let me abandon it. You have been there for me every step of the way with your wisdom, your hard-hitting questions that make me reconsider my positions, and your constant message reminding me to "spread love". I cannot thank you enough.

Dr. Wilgar, thank you for being my biggest fan on campus. Your class served as my inspiration to write this book. When I came to you with the idea of writing the book, you didn't think twice before telling me that I can and will do it. Thank you for dedicating so much time to helping me nail down my thesis in those early months and thank you for your continued support ever since.

If Only We Knew

To Glenn Llopis, Reggie Marra, Brother Stephen Balletta, Dr. Brunn-Bevel, Dr. Cansoy, Dr. Bayne, Dr. Harriott, Dr. Rodrigues, Dr. Howe, Dr. Mielants, Dr. Nash, and Dr. Pilkington, thank you for encouraging me to think deeply.

To my friends, thank you for your enduring support. Throughout this journey you have always let me know that you were by my side, and without your support, this book would not have been published.

I especially want to thank my friends, Daniel Garcia and Renée Levesque. Thank you for your feedback and your support.

Above all, this book would not have been possible without the support of my loved ones. Thank you, Mom, for being my role model. Your work ethic and dedication to making a difference in the world inspires me every day. Dad, thank you for being my personal full-time editor. Thank you for our long conversations discussing the ideas I had for this book and thank you for challenging me when my ideas did not make sense or were not expressed clearly. Your feedback was invaluable. I am so grateful to have you both in my life.

To my brother Eddie, as I sit down to write these acknowledgements, I'm reminded of a quote by Marcus Aurelius in *Meditations*: "That I had the kind of brother I did. One whose character challenged me to improve my own. One whose love and affection enriched my life." Thank you, Eddie, for your wisdom, your humor, and your genuine love—and thank you for being my brother.

Finally, to my grandparents, thank you being there for me in person and in spirit. Grandma Vio, thank you for showing me endless love. Your unwavering faith inspires me to accept whatever life throws at me. Papa Peter, thank you for your compassion and understanding. Every day I try to live up to your example and treat people how you treated people. Grandma LaLa, thank you for being my cheerleader and the biggest literary fan in the world. Your smiles and your love made me who I am today. Finally, thank you Papa Sandy. You always said, "You can never do wrong, doing the right thing." I never forgot that while writing this book.

Thank you to all of you.